Nothing But My Sword

Nothing But My Sword

The life of
Field Marshal James Francis Edward Keith

Sam Coull

Birlinn

First published in Great Britain, 2000 by
Birlinn Limited
8 Canongate Venture
5 New Street
Edinburgh
EH8 8BH

British Library Cataloguing-in-Publication Data
A catalogue record for this book is available from the British Library

ISBN 1 84158 024 4

Cover pictures reproduced with permission from
Mary Evans Picture Library, London

Typeset by LBJ Typesetting Ltd of Kingsclere
Printed and bound in Finland by WSOY

To Henriette

Contents

Foreword

·

Many years have passed since I was first swung high within a parent's grip to get a better look at a grey statue, a figure of a man dramatically giving direction with his baton. From the riding boots my gaze travelled upwards, past the three-quarter length coat with sword peeking out until, under a wonderful hat, my young eyes settled on a square jawed face. It is a face with a softly smiling mouth and eyes that stare sightlessly out over nearby rooftops towards the cold North Sea and northern Europe.

This Peterhead memorial to Field Marshal James Keith is a copy of one created for Wilhelm I of Prussia by the artist Taesart. The original stands in Berlin along with images of Keith's military contemporaries, who are also frozen in stone for posterity. Wilhelm gifted this copy to Peterhead upon request from the town's magistrates.

Today, the statue hardly gets a glance from those who have grown used to its presence, but visiting groups of Polish or Russian seamen can often be seen in discussion around its base. They give every appearance of knowing more about James Keith than the locals, and perhaps they do, for Keith led armies over much of Europe and is a shared part of our history.

Shortly after James Keith's death at Hochkirch on 14 October 1758, a German doctor asked Keith's brother, the Earl Marischal, if he could write the Field Marshal's story; he received a coldly negative reply. Rousseau, the philosopher and writer, also wanted to be Keith's biographer, to repay Marischal for his food and lodging as the Earl's penniless guest – he was also bluntly told to forget it.

And now those days of distractedly swinging from a parent's hand have long gone, although the smile on the statue's face appears to have stayed with me down through the years. So, more than fifty years on and just weeks after the 300th anniversary of Keith's birth at Inverugie Castle, I have started to write the story of this brave and cultivated man.

Sam Coull

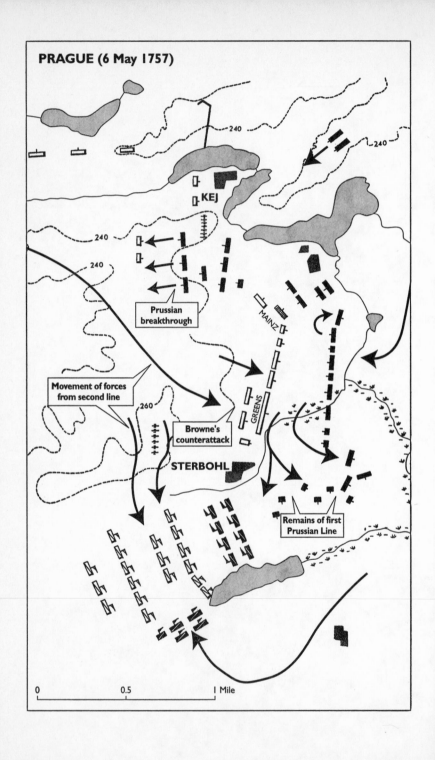

PRAGUE (6 May 1757)

240

240

KEJ

240

240

Prussian
breakthrough

MAINZ

Movement of forces
from second line

260

GREENS

Browne's
counterattack

STERBOHL

Remains of first
Prussian Line

0   0.5   1 Mile

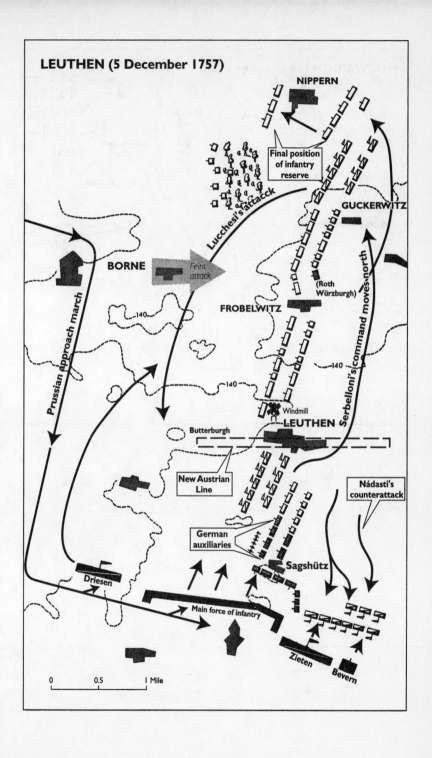

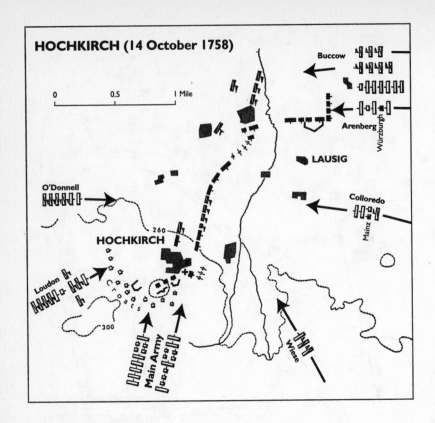

HOCHKIRCH (14 October 1758)

0   0.5   1 Mile

Buccow

Arenberg

Würzburgh

LAUSIG

O'Donnell

Colloredo

Mainz

260

HOCHKIRCH

Loudon

Croats

300

Main Army

Wiese

1
.

The Earls Marischal

.

SOME TWO MILES WEST of Peterhead, the River Ugie formed a natural part of the defences of Inverugie Castle. Built high up on the north bank, the river looped around the castle home of the Keith family[†] giving all the security and protection of a moat but presenting a much more dangerous obstacle to uninvited visitors during the winter months, when floodwater surged around the castle on its way to the sea.

The month was April, and, although morning had long broken, a light mist still hung around the river and worked its way upwards to shroud the castle in damp. Mixing with the mist was the heavy scent of peat and woodsmoke from castle cooking fires which permeated the air in and around the Keith home. As usual, Inverugie Castle had come to life just before 5 a.m., when castle servants began preparations for a new day and a day moreover when its owner, Sir William Keith, was about to set out for London and the opening of a new Parliament, scheduled to sit on 6 May 1703.

Sir William was making preparations for his long journey south and had just finished a breakfast of porridge, oatcakes and barley

[†] 'Memoires are commonly so tedious in the beginning, by the recital of genealogies, trifling accidents which happen'd in childhood, and relatione of minucies (hardly fit to be imparted to the most intimate friend), that it renders them not only uninstructive to the reader, but often loathsome to those who wish to employ their time in any usefull way'. *Memoir of Field Marshal Keith.*

bannocks, washed down with a couple of mutchkins (or half-pints) of ale. Outside the great hall and down on the flagstones of the courtyard below he could hear the clatter of horses' hooves and the voices of the escorts accompanying him to London. Pulling on his riding boots, Sir William straightened up to see the retreating figure of his youngest son from the corner of his eye – the Hon. James Francis Edward Keith – hurriedly crossing the hall from his tower bedroom towards the stairway down to the kitchens. As Sir William watched his son disappear downstairs, he fleetingly wondered what he was up to, half expecting to hear some shouts or screams echoing from below.†

The seven-year-old was forever in hot water because of his pranks, constantly on the receiving end of dire warnings and threats from his parents – none of which had the slightest effect. The boy could only be described as 'ill-tricked'. Every so often Sir William had to listen to complaints from servants who had fallen victim to his pranks and wearily promised severe punishment in retribution, but none of it ever seemed to make the slightest difference to the Hon. James. One crusty old retainer, who had served the Keith family for many years, was overheard to tell the Hon. James: 'gin ye ivver mak a pudden laddie, I'll ate the prick,' the 'prick' being the sliver of stick used to pin the 'pudden'

---

† 'Inverugie Castle is situated about two miles from Peterhead, on the high northern bank overlooking the river Ugie . . . the castle is an oblong building with two round towers, one at the south-east, and the other at the north-east corner. This is an unusual arrangement, as the round towers are generally at diagonally opposite angles. The buildings are four storeys high, and there was probably one extra storey in the round towers which are now ruinous at the top. On the vaulted ground floor is the kitchen entering from the courtyard, and having a stair communication in the thickness of the wall to the hall above. The entrance to the hall is by an outside or fore stair, having a vaulted roof with rib mouldings. This is likewise unusual. The hall which is on the first floor is a spacious apartment with lofty arched window recesses and with a large fireplace at one end. Entering from it are the square shaped rooms in the round towers, adjoining to which is a wheel stair in each tower.' Inverugie Castle from *Castles and Domestic Architecture in Scotland* Vol. 2 (1887) Gibbon and Ross.

together. His mother, Lady Mary Keith, Countess Marischal also admonished him but that was about all: after a stern lecture to her favourite son had ended the incident was soon closed, forgotten and forgiven. Her son James was taller than his older brother, and had the squarish, heavy build and dark, swarthy complexion that came from the Countess's side of the family.

James Keith's brother George was three years older and the pair were inseparable. George was much more academically inclined and cast in the Keith mould. His loyalty and love for his younger brother constantly brought George before his parents, pleading for leniency or making excuses like a defence lawyer for the Hon. James after he had been caught once again in an escapade. There were also two sisters, Lady Mary and Lady Anne. Mary, the eldest, was more like her mother while Anne, the prettier, wittier and more lively of the two, enjoyed her brother's pranks and punishments.

The thirty-eight-year-old Sir William Keith had married Lady Mary Drummond, daughter of the fourth Earl of Perth, in 1690. George was born on 2 April 1693 and James on 11 June 1696, with Mary and Anne following later.

It was now time for Sir William to say his goodbyes, join his men waiting in the saddle and go, leaving Lady Mary to take over family affairs and run the estate, as she had to do all too frequently in his absence. There were only two routes from Inverugie open to him at the start of his journey in 1703. One was over by Howe o' Buchan and Cowsrieve to Hedderbridges (today's Black Hills) and the Kirk of Cruden; an alternative route went by Peterhead and crossed the new 'stone and lyme' bridge of two arches which replaced a wooden structure swept away in a spate. This new bridge had been constructed after an Act of Parliament was pushed through by the Keith family and made law in 1686. Soon afterwards, the wooden bridge was lost to the surging floodwaters of the River Ugie.

Sir William took the road by Peterhead – scarcely a road, more of a beaten path and similar to all the others of its time in Scotland. These 'roads' evolved through constant usage by travellers, who bent their way to fords above tidewater inland while avoiding bogs and at the same time seeking inns and stopping places where a dry bed and quality ale might be found. Even on horseback, Sir William faced a journey of some three weeks. A coach from Edinburgh to London took no less than a fortnight to arrive. And in any case he had to see Thomas Arbuthnot, his Baron Baillie in Peterhead, about pressing matters in the town and planned to break his journey at his Aberdeen mansion, fronting onto the Castlegate, with another stop at Dunnottar Castle where he would spend the night. Dunnottar was the Keith family's clifftop stronghold, impregnably jutting out into the sea south of Stonehaven (or Steenhive as it was then known).

We will leave Sir William to his journey only to comment briefly on the trials and tribulations of seventeenth and eighteenth-century travellers in Scotland. There are no words to adequately describe the broken paths that passed for roads. A horror-struck traveller of the times reports: 'Stage coaches they have none . . . the truth is the roads will hardly allow 'em these conveniences, which is the reason that their gentry, men and women, chuse rather to use their horses. However, their great men often travel with a coach and six, but with so much caution that, beside their other attendance, they have a lusty, running footman on each side of the coach to manage to keep it in rough places.' The road from Aberdeen to Stonehaven was so poor that a traveller in 1656 was moved to describe it thus: 'Cawses uncartable and pavements unpracticable, pointed with rocky, stumpy stones and dawbed all over with dungy dirt that makes it unpassible. And the fields, as I conceive, are ten times worse, because o'erspread with miry clay and encumbered with bogs that will bury a horse'.

Despite numerous Acts of Parliament with duties imposed on Justices of the Peace – not to mention committees composed of nobility and other worthies, nothing was really done to improve Scottish roads until well into the eighteenth century.† One obvious

---

† 'No public coach appeared in Aberdeenshire until the last decade of the eighteenth century.'
The Statute Labour Period: An Act in 1669 began a century-long struggle to get roads provided by statute labour – The Sheriff, one of his deputes and Justices of the Peace were to convene at the head burgh of the shire each Tuesday of May yearly to list the highways, apportion the

explanation was that these self-same gentlemen and nobility would have lost the services of their own estate workers in doing what was known as a 'stent', or unpaid work of an annual, fixed duration spent on mending roads. Clearly, when the choice was that of either obeying statutory obligations requiring work on Scottish roads and losing the services of tenants and estate workers or having these same people producing for themselves, noble lords and gentry had no difficulty in arriving at a decision. The roads could just get worse . . .

Despite the condition of these roads Sir William duly arrived in London. He was more than familiar with the city, and streetwise, in both a geographical and political sense. Charles II, that libertarian, womanising and hugely popular monarch, had been a great friend of the Keith family and had been entertained by them at Dunnottar. It is possible that Sir William hired a coach and six for the last stage of his journey to Parliament – like all of his family before him, he was conscious of his own position among the ranks of nobles surrounding him.

All sixteen of Scotland's noble representatives in that London Parliament spoke a brand of Doric which was largely unintelligible

work on the roads in each parish and to appoint overseers and surveyors for the roads in each parish. These overseers and surveyors were to have intimation made at the Parish Kirk on the Sabbath day immediately after the first sermon, calling on all tenants, cottars and servants to have in readiness 'horses, carts, sleds, spades, shovells, picks, mattocks and such other instruments as shall be required for repairing roads.' The more skilful were to be placed in charge at fit wages. Every person was to give six days labour for man and horse for the first three years and four days yearly thereafter, between seedtime and harvest; those failing to attend to have their goods poinded to the value of twenty shillings Scots for each man daily and thirty shillings for each man and horse, or, where there were no goods to poind the Justices could 'punish them in their persons as they shall see cause.'

1759: The unwillingness of the men to do the work. In the Parish of Peterhead, for example, 388 men did 1420 ells (1459 yards) in six days, or less than two feet of road per day.

See D.G. Moir, Buchan Field Club Vol. XV. Paper on the Old Roads of Buchan, July 1935.

to the ears of their English colleagues.† As we see even today when Scottish business comes before Parliament, the Chamber would have begun to empty and, as the incomprehensible Doric fell on English ears, it is likely that the exodus became even more hurried. But Sir William ploughed on undaunted: he protested against any of the other earls being called to speak before himself and reminded Parliament of 700 years of Keith family history. Having established his credentials, he went on to make his position clear and spoke in unequivocal terms of his outright opposition to the Union, scheduled to take place in 1707 – his vocal opposition was augmented in writing, for Sir William then entered a solemn protest against the Union of England and Scotland in the Rolls of Parliament.

His dislike of progress towards union between England and Scotland was quite understandable, for there was no guarantee that it would leave his family placed near to the throne of Britain and its occupant. His family's place in history did indeed go back a long time – more than the 700 years quoted by Sir William.

As Earls Marischal, the Keiths shared a joint public position as Scotland's second family – after the royal Stuarts – with the neighbouring Hays of Slains, High Constables of Scotland. So jealous of each other were the Keiths and Hays that they went to court for a decision on disputed powers that each thought rightly belonged to them. The fact that the Keiths had long embraced the Protestant faith, while the Hays were Catholic, didn't help matters and probably only fuelled resentment between the two families.

James Keith's father, the ninth Earl Marischal, was obsessed by the Stuarts but whether he shared their belief in the divine right of Kings is not clear. According to one source, not only was he opposed to the union but 'always opposed the measures of King William's reign' while still 'waiting on the Queen at her accession

---

† Doric is a unique blend of Scots and European words, incorporated into this North-east of Scotland dialect due to trade with France and the Hanseatic ports of Europe. Although spellings may differ, the phonetic pronunciation clearly points to their origin. For example, while the French equivalent of partridges is *perdrix*, the phonetic spelling in Doric is 'pairtricks'.

to the throne and acknowledged her government'. This same historian was somewhat contemptuous in his admiration for him – 'he had an abundance of flashy wit, and by reason of his quality, hath good interest in the country.' He was 'a thorough libertine, yet sets up mightily for the Episcopacy: a hard drinker . . .' Another observer, the adventurous Colonel Hooke, found 'his manners insinuating: his temper of mind full of vivacity', and describes him as 'the most active of all the King of England's friends.'

Given that the Stuarts were devoutly Catholic, the affection the Keiths had for them sets a question mark against their own religious beliefs and what part they let religion play in their politics.

The Keiths traced their origins back to an ancient Rhineland tribe called the Catti.[†] Sometime in the first century BC, so the legend goes, the Catti fought the Romans in the Hercynian forest: their retreat took them by Katwyck on the Rhine to embark for Scotland from the coast of Holland. Just how many Catti took to the boats in this exodus is not known but they eventually made landfall in Caithness or – as it was perhaps more recognisably known in first-century Scotland – Cattiness.

From the time they landed the Catti began to multiply significantly and adopted the local ways by joining the clan system as Clan Chattan. The clan spread throughout the north of Scotland and, as with all success stories of their time, what the Catti couldn't win with the sword they won by marriage. Most of all they seemed to have had a sixth sense when it came to making a decision about which side to support in the wars and power struggles of the coming centuries. By this time the family name had changed to Keth or Keith.

History tells us that the first Keith to draw a sword for his sovereign and profit by it was Robert Keith: he slew Cammus, a Danish invader, in single combat at the Battle of Barras in Angus in 1010. Rewards quickly followed with the grant of lands in East

---

[†] See Peter Anderson, 'Records of the Marischal College and University of Aberdeen', Leopard Magazine 1985–86. Also J.M. Bulloch, 'Studies in the History of the University', Aberdeen Quatercentenary Studies, 1906.

Lothian and Robert's appointment as hereditary Grand Marischal of Scotland. With his title came a motto *Veritas Vincit* or 'truth conquers' and a coat of arms. Concerning the origins of this heraldic device, the story goes that when the Battle of Barras was over, the King came to look at the dead body of Cammus the Dane and, pleased with what he saw, bent down and dipped his fingers in the Dane's still-warm blood to make three strokes, or pales, on Keith's shield. Yet another version tells that a noble combatant disputed the Keith claim of having killed Cammus and was then himself challenged to single combat on this point of honour. This dispute was resolved when Keith killed the nobleman and it was this noble's blood which decorated Keith's shield in three pales – this is perhaps a better and more satisfying explanation of the motto and coat of arms. Robert Keith went on to marry Margaret Fraser of Tweeddale and founded the Keith family which was to impact on so much of Scottish history.

We are centuries still from the little boy playing around Inverugie Castle with his brother, wheezing and coughing from periodic bouts of chronic asthma, a condition that was to plague him for the rest of his life, but that small boy was driven by the history of his powerful family – a history that matched Scotland's own.

In the fourteenth century, Sir Robert Keith was held in some esteem by King Edward I of England – known to history as the Hammer of the Scots. In classic and impeccable Keith style, he judged that it was the right moment to switch sides and joined King Robert the Bruce in time for the Battle of Bannockburn in 1314. In what was to become a family tradition, Robert Keith was to be found in the thick of the Bannockburn bloodbath, leading his light cavalry in a well-timed charge that scattered the deadly English archers and contributed in no small way to the Scots victory. Bruce rewarded the Keiths for this by giving them the lands of Buchan – satisfyingly, these had formerly belonged to their enemy the Comyn. At a stroke, King Robert the Bruce had secured a hostile part of the country for himself and bound the Keiths to the Scottish crown. When the King died, he gave instructions that his heart was to be cut from his body and taken on a crusade against 'the enemies of Christ': Sir James Douglas – or the Black Douglas as he was better known – went off to expedite his late King's dying wish. Sir James Douglas himself died fighting hopeless odds in a pitched battle against a Moorish enemy in Spain, where he threw the casket containing the heart of Bruce in front of him before charging after it to his death. Ancient stories suggest that it was a Sir William Keith[†] who recovered the casket and brought it back to Scotland for interment before the high altar of Melrose Abbey.

The family's rise to power was not all accomplished by the sword: with a marriage to an heiress of Sir Alexander Fraser, Chamberlain of Scotland and Bruce's brother-in-law, the Keiths gained great estates in Kincardineshire, in which county they proceeded to build their grim and impregnable family seat – Dunnottar Castle.

In 1458 the family title changed when the Sir William Keith of that time was made Earl Marischal and Lord Keith. His great-great-grandson, the fourth Earl, was known as William of the Tower because of his near hermit-like existence at Dunnottar. His contribution to the Keith fortunes came from his marriage to a kinswoman, the heiress of Inverugie, by which he nearly doubled the family lands – now reaching into seven shires: Haddington. Linlithgow, Kincardine, Aberdeen, Banff, Elgin and Caithness. He was reckoned to be the wealthiest peer in Scotland, receiving rents of 270 000 merks a year. It appears religion was also one of his strengths for, by the exact timing of a speech to Parliament, he helped the Confession of Faith over its last hurdle during the Reformation. As well as being a very wealthy man, according to accounts he liked to live like one. It is reported that by his 'magnificent living, and the vast charges he had been at in public office, he had drawn his estate into considerable burden.' When the realisation of how much he had spent and how much the fortune of a great family had depreciated during his stewardship sank in, he retreated to his Dunnottar stronghold until he had resolved his debts. This self-imposed incarceration lasted for over seventeen years, until all the debts were cleared.

[†] The Keiths were not terribly original in the names they chose for their eldest sons. In fact, they chose only William, Robert or George as first names, in much the same way as royalty tend to stick to just a few 'approved' names.

The beneficiary of this financial rectitude was the fifth Earl, George, who had spent sometime on the Continent in a mind-broadening exercise: all the civilised qualities which were manifest in James Keith and his brother George, more than 150 years later, were present in the fifth Earl Marischal. An oil painting now owned by the University of Aberdeen, shows this earlier George in a pose that was also to be adopted by his descendants, the tenth Earl and his brother James Keith. The Keiths were depicted 'head-on' so that the characteristic acquiline nose could be camouflaged and its size partially hidden for prosperity. Whether this was done at the direction of the sitters or because the artists were afraid either for their commission fee or their liberty is not known. A strong sense of humour may have been a Keith characteristic but so also was their sense of history. Paintings tend to survive long, long after the subjects have departed this life and James Keith could have had only one reason for having his own portrait painted so often and for being so sensitive to the eyes of future generations.

If any evidence is needed that the Keiths were intellectually above their noble counterparts, then George Keith, the fifth Earl Marischal, was a living proof. While his altruism in founding Marischal College was undoubted, it must be borne in mind that he had also done so to establish a rival institution to King's College, Aberdeen, which had been founded by the Church of Rome.

Marischal College was granted a charter on 2 April 1593, when the Earl – 'greeting true Christians all and each' – gave instructions for the building of his college. Perhaps to make some sort of point, he built it on lands and property that had until shortly beforehand belonged to the Franciscan Grey Friars of Aberdeen. This gift was made possible by the King who, on 20 September 1592 granted in life rent not only of the Aberdeen property and lands of the Grey Friars, but also the lands and Barony of Altrie which had formerly belonged to the Monastery of Deer. As the Earl's charter for a college instructed, it was to build a 'Gymnasium, in the buildings formerly belonging to the Franciscans where young men may be thoroughly trained and instructed both in the other humane arts and also in Philosophy and a purer piety.'

With the foundation stone came other fundamentals, such as: 'The nomination of all the teachers, or presentation as it is called, whenever a place is vacant by death, dismissal or resignation, shall be in the hands of the Earl Marischal, the Founder or his heirs.' Most interestingly, given the times, part of the college charter provided for 'having a care to provide for poverty' and the Earl not only allowed for six bursars but stipulated that in the matter of fees 'the poor shall be altogether exempt'. As Carlyle puts it, 'diviner pursuits were made possible on frugal oatmeal.'

Marischal College was a huge advance for education in the north of Scotland. The Earl also endowed his college with the privileges of a degree-conferring university and, out of his own pocket, endowed his creation with a sum to fund the maintenance of a principal and three professors. At this same time he gave a charter to the town of Peterhead itself, which could only have been given with the intention of boosting trade between that port and continental Europe.

Although the city of Aberdeen has had centuries to show some gratitude for Marischal College, other than a street name there is now nothing else to commemorate the city's benefactor.

As with his descendant James Keith, the fifth earl's Protestantism must have been a hardy plant to survive, and also like James Keith, his mother was a Catholic; she was Lady Elizabeth Hay from the neighbouring Errol family. He had been born about 1553 and into that tumult when a new Protestant faith was being forged; to cap it all, he went to the Catholic King's College, which must have been an extremely uncomfortable place for someone who declared himself to be a Protestant.

The fifth earl was very interested in culture and, we are told, applied himself to the study of many disciplines. He made progress in Latin, Greek and Hebrew, as well as developing an interest in history, antiquities and literature. This interest took him to Geneva, where he met Theodore Beza, a disciple of Calvin's, before going on a tour of the principal courts of Europe where it is said he made an excellent impression.

George's father died in 1580 and his grandfather the year after so, with his educational background and an inherited 270 000 merks from his estates, he was well equipped for the path he was to take in life. With his knowledge of languages and foreign

11

protocol he was an obvious choice to be sent to Denmark in July 1589 as King James's special ambassador to conclude details of the marriage between the King and Princess Anne. With characteristic Keith generosity, he took responsibility for the massive expense involved in this diplomatic mission. It was for this mission (and no doubt the fact that Keith picked up the tab) that the grateful King gave him the lands of the historic Abbey of Deer, as part of a reward that made Marischal College possible.

After his appointment as Lieutenant of the North by the King in 1593, and during disturbances caused by a Spanish plot – Keith acted with such firmness and calculation that the insurrection was quashed without bloodshed. For this he won the praise of the King and whole country and became Commissioner of the Scottish Parliament in 1609.

His private life was, however, less successful. His first wife was a daughter of the Protestant Earl of Home, by whom he had one son and two daughters. His second venture into marriage was with Margaret, daughter of the sixth Lord Ogilvy of Airlie, by whom he had two sons, one of which was James of Benholm. Family relations so deteriorated that he was forced to go to court against Benholm to complain:

> Maist unkyndlie and unnaturalie schaikin af these respective dewiteis of consideration quhairin in conscience befoir God and be the strait bandis of nattur he standis bund unto me and being unthankfull of the grite cair that I have had of his educatiouin & of the estait and leiving quhairunto I haue provydit him, he hes withdrawne himselff fra me and assotiat himselff with some personis, enimeis to my house, and quha huntis by all occasionis to mak thair advantage of this fyre of divisioun, quilk thay have raisit in my hous, and by thair counall he hes committit a number of insolencyes aganis me, quhairof some will resolve in criminall persutes, and utheris in civile persutes.

Family disputes surfaced once again after the fifth earl's death, when the Lady Marischal, who very quickly remarried, was impeached for having taken the Earl's 'goods, silver work and tapestry'. George, the fifth earl, had died at Dunnottar on 23 April 1623, after which the King intervened in what had become a huge and very public scandal, blotting a great public career. In a biting letter to the Privy Council in 1624, the King spoke of the 'unkynde, ingrate and insolent behaviour of the late Erle Merschels wyfe to hir lord and husband, who with hir sone Benholm, the Laird of Thorntowne [Strachan, whom she married soon after the Earl's death] and utheris, beside uther indigniteis, had in a thrifteous maner robbed the said Erle of writtis, money, plate, furnitour of his houses and uther things.' The King went on to explain his intervention as arising 'out of the regaird we had to the memories of that man who had to our honour and contentment served us at home and abroad in greatest charges.'

William Guild, Principal of King's College, composed a tribute to the fifth Earl's memory which played upon the family motto:

> As Trueth ov'rcomes and doth victorious rest,
> Thy loue to It hath made thee now most blest,
> Which with Thine happie Off-spring to remaine,
> Shall bee to them their onlie Glore and Gaine.

This interest in culture and languages and a generally academic quality of mind was handed down through the Keith generations: by the age of five, James Keith was already receiving tuition from a relative, and the later Bishop Keith. As he absorbed all that was going on around his family estates, the boy would already be learning Latin and Greek: both languages being essential for entry to Marischal College, since all the lectures at that time were given in either one language or the other. How the Keith churchman coped with the 'happie offspring' and his pranks is a matter for conjecture but James Keith did go on to Marischal College to take a degree.

An anecdote concerning George, the fifth Earl, highlights the degree of informality which existed at this time between the Scottish king, his nobles and subjects.

A country gentleman recorded in his diary that in July or August 1589, King James VI was attending this laird's daughter's marriage at the Craig of Inverugie. Other historical records bear out that the King was in the area at this time, having marched an army into Aberdeen to put down a serious revolt which had broken out in the north. Part of the military manoeuvres were in Buchan, where he took and garrisoned the Castle of Slains, principal seat of the Earl of Erroll, who was a main player in the insurrection. Now lost to the centuries, this visit by the King was commemorated by an annual, prolonged bout of revelry and high jinks at the Craig.

13

The King having taken that other castle road, the one which led to the south bank of the River Ugie opposite the castle, called on a shoemaker whose cottage stood on the edge of a deep pool known to today's anglers as the Sutor's Pot. Perhaps enjoying a lark or, playing to what he probably knew well of Marischal's sense of humour, he said 'Gang o'er and tell Geordie Marischal to come and speak wi' Jamie Stewart.' The sutor crossed the Ugie to the castle where he dutifully delivered the royal summons to the Earl who responded 'Man, the King's dune you mair honour than he's dune me.'

Of the sixth Earl Marischal we know little, except that with a classic Keith disregard for expense and an ongoing family interest in continental affairs, he set out in 1634 to intervene in European power politics by helping King Ladislas VII of Poland equip a fleet. At this time Poland was in a constant state of turmoil and formed a break in the Swedish-controlled Baltic. Why the sixth Earl should have wanted to involve himself in the troubled affairs of Poland is a question to which there may be no answer. In any event, he survived only until the following year, leaving three sons behind him: two of whom went on to claim the title and a third who became Earl of Kintore.

The seventh Earl was a rabid supporter of King Charles I and raised a troop of horse for the King's rescue during the English Civil War in 1648. He managed to escape from the rout at Preston and was able to welcome the King at Dunnottar – but he had chosen the wrong side and paid for it. For this mistaken allegiance he spent nine years in the Tower of London from 1651 until 1660.

The eighth Earl was the seventh's brother and like his immediate predecessors was drawn to Europe. For a time he soldiered in the French army where he gained a military experience which was put to good use in the Civil War battles of Preston and Worcester.

It is likely that both Dunnottar and Inverugie were well stocked with books and Keith family papers collected over generations. Certainly, young James Keith would have become aware of his family's history from early childhood and had extensive libraries at his disposal to fill in the detail.

For any child of the Keith family, the libraries and their documentation would have provided gripping reading and given the reader a sense of belonging to both a family and a national institution. Leafing through the books and documents, it must have soon become clear to James Keith just how much Keith blood had been shed for King and country.

For example, his history instruction would have told how Keiths marched with James IV of Scotland to meet the Earl of Surrey on 9 September 1513 at Flodden. Alongside their king, twelve Scottish earls, thirteen lords and five eldest sons of peers plus fifty chiefs, knights and around 10 000 men died in battle that day. Among the dead lying on Flodden field were two Keiths, the third Earl's two eldest sons. The bodies of the Keith brothers were discovered in a circle of nobles who had died in a 'last stand' around their king. Of all the factors that influenced and shaped the future of James Keith, his family's history has to be a major consideration.

But the Keiths were men of their times and any impression that they were islands of civilisation in a sea of barbarism, or indeed paragons of virtue would be mistaken. They seem to have had quick tempers and a disposition to react swiftly to events – sometimes too swiftly. For all his altruism and learning, even the fifth Earl Marischal was no exception. His early life was turbulent and he had been forced to seek a royal pardon for being 'art and part' in the slaughter of William Keith of Luquharn, his near relative. Getting away with murder, even in those days, involved him in the costly business of bribes. Only a little later he was arraigned before the King and Council for conducting a deadly feud with the Earl of Meldum – there were two sides to the Keiths.

Given the times, it is natural that the men of the family dominated events: but many of the women had strong personalities too. Sir William Keith, the ninth Earl, had two daughters – Mary and Anne. It is most unlikely that the girls received anything other than a basic education, if that, and would mainly have received instruction on how to run a castle household, entertain guests and support a future noble husband. Most of this tuition would have come from their mother. Lady Mary Keith, James's eldest sister, went on to marry John, sixth Earl of Wigtoun, and died in 1721. Bright, witty Anne, the youngest of the family, married Alexander, sixth Earl of Galloway, and died in 1728, one year before her mother.[†]

† The Scots Peerage.

15

Any idea that noble women only had a decorative role to play can be quickly put aside, certainly in the case of Sir William Keith's wife. She had been Lady Mary Drummond, eldest daughter of James, fourth Earl of Perth, High Chancellor of Scotland, and her family pedigree was very similar to that of the Keiths. Her family had also fought alongside Robert the Bruce during the Scottish Wars of Independence and had been rewarded with lands in Perthshire. At the Battle of Bannockburn, while Sir Robert Keith had led the Scots cavalry in a charge which wrecked the assembled ranks of English bowmen, the English cavalry was crippled by Malcolm Drummond, Lady Mary's ancestor, who was accredited with the strategic spreading of caltrops around the battlefield (spiked clusters for disabling enemy cavalry).[†] This Malcolm Drummond gave his daughter Margaret in marriage to Bruce's son King David II. Robert III of Scotland (1390–1406) married Annabella, the daughter of John Drummond of Stobhall and out of that marriage came their third son and Scotland's James I, who reigned from 1406 to 1437. During 1488 Sir John Drummond was made a baron. The fourth Baron became the first Earl of Perth and during the reign of Charles II was Commander-in-Chief of the Scottish army (from 1660 to 1685). During the period of the Commonwealth (1649–1659) Drummond spent some years in Russia, where he became a lieutenant general and military governor of Smolensk; on his return, he was granted the title of Viscount Strathallan. One of his descendants was mortally wounded at Culloden in 1746. On both parents' sides of the family, James Keith had antecedents almost fanatically loyal to the Stuart cause with long, impeccable military pedigrees and something of an instinctive Scottish nationalism: this history fired the blood of Lady Mary, her husband and their sons. The Countess Marischal's own family home was at Drummond Castle, some ten miles north of Sheriffmuir and a few miles south of Crieff near the village of Muthill. Lady Mary was a formidable woman by anyone's reckoning and a fanatical Jacobite supporter to boot. Her father, the Earl of Perth, was also intensely supportive of the Jacobite cause and at the instance of his monarch in exile had converted to the Catholic

[†] Michell MacDonald, *The Clans of Scotland*.

faith – going against the tide of religious feeling at the time. It was a faith which Lady Mary also shared.

Among those employed by the Keiths at Inverugie Castle was a chaplain, even though the Earl was given to attending the Kirk, near to where Peterhead Links are now, from time to time. It appears that Kirk services were taken on alternate Sundays by a Presbyterian minister and an Episcopalian minister; it is anybody's guess what faith the chaplain preached at the castle. Just how the Countess Marischal managed to observe the demands of her Catholic faith is hidden from us.

So much then for Keith family life at Inverugie. Sir William was engaged on matters of state in Parliament and ran his estates through trusted employees like Thomas Arbuthnot, his Baron Baillie in Peterhead. Lady Mary ran the castle while casting her eye around contemporary nobility in search of suitable husbands for her daughters, while the daughters themselves got on with whatever young ladies of quality did with their time, hoping no doubt that their husbands in an arranged marriage would meet their expectations in all departments. Lastly, James Keith and his brother began their days at 5 a.m. with studies under the supervision of a tutor in preparation for university entry.

2
·
A Power Behind the Throne
·

THE KEITH FAMILY OWNED many properties and estates throughout Scotland but they had two principal homes: Dunnottar, a castle stronghold perched on sea cliffs south of Stonehaven, and Inverugie Castle, birthplace of James Keith. Of all the Keith properties, Inverugie Castle was the place which James Keith and his brother and sisters were most likely to have called home – and counted their loyal support from the inhabitants of the surrounding countryside.

An earlier Sir William Keith, Grand Marischal of Scotland in the fourteenth century, had owned the Dunnottar headland site and decided he wanted to build a castle on it. Unfortunately for him, others had previously occupied the site and broken remnants of a Catholic church with its graveyard were a visible obstacle to the Marischal's building plans. Taking the view that it was his land and he would do what he wanted with it, Sir William went ahead – even though he knew that he was provoking the Church of Rome.

He then built his castle on what the church regarded as sanctified ground and for this impudence was duly excommunicated by the Bishop of St Andrews. In his defence against Catholic wrath he complained that he had only acted out of the necessity 'to protect himself from the tribulations and from the malice of the tyrants of the kingdom, and in order to obtain security for the persons and goods of his dependents.' On 17 August 1395 Pope Benedict XIII intervened to tell the Bishop of St Andrews to hold an enquiry and, if Keith's case was found to be reasonable, to lift his excommunication – on condition that the Catholic church be recompensed for Dunnottar's change of use (which is not to say they ever received a penny).

A new family seat now decorated the Kincardineshire coast and from then on it would prove to be a place of refuge from Keith enemies with superior armies: a place where the Regalia of Scotland would also be safely kept. Dunnottar was where kings of Scotland visited to be entertained at banquets while others less fortunate found themselves locked up in dungeons or awaited execution.

On 15 October 1504, King James IV was a visitor and there is a record saying that 'the cheild playit on the monocordis' and was paid eighteen shillings for the entertainment provided. Queen Mary visited Dunnottar twice, on 4 November 1562 and again on 5 September 1564. Her son James VI – whose visit to Inverugie is recorded in Chapter 1 – was also a guest at Dunnottar in June 1580. 'The kyngis grace,' goes the report, 'coyme to Dunnottar the 18th day of June, the yeir of God 1580 yeiris; and the fyrst time that I, Walter Cullen, reder of Aberden, sehit his graice, was the xx day of the said monett of June 1580 yeris, and that at the woid of Fetteresso, he beand at the huntis with sertanne of his lordis; and thair eftir I paist further to Dunnottar, fair I beheld his grace at supar, quhill he paist to his chalmer; and thair efter his grace paist furtht of Dunnotte, the xxviii day of June, 1580 yeris, to Egaill' [Edzell]. James returned again to Dunnottar Castle in April 1589, to receive the submission of disaffected Catholic lords. Three years later these same 'disaffected' lords had forgotten their submission and, when they again took arms against the King, Dunnottar fell to them but only for a month. It was again restored to the Keith family and was still theirs when James called for a third visit in 1594.

The year 1596 saw the north-east of Scotland in a frenzy of witch hunting and one John Crichton was sent to Dunnottar where he was to perish at the stake. If this was an age of strong religious faith, it was also a time of superstition, of ghosts, fairies, witches and demons. It has been estimated that between the fifteenth and seventeenth centuries more than 30 000 people, mostly women, were executed for witchcraft in Britain. The last known went to the stake in Essex during 1676, when eighteen 'witches' were executed. The last hanging for witchcraft in England took place in

1716, while the last execution in Scotland took place in 1722. It was to take until 1736 for the law allowing execution for witchcraft to the repealed.

You didn't have to be a witch to find yourself in trouble and locked up in Dunnottar: debt could just as easily be the reason for occupying a cell. On 6 November 1629 a certain James Keith of Craig, doing time in Dunnottar for debt, decided to attempt an escape, the details of which are described in a Privy Council minute. The minute tells us that Keith of Craig:

> craftelie perswaded all his keepers except one Johne Hamptoun to goe that day to the sermoun, quhilk they accordinglie did, and the said Johne, having according to his usual maner prepared some meate to the said James Keith, and having opened the doore of the prisoun to give the same to the said James, he in the meane tyme fiercelie sett upoun the said Johne, being ane old weaklie persoun, gave him three or four great strailes on the head with ane whinger and ane great straike on the right arme and brake his left arme in twa peeces and left the poor man for dead, and then he tooke up the keyes of the Castell, the whole people being at the kirk, and so escaped and brake waird.

Dunnottar grew along with the wealth of successive Earls Marischal and reached its peak in grandeur and fortification during the sixteenth century before the slow process of decline began.

During the Wars of the Covenanters the Keiths quickly fixed their flag in support of the new creed – almost. On 15 February 1639, the seventh Earl Marischal met with a committee of gentlemen at Dunnottar and 'thair declarit him self cleirlie to be ane covenanter, quhilk wes doubtful befoir.' In June of that same year, Aboyne made his 'Raid on Stanehive', only to be given a thorough beating by both Marischal and the Duke of Montrose, who had yet to change sides.

While Marischal dithered about his membership of the Covenanters and had on balance been more anti- than pro-, his dungeons at Dunnottar had been jail to those of the new faith.[†] Now, with his mind made up, the change was as sudden as it was decisive and a first batch of three anti-Covenanters found themselves swopping places with the opposition at Dunnottar. They:

† W. Douglas Simpson, *Dunnottar Castle Guide Book* Vol. 11 pp. 459–60.

had all thrie, to Dunnottar as antecovenateris, and wairdit in ane strait dvngeoun, put in ironis, but ony offens bot being the Kingis servandis. No comfort thay had of fyre or candle, meit or drink, or bedding bot lay fast in the ironis, day and nicht, without syunschyne or licht of the hevi, and wes miserable fed vpon broun bred and small drink during the space of fourteen dayis whill it pleissit the Lord to relieve thame.[†]

But Marischal's friend and fellow Covenanter, Montrose, took a decision to change sides. After beating Argyle's army at Inverlochy on 2 February 1645, Montrose marched on Elgin before turning his attention to Stonehaven. Montrose was the Rommel of the mid-1600s and regularly took on and defeated much greater forces than he had under his own command. Wisely Marischal retreated into Dunnottar along with some sixteen ministers who had of late preached the new religion from their pulpits. It was the custom for all the folks in the countryside around Dunnottar to lodge their valuables at the castle for safe-keeping in times of trouble; this was now one of those times. But while the valuables of these ordinary folk were taken into the castle, they themselves were left to face Montrose after Marischal refused to negotiate with him from inside Dunnottar.

When a royalist captain brought back the news of Marischal's refusal 'Montrose wes heichlie offendit'. So 'heichlie offendit' was Montrose that while Marischal watched from the safety of Dunnottar's battlements, Montrose proceeded to go on a rampage all over Marischal's lands. As a contemporary report of the times puts it

'Quhairvpone [whereupon] Montroiss, on 21st Merche, began and brynt wp the barneyairdis of Dunnotter, houssis, cornes, and all, quhilk the erll, his ladie and the rest within the place saw; syne fyris the tolbuith of Stanehevin, quhairin thair wes stoir of beir and cornes, and

---

[†] 'At that time, the Earl Marischal had a mansion on the north side of the Castlegate (from which the modern Marischal Street takes its name) and this house was occupied by Lady Pitsligo, a fast adherent of the Covenant. On the galleries in the court of this mansion, the bold Covenanters, nothing daunted, took their station on Sabbath morning; and first Dickson, next Henderson and lastly Cant in that fiery eloquence by which they were characterised – addressed the crowds that flocked to hear them, during the intervals of the church services.' King, *The Covenanters in the North* (c. 1644).

haill toun also, being the Kingis royall brughe, with the haill cornyairdis, houses, and bigginges, except the said James Clerkis bigging, quhairin [wherein] Monroiss himself wes quarterit. They plunderit ane schip lying in the harberie, syne set hir in fyre, with the fisher boitis lying thair. Thay brynt wp the haill toune of Cowie, houssis, biggings, cornis and corynairdis, and siclike; plunderit the haill gooodis, geir, horss, nolt, scheip, quhilk they cud get. Thay plunderit the persone of Dunnotteris houss, syne set the same on fyre. It is said the people of Stanehevin and Cowiy cam out, man and woman, children at thair foot, and children in thair armes, crying, houlling and weiping, praying the erll for Godis causs to saif them from this fyre, howsone it wed kendlit. Bot the poor people gat no ansuer, nor knew thay quhair to go with thair children. Lamentabill to sie! Fetteresso also wes fyrit, and ane quarter thairof byrnt; bot the haill lauche bigging and cornyairdis vtterlie distroyit and brynt up. Thay fyrit the plesant park of Fetteresso.s treis brynt, vtheris being grein could well not burne. Bot the hart, the hynd, the deir, the rae, skirlit at the sicht of this fyre; bot they warall tane and slayne. The horss, meiris, oxin, and ky war all lykuaies killit; and haill barrony of Dunnotter and Fetteresso vierlie spoilzeit, plunderit, and vndone.'[†]

This seventeenth-century report graphically details the miseries of ordinary people caught up in wars of which they knew nothing and cared even less. Even with spring about to begin, one wonders how many starved to death that year and in the following winter.

Chapter 1 described the friendship between the Marischals and Charles II and, indeed, on 8 July 1650 we find him being entertained by the Earl Marischal, with fresh salmon costing £4 12 shillings Scots, prior to heading south to fight for his father's kingdom. When he called again, a year later, seven lambs were on the menu, having been bought for the royal guest at a cost of £9 6 shillings and 8 pence Scots. After the Battle of Worcester on 3 September 1651, Dunnottar was the chosen repository for the Crown Jewels, the Earl Marischal being the hereditary Warden of the Regalia.[‡]

[†] Fetteresso was another Marischal estate.
[‡] The extent to which the Keiths were the power brokers of their time is highlighted by the clandestine visits made to Dunnottar by the exiled Charles II in both 1650 and 1651. Years before the monarchy was restored, Charles deemed it vital to solicit the Earl Marischal's support for a planned attempt to re-take his throne.

In early September 1651 one of Cromwell's generals, Overton, appeared on the Blackhills between Dunnottar and Stonehaven; Overton and his troops started battering the castle with their siege cannon. The castle was shorthanded during the siege and only thirty-five men rallied behind the walls. From his vantage point on the Blackhills Overton poured fire into the castle until, after taking all the Roundheads could throw at them for eight months, Dunnottar at last capitulated on 24 May 1652.

The main trophy sought by the Roundheads was the Regalia of Scotland and King Charles' papers but when the conquerors finally walked into Dunnottar there was nothing for them. All the papers 'aucht score sexteine severall peises' had been smuggled out stitched into a belt around a lady's waist. The Regalia had been lowered over the castle walls to the seaward side and taken away by a woman pretending to gather dulce and tangle in her creel. She then took them to Kineff parish church where they were concealed under the floor until the Restoration of the monarchy in 1660.

The thwarted Roundheads went on to create havoc in the fallen castle by demolishing the chapel; 'the famous Library also suffered prejudices by the Rebels.'

Dunnottar's dungeons remained in use and in May 1685 Covenanter prisoners, numbering 112 men and forty-five women, were pushed into what is known today as the Whig's vault, to remain there for the next two months. From Wodrow, historian of the sufferings of the Kirk of Scotland, there comes a sorry tale:

At Dunnottar, they were received by George Keith of White-ridge, sheriff-depute of the Mearns. This large company was thrust into a dark vault underground, one of the most uncomfortable places poor people could be in. It was full of mire, ankle deep, and had but one window towards the sea.

So throng were they in it, that they could not sit without leaning, or lying, and were perfectly stifled for want of air. They had no access to ease nature, and many of them were faint and sickly. Indeed all their lives were in great danger. In this miserable vault about a hundred of them were pent up all summer; and it was a miracle of mercy not all were killed. The barbarities of their keepers and the soldiers are beyond expression. The prisoners had nothing allowed them but what was paid for, and money was paid for cold water. And when the soldiers brought in barrels of water, and had sold it out in parcels to them until they began to weary of it, they would pour it into the vault to incommode them the more. Considerable numbers of them died, and no wonder, through such hardships; and it was boasted of as an undeserved favour by the soldiers, that they received the dead corps and disposed of them as they pleased, for none of their fellow prisoners were allowed to see them interred; it was too great a favour to allow them so much of the free air.

When the whole number had continued for some days in the great vault, the governor was pleased to remove about forty of the men to another small vault, which being narrow and low they were not much less straitened than in the great vault, and they were in hazard to be stifled, there being no air nor light there, but what came in by a very small slit or chink. The walls, it seems, were a little decayed, and some air came in at the bottom of the vault; and they used one by one to lie down on their belly on the bottom of the vault; that they might have some of the fresh air. By this means some of them, particularly the Reverend Mr Frazer, contracted a violent cold and dysentery. . . after some time spent in this melancholy posture, the governor's lady came in to see the prisoners in the two vaults and prevailed with her husband to make them a little more easy. Twelve of the men were removed from the forty to a better place, where they had room and air enough, and the women were removed from the large vault, and put into several rooms. This was indeed a great kindness, but they had an abundance of hardships remaining. . .'

After deciding that anything was preferable to their prison, some twenty-five broke out of the large vault through a small window over the sea and, at the risk of their lives, crept along a ledge to freedom. Only ten were to make it, while the other fifteen were retaken: after a savage beating, they then had burning matches put between their fingers. Some died of the pain and others had the flesh of their fingers burnt off to the bone.

During the spring of 1689, Dunnottar housed a garrison of sixty men with James Keith's father as their captain, holding the castle for the monarchs William and Mary. His appointment must have faced him with a special problem, for on 23 August of that year, the ninth Earl Marischal had seventeen Aberdonians in his custody, one of whom was a George Liddel, one of his own appointees at Marischal College, who was locked up with the rest as Jacobite suspects. These suspects remained under lock and key until 12 September of the next year and were then liberated under an Act of Indemnity by order of the Privy Council. As a fairly rabid Jacobite himself, it is easy to guess at Marischal's efforts on behalf of his friends locked up under his own roof. No doubt they received a more humane treatment than the Covenanter prisoners before them at Dunnottar.

The Keiths' principal home may be regarded as Inverugie Castle. Although work on the castle had begun in the 1500s, it seems likely that at least some of it was built by Keith's father William, completing the previous construction efforts of the big-spending founder of Marischal College.

Looking at the ruined castle today, with so much demolished or removed, it is difficult to visualise what was once a four-storey building. Castles such as Inverugie normally followed a similar design which meant that the towers faced diagonally across from each other. Perhaps this change in normal design was the result of an overweening confidence in the defence barrier posed by the river and high bank to the castle's rear. The great hall, which was on the first floor, had entry by an outside or forestair and had a vaulted roof with rib mouldings. This hall was itself spacious and had lofty arched window recesses with a large fireplace at one end. The kitchens were entered from the courtyard below and communicated by an internal stair in the thickness of the wall with the hall above. Leading off the hall were the entrances to the round towers which contained square-shaped rooms that had their access from a wheel stair winding up within each tower.

Today, we would shudder to think of some poor wretch lying in a dungeon below us while we had a meal, a bath or watched television; it is difficult to imagine a home with a dungeon. But Inverugie Castle had a dungeon, where offenders were kept to await the pleasure of m'Lord Marischal.

The power of the Earls Marischal over those around them was absolute – they controlled everything† from employment to the courts, where they dispensed justice and which could mean handing out a death sentence. Although death sentences were undoubtedly carried out, nothing survives either in books or local legend to

---

† 'On the creation of Peterhead into a Burgh of Barony, judicial power both civil and criminal within the Burgh became vested in the Earl Marischal and could be exercised either in his own person or by his Baron Baillie. As feudal Baron, the Earl Marischal held "power over pot and gallows" throughout his domain.' Neish, *Peterhead* p. 216.

tell us who met their end at Gallowhill, a few hundred yards from the castle, or how often the gibbet had a body swinging from it in full view of travellers journeying up the coast towards Fraserburgh.

Inverugie is only some two miles from the town of Peterhead which was within the overall supervision of the Earls Marischal and their Baron Baillies. The reader should also remember that the Keiths had a hand in church affairs, appointed teachers in the local school, levied taxes and customs and collected rent from tenants all over their extensive estates. No one transported in time from the Peterhead of the 1600s, with a population of between 800 and 1000, could look at the town today and recognise very much of what they saw. The population of Peterhead was decimated after flea-carrying rats brought bubonic plague ashore from foreign ships in 1645. The disease, with its symptomatic infected boils, delirium and vomited blood, ended the lives of 300 in just six weeks.† Some 500 of Cromwell's soldiers had been garrisoned on Keith Inch from where they had conducted a rule of terror; they also lost soldiers to the plague along with the locals.

Given the plague and the succession of failed harvests and famines which characterised the final decades of the seventeenth century, it is unlikely that Peterhead had a population of even 1000 by the century's end.

The town's Backgate really was just that and, from the harbour up the Backgate, along a line from Back Street and Marischal Street to the Kirkyard, lay the western boundary. All that there was of Peterhead lay between that line and the sea. Only two roads led out of the town, one skirting a heather bog – now the Links – on up Cairntrodlie before veering south to Longhaven and Cruden Kirk. The other road went westwards towards Inverugie Castle and up the coast.

Fishing was the principal industry even then, but the Earl Marischal owned the boats just as he 'owned' the vassal fishermen

---

† 'In 1644 some 500 of Cromwell's soldiers were encamped on Keith Insch with their headquarters in the 'castle' from where they conducted a reign of terror. In 1645 came the plague, carried by shipborne, flea-carrying rats from the Far East. Bubonic plague swept the town bringing boils, delirium and vomiting of blood. In just six weeks over 300 died with Cromwell's soldiers among the dead.' Neish, *Peterhead*.

who sailed them and the fishermen's tenement block accommodation which occupied an area from the Longate down to the harbour. Needless to add, the Earl also claimed the greater part of the catch. Instead of a bank pushing fishermen out to sea to repay a loan on their boat, as happens today, there was the Earl, or his Baillie to see that, weather permitting, his boats were out catching fish. If a fisherman didn't go out as often as the Earl would have liked then there was always the 'jougs', or iron manacles, from which he could contemplate his idleness. As late as the beginning of the nineteenth century a set of these 'jougs' could be seen attached to a house on the east side of the burn of Buckie in Banffshire.

Between Peterhead and Inverugie there were only two other clusters of dwellings, one at Almanythie, now integrated into the town, and another hamlet called Peterugie, just west of what is the Buchanhaven port of Peterhead.

The poorer houses in Peterhead would have been built from stones either carted up from the shore or from a quarry on Keith Inch and taken across a connecting neck of sand and gravel called the Quinzie, where a bridge now stands. These houses were constructed by bedding layers of stones in clay mixed with chopped straw or heather. Inside, the walls were plastered with clay and whitewashed with lime, while the roof was closed to the elements by divots and a heather thatch. Among the better off, houses would have been of the granite stone and lime variety, such as the Keith castle, which was little more than a fortified house standing guard over everything that came into or went out of the harbour over on the Inch.

Ships from Peterhead carried on a thriving trade with the Continent and brought back timber from Norway. In 1631 the Earl Marischal got permission to export twenty chalders of victual, half-beer and meal from the Privy Council. By the middle of the seventeenth century, Peterhead had gained some fame for the quality of its butcher meat and a Flesh Mercat with a slaughterhouse was built near the shore to take advantage of the seawater.

Burgeoning trade also helped to swell the numbers of skilled craftsmen whose talents came to be appreciated far beyond the town's boundaries. Since the Earl had a tight grip on all around him, it is easy to guess that, as part of a feu agreement, these craftsmen would have had to work on the Keith estates.

Peterhead became a port of call for windbound vessels from Europe and America. Coasters called with their holds full of wines, provisions, lime, slates, coal, hemp and timber. The harbour being shallow, imports had to be hurriedly deposited on the beach for those awaiting delivery as the ships themselves must have been anxious to unload and catch the tide. In times of boom and bustle the quays and beaches could only have been a shambles as goods piled up everywhere – a lot of it being moved off and disappearing in carts without any duty being paid. Nothing escaped the eye of m'Lord Marischal; so to put an end to this haemorrhaging of his revenues, a Public Warehouse thirty-eight feet long by twenty-two feet wide was built at the harbour.

By 1688 episcopacy in Scotland was on the way out but it was not until 1699 that the Episcopalian minister in Peterhead got his marching orders. The Keiths had been solidly behind this faith but now the minister, a neighbour of the Marischals in Brook Lane, had to go and be replaced by a Presbyterian. It is doubtful whether this change was anything more than a gesture and smokescreen thrown up by Sir William and his Catholic wife Mary for the benefit of others watching him from around Scotland. In any case, this same Episcopalian minister intruded into the little Kirk near the Links at the outbreak of the 1715 rebellion to occupy the pulpit. He read a proclamation levying men for the Pretender's service and a further proclamation declaring a Thanksgiving for the Pretender's safe arrival in Scotland. The minister took this Thanksgiving service on 2 February 1716 and prayed publicly for the Pretender under the name and title of King James VIII.

When it came to politics, it seems, religion was not and never could be an obstacle to the Keiths. Here we have James Keith's father, an Episcopalian, his mother a Catholic and James Keith himself a Protestant, all of them desperate to have a Catholic Stuart King on the throne.[†]

† In 1602 Gilbert Keith, son of the third Earl Marischal, fell foul of Kirk discipline and was charged with an incident involving fornication. He

The Keiths' dedication to education is beyond dispute and the young of Peterhead benefited from their enthusiasm to improve the schooling in the town. As with Marischal College, it was teachers chosen by the Keith family who taught, while the Kirk session supervised the day-to-day running of the school.

It is clear that the Keith family's grip on everyday life around them was tight. Nothing, it seems, escaped the eye of the Earl Marischal and the trickledown of power from the King to his loyal servant, the Marischal, continued its downward path to the Marischal's own servants. The system was based on loyalty and trust – with some fear as well.

It must be entirely possible that the distinguished career of another Scottish soldier had a great influence on the decisions made in adult life by James Keith. This was General Patrick Gordon, whose service in Russia James Keith mirrored almost exactly. The parallel of careers seems too much of a coincidence to have happened by sheer chance – rather it seems calculated choice aided by good luck.

Patrick Gordon was born in 1635 on his family estate at Auchleuchries, Aberdeenshire, into a staunchly Catholic family who were devoted to the Stuart cause. Like James Keith, he had an elder brother who was going to inherit the estates while Patrick was merely the 'spare' to the heir. With his Catholic faith there was no chance of Gordon entering university or finding a career in the army, so he went off to the Continent and was recruited into the Swedish army. After various adventures he was about to return to Scotland in 1660 at the Restoration of the new Stuart King, Charles II, when fate intervened and a Russian diplomat offered

---

told his accusers that had they but come to him sooner he could have told of them of fifty more faults. Refusing to submit to church discipline, he remained a pain to the church elders: for years he stayed away from the church – lighting fires in the streets at Midsummer eve (regarded as a superstitious custom), breaking windows of the Kirk and shooting bullets into its door. It took until 1609 for him to finally stand before the congregation and 'in maist humble maner . . . craif first God, then the ministrie and magistrattis, pardoun and forgiffness.' T.C. Smout, *A History of the Scottish People*.

him a commission as a major in the Russian army. He accepted the offer, and being a man of high principles and integrity, his rise in the esteem of Peter the Great was soon matched by rapid promotion.

He also served the Tsars Alexis and Fedor and the Regent Sophie, reaching the rank of general after wars against Poles, Turks, Tartars and Bashkirs. He returned to England in 1686 and so impressed King James II that the King did his utmost to free him from his Russian service to have him for his own employment. Patrick Gordon had come home to settle family business: both his father and elder brother had died and the family estate now fell to him. But to make sure he returned to Russia, his wife and family had been refused permission to accompany him back to Scotland and were to all intents and purposes held hostage.

General Gordon had come home to claim his own, although he hardly needed the Auchleuchries estate with what he already owned in Russia and his annual salary of 1000 roubles (to put that into perspective a Lutheran pastor of the time was only paid sixty roubles per annum). On his arrival in England he was met by King James, to be fêted in high society as a hugely successful and interesting personality. In due course he escaped the adulation of London and made his way up to Scotland: this time a victim of inquisitive Scottish society. As such, he was an invited guest at the Earl Marischal's mansion on the Castlegate in Aberdeen on 12 July 1686.

It requires but a little imagination to see in the mind's eye, Marischal and his guest talking over a leisurely meal before settling down in comfortable chairs thereafter to glasses of claret and hours of question and answer about Russia. It is only reasonable to assume that Sir George Keith, James Keith's grandfather, went back to Inverugie Castle and retold to his family what he had heard from General Gordon; about Russia, the prospects of career advancement and the attendant wealth.[†]

---

† 'In the evening, the Earle Marshall came to town, whom I visited, he comeing over to my lodging where we supped, and were merry. In the morning, I tooke my leave of the Earle Marshall, who went north.' *Diary*

Even more likely, when winter took its grip on the exposed north-east shoulder of Scotland and Inverugie castle was battered by gales or locked in by drifting snow, the tales of Patrick Gordon's Russia would have been heard again at the fireside by a wide-eyed James Keith. The Patrick Gordon story, that of a local boy making good, would have had a special interest in that Gordon's Auchleuchries estate neighboured that of the Keiths.

When Patrick Gordon came home, James Keith's mother Mary Drummond was still four years away from her marriage to Sir William but there would still have been contact between the small, noble group of Catholic diehards sharing the difficulties of belonging to an embattled faith. Who can say that Lady Mary did not hold Patrick Gordon up as a shining example of someone who succeeded by his enterprise and promotion of Catholic virtues probably linked with her own family's John Drummond, who also had a meteoric career in Russia.

of General Patrick Gordon.
(George, eighth Earl Marischal, succeeded his brother in 1661 and died in 1694. He had served in the French army and distinguished himself at the Battle of Worcester in 1651.)

3

·

A Jacobite Youth

·

THE FIRST OF THE children born to Sir William and Lady Mary appeared on 2 April 1693, some three years after their marriage. He was given the name George and was destined to be the tenth and last Earl Marischal. In future years the bells at Longside would annually and dutifully ring out to remind everyone of his birthday. The proud parents gave their firstborn the same name as the most illustrious of the Keith family, carrying on the naming tradition of choosing from a strictly limited list of historically significant names.

When his brother was born three years later on 11 June 1696, his father thus already had his heir. By the Scottish law of primogeniture this new arrival to the Keith family at Inverugie didn't stand to inherit very much but was a ready standby in case of the early and unexpected death of Sir William's eldest son: the old 'heir and spare' tradition of the aristocracy. Five days after his birth at Inverugie Castle he was christened James Francis Edward Keith, linking him from birth and by name with the Stuart cause and the Pretender, James VIII – for whom he and his family were to lose everything.

James Keith's immediate future was already mapped out for him. While developing an awareness of his status and acquiring all the social skills and graces necessary to young men of quality, he would have been plunged into his education from the age of five or even earlier. A near relative, later to become Bishop Keith, was drafted in to prepare the educational groundwork for entry into

University.[†] Long before he was ten years old James Keith would have been immersed in Latin and Greek syntax. Lecturers spoke Latin every working day with students replying in kind and it is probably no exaggeration to say that most were better at Latin than they were at English.

James would have had the attention of castle servants and all the other privileges and trappings of his high birth. He would have had a pony to roam all over the Keith estates; he most likely played around the boats in Peterhead harbour – it is known that James and his brother were often seen fishing together in the river.

In 1711 James entered Marischal College to take a law degree, just as his brother had done a few years before him. It seems that the problems of funding and accommodation were then as bad as or worse than they are today. A contemporary source tells us, 'For scarstie of chamberis and want of beddis to serve the haill studentis within the Colledge, sindrie of the schollaris were forceit to ly in the Town house quhair they were buirdit, to the great hindrance of their studies.'[‡] In the Marischal College of 1699 the university's poverty was marked and recorded thus: 'The Hall, in particular, lay for many years without windows.' When James Keith arrived Marischal College had an ambience of piety coupled with a Jacobite sympathy that was altogether understandable when five of its seven key posts were held by Keith appointees. Jacobitism was much stronger at Marischal than at its sister university of King's. By 1700 most of the students and lecturers must have been outspokenly Jacobite and we are told that they burned an effigy of the Pope as a demonstration of Protestant fervour. It may well be that James Keith found his Protestant faith while at university.

[†] 'His education as a boy was, from 1703 to 1710 – that is from his seventh to his fourteenth year – supervised and directed by his young kinsman, Robert Keith, who afterwards became Bishop of Fife and Primate of the Scottish Episcopal Church (1743–57).' Robert Anderson, *Memoir of Marshal Keith*.

[‡] Jennifer J. Carter and Colin A. McLaren, *Crown and Gown*; Shewen, J.S. Brown and C.I. Beattie, *Marischal College Buildings 1594–1844*.

At the beginning of his degree course in 1711 James would have studied Greek in the first year, logic in the second, ethics in the third and physics in the fourth. Unlike most of his fellow students, there would have been no problem with accommodation, food or clothes: his family happened to own a mansion in Aberdeen, and a lot of other property surrounding it.

It is difficult to believe that with his nature, his Jacobitism and his privileged position James would have plunged himself into his studies and been lost to the politics of his time in cloistered academia. A more easily acceptable picture would be one of a teenaged James Keith agitating among his student friends and arguing for the return of his namesake James VIII. Before the end of his course at Marischal College the Jacobite rebellion against King George I erupted; in 1715 teaching was suspended for two sessions and all but one lecturer was removed from their posts. How diligently James Keith attended to his studies can only be guessed at but we know his mother employed an additional tutor for him – a tutor as rabidly Jacobite as Lady Mary herself, one William Meston A.M. (Artium Magister).[†]

Meston was also a friend of Keith's brother George who appears in the Marischal College records as a magistrand in 1712. Meston was a regular at the inns and taverns, a leisure-time politician who didn't need too much drink before raising his tankard for a toast to the Pretender. He had a quick wit which would have immediately endeared him to the Keith family and was a raconteur of some note, with rhyming propensities. With Meston at her son's side exerting a Jacobite influence, Lady Mary herself continued to control Keith's teenage years.

William Meston resigned from his position at the Aberdeen Grammar School on 27 May 1713, to take up his new appointment as Keith's tutor – exactly one year to the day after Keith's father had died.[‡] Meston's job entailed being with his young charge on a day-to-day basis, supervising and helping with his studies, for

---

[†] J. T. Findlay, *William Meston A.M.* Buchan Field Club 1902–1903.
[‡] Sir William Keith's death on 27 May 1712 is unremarked upon by any historian.

which he would have had grace and favour accommodation. The name of James Keith appears as a magistrand in 1715, when he was about eighteen years old. It must have been a cosy employment for Meston, with holiday breaks to the Keith castles of Dunnottar, Inverugie and Fetteresso. To broaden James Keith's political and cultural interests it is only reasonable to suppose the pair went off to London to see the sights. James Keith could have found no better companion that Meston to accompany him around the drinking houses, meeting a rich mix of company and 'broadening his outlook'. For his loyal services and support to the Keith family Meston was appointed Professor of Philosophy at Marischal College in November 1715, but he was never to do very much in that last appointment.

As 1714 drew to a close disruption at Marischal College grew and Jacobite activity increased. It was reported that 'Ill disposed persons at Aberdeen did in the night time, and under the disguise of women's apparrell, proclaim the Pretender'; and that 'On August 10th after midnight some young men, attended by several women, went through the streets with two viollers playing to them, who played seall tunnes, one whereof was "Lett the King enjoy his own again". And they came to a fountaine a little above the Cross and took water in their hatts and drank the pretender, King James his health; but cannot learn of any proclamation.' These demonstrators were, however, warned of the approach of authority and managed to avoid arrest. It is tempting to assume that James Keith was a part of these disturbances, which were largely a reaction of the death of Queen Anne in London on 1 August.[†]

The ailing monarch, long plagued by ill health, had no living heir, despite seventeen pregnancies. Well before her death a power struggle had been taking place between the Tories, who favoured the succession of James Edward Stuart (the Old Pretender) and the Whigs, who supported the Protestant Elector of Hanover. As Colonel of the Guards and close to the sovereign, George Keith was drawn into the intrigue surrounding the royal succession.

---

† Gila Curtis, *The Life and Times of Queen Anne.*

Blatant support for the Stuart cause from staff and students almost wholly Jacobite in sympathy led to the closure of Marischal College just as James Keith should have been graduating. There is no clear record of him receiving a degree but his military records from Berlin say that he did. What seems likely is that he left university early in 1715 and set out for Edinburgh to take up a law apprenticeship but decided in short order that the law was not for him. An altogether different life now appealed to him: he wanted a military career, having chosen to follow the path of his brother George. His mind made up, he set out for London to seek a commission in the British army, little knowing that before the year's end he would be fighting against that same army at Sheriffmuir. As James Keith left Edinburgh to make his way south to London, his brother George had already left London and was even then on the road north to Scotland.

George had taken his degree at Marischal College and gone straight into the army, serving with Marlborough in the Netherlands and elsewhere on the Continent and distinguishing himself as a soldier. Throughout their lives the two brothers were in continuous correspondence with each other so we can assume that there were regular letters home to Inverugie Castle and to James Keith at university, telling of battles won and brave deeds done. George had first joined the Scots Grenadier Guards in Edinburgh where old Keith/Hay animosities had at one time flared into a messroom brawl – the climax came when George was injured by a bottle flung at him by the Earl of Errol.

When the Jacobite Lord Ormonde replaced Marlborough he appointed George Keith as his senior brigadier with a rank of Lieutenant General. Later still, Queen Anne appointed him Colonel of the Second Scots Troop of the Horse Grenadier Guards. Through all the scheming and plotting leading up to Anne's death, George Keith was there in the middle of it and immediately after her death George, Ormonde and others huddled in discussions as to how they could ensure a Jacobite succession. It seems clear that with characteristic Keith impulsiveness George proposed using his troops to stage a coup, since at that time there was only one other regiment stationed in London (belonging to the Whig Duke of Argyle) that was likely to offer any opposition.

From what we know of George Keith there is no way that he would have been indiscreet or proclaimed his proposal to the world: a much more likely probability is that a Jacobite party which 'leaked' badly and was under constant surveillance made the Keith offer known to the Whig opposition. Not surprisingly, when Marlborough returned in June 1715 to resume command from Ormonde and instigate a general 'clean-up', George Keith had his command taken away from him. His career in tatters and with nowhere else to go, George Keith started on his way up the road to Scotland and home.

Three years had come and gone since Sir William Keith had died, leaving his estates to be run and rents collected for the family by his widow. These estates were scattered the length and breadth of Scotland and the problems of administration must have been an added burden for the Countess. Whatever her talents the widow must have found it a difficult if not an impossible job on top of all the other demands on her time: she had standards to maintain, servants to pay, two daughters for whom she had to find suitable husbands and James Keith's university expenses, not to mention the huge costs of George Keith's commission in the army and the crippling costs of maintaining him at Queen Anne's court. The Keith family lived like royalty and had an aristocratic disregard for matters of finance which amounted almost to contempt. It could well be that while the Keith family still had extensive land and property holdings, they were strapped for cash because of a lack of management in their financial affairs. They were never any good at business and burdened by a simple generosity, or *noblesse oblige*, which led them constantly to give sympathetic and generous handouts whenever the occasion offered itself.

Sometime in July 1715 the Keith brothers met at an inn in York. This meeting has been related elsewhere as if it were some sort of coincidence, when in fact it could well have come about by arrangement. Sitting down to discuss their future, it was obvious to both that George's army days were over: his bitterness must have communicated itself to James. Equally obvious was the fact that James Keith's own Jacobite sympathies and his brother's recent loss of job did not do very much for the younger brother's prospects of a career in the British army. Power and money went with high office and it must have seemed to the Keith brothers that their present position – out of favour and out in the cold – spelled disaster. With a Whig government and a Hanovarian monarch about to ascend the throne everything pointed down a disastrous road to financial ruin. This conclusion must have been clear to the brothers if cash flow from the Keith estates was also drying up.

A clue as to the parlous state of the Keith finances is given to us by John St Clair of Sinclair whose explanation of how the Keiths were drawn into the 1715 uprising runs:

> Next thing to be done was to draw into the affair some one who had the character of a general to give the thing a name. He [the Earl of Mar] knew the Earl Marischall, who had little or no estate, was a younge man of ambition; and though his familie was sunk, yet the name of it had influence in this countrie, which he'd readilie make use of to resent the injurie done to him in taking away his regiment, and it being uneasie to him to accomodate himself to the way of liveing that his necessities reduced him after haveing so latelie tasted the sweets of a regiment.

Sinclair was related by marriage to the Keiths: he could well have been speaking the truth. We have this picture then of the two brothers talking over their difficulties and options in that York inn, struggling to find a way forward. When going home to build up the family estates and in time regaining favour in London – when the dust had settled – should have seemed the best solution, it was not to be the one they chose. The Keiths had always prospered under and enjoyed the goodwill of Stuart monarchs; besides, the Pretender had promised to turn the clock back by giving an undertaking to repeal the Treaty of Union if he were to win the British throne. It must all have appeared dazzlingly simple: the Stuarts had to make a comeback and the Pretender had to be made King, while the Keiths as kingmakers and powerbrokers would also be back behind the throne.

James Keith not only belonged to a powerful family: his whole upbringing had emphasised a duty to support that family and give direct and unquestioning help to the head of the family – at this time his brother George. James Keith was always loyal, with a sense of duty and an ability to focus on what immediately needed doing which went hand in hand with a capacity for quick decision making. Such qualities made him a natural soldier.

A decision had been taken at York from which there would be no turning back. Mounting their horses, George and James Keith took the road back to Scotland to stake their all with the Jacobite uprising of 1715.

4

.

1715: Defeat at Sheriffmuir

.

A s THE KEITH BROTHERS hurriedly rode north another angry man, in the person of the Earl of Mar, was also making his way to Scotland to take a leading role in the Jacobite rebellion – although with much less speed and in a much more sedate and cautious manner. In the preceding months Mar had exerted himself to cultivate George Keith and succeeded in recruiting him as an active rebel in the Jacobite cause; George Keith was now much too committed and in far too deep to extricate himself – had he even wanted to. In stark contrast to the Keith brothers' progress north, Mar's journey was both hesitant and unsure, almost as though he would have welcomed an excuse to change his mind and abandon his plans for a rebellion.

Accompanied by Major-General Hamilton and Colonel Hay plus two servants, Mar first changed his usual clothes to make sure he wouldn't be easily recognised, before slipping out of Gravesend on 2 August on board a ship bound for Newcastle. Transferring vessels at Newcastle, this party of five eventually entered the Firth of Forth and landed at the Port of Elie on the Fife coast. With no great hurry or urgency, Mar went along the coast to Crail, where he met with Sir Alexander Erskine, the Lord Lyon, and other Jacobites at the house of John Balfour, where he spent a few days before going on to visit his brother-in-law, the Earl of Kinnoul, at Dupplin in Perthshire. It was to take Mar until Thursday 18 August before he finally said his goodbyes to Kinnoul and left for his home at Kildrummy Castle, accompanied by forty horsemen and crossing the Tay about two miles below Perth.

On 19 August Mar despatched letters to all the leading Jacobites, requesting their presence at a grand hunt to be held over
many days from 27 August at Braemar. The hunt stratagem was a
well-used cover previously employed by the Jacobites when they
wanted to meet – their actions were under constant surveillance by
a watchful government.

While Mar's letters were winging their way to influential
Jacobites the Keith brothers, with their old friend and mentor
Meston, entered Aberdeen and proclaimed the Pretender at the
Market Cross on 20 August 1715. After York they had wasted no
time and by this direct action they effectively forced the pace of
rebellion, setting in train an inevitable sequence of events which
pushed all the other main players into quickening pace.

By the following day George Keith, James and Meston had left
Aberdeen for Inverugie and made another proclamation for the
Pretender at Peterhead. This ceremony took place somewhere near
and to the rear of where James Keith's statue stands today.

What has been described so far may appear to be the ill-
considered actions of two hot-headed young men but the truth is
their adventure had every chance of success with only a modicum of
good luck and decisive action. During the reign of Queen Anne the
strength of British army had been allowed to drop to around 30 000
men, something of which George Keith must have been very well
aware. Most of Scotland was heartily sick of the Union, blaming it
for a devalued currency and the prevalence of poverty and misery.
The first part of the seventeenth century had seen plagues which
cut down large sections of the population, and the last ten years of
the century records a succession of failed harvests. The turn of the
seventeenth century saw huge numbers of starving, destitute people
wandering the roads looking for help and food, while many simply
fell and died at the roadside. Although modern science can look
back and tell us that this famine was worldwide because of a 'mini
Ice Age', in an age of witchcraft, omens and curses, it was likely that
the Union took more than its share of the blame for this time of
tragedy in Scottish history. Population figures suggest there were
only about one and a quarter million people in Scotland at this time,
with about eight in every ten working on the land.

It was a far different Scotland from that which we know today: it
had no fenced-off fields or roadside dykes and was almost treeless,

with only gorse and broom affording some cover over what we would describe as moorland. Currency was a huge disaster, with the Scots pound worth only one-twelfth of a pound sterling, further undermining cross-border trade. The century's most spectacular financial crash was the Darien scheme – an all or nothing, do-or-die speculative venture which lost family fortunes throughout the land. It has been estimated that the £400 000 sterling invested from Scotland, and lost in the doomed project, accounted for half of the country's entire capital funds. Money was so short around 1700 that one in every seven Scots noblemen was marrying an English bride with the rather less than noble thought of a fat dowry paid in pounds sterling.

Agriculture was in a similarly sorry state; the linen industry was idle and new taxes were levied on malt at six pence per bushel and customs were being imposed on imports such as claret where none had been payable before.[†] To put it baldly, Scotland was broke and in a very bad way as poverty and a cash crisis worked its way through all levels of society. Although the nobility had its pride and struggled to keep up appearances, most of them were as penniless as the lower ranks.

The Keiths now had real financial problems, faced with an urgent need for cash to equip and feed the rebels. A focal point for recruitment, where at least some of the manpower shortage could be addressed, was to be Inverugie Castle where a Buchan ballad tells us:

> With a cheer, the brave retainers
> Heard the words of noble Keith;
> With a cheer they quickly mustered
> Bent on victory or death.
> With a cheer they drain their goblets,
> And the glasses from them fling,
> Marching out from Inverugie,
> To the standard of their King.

The estates around Inverugie were rabidly Jacobite but just how many did in fact march out of Inverugie with the Keiths is not

---

[†] See Bruce Lenman, *An Economic History of Modern Scotland*; also L.M. Cullen and T.C. Smout, *Comparative Aspects of Scottish and Irish Economic and Social History 1600–1900*.

known. There is nothing in local history books, or even folklore, to suggest that the Keith brothers drove tenants and servants out to join the rebellion with dire threats, as Mar and some other Jacobite leaders were to do. What evidence there is seems to indicate that the men from Buchan who joined the rebellion did so from conviction and were true volunteers.

We can assume that the Countess Marischal would have assembled all the funds she could lay her hands on to help her sons and the cause she held dear. Even so, money must have been a real headache and it is likely that an appeal would have been made for everyone to give whatever they could spare. Years later we read that the Earl Marischal's nanny, a Mrs Gordon, was handed a poke of gold coins by a tearful George, as he remembered how she had sold her cow to finance his later rebellion in 1719.

Time was now pressing and by 26 August 1715 the brothers were back in Aberdeen with their men, where they replaced the magistrates and council with their own appointees who then raised more cash for the cause by levying a special tax on the city. From this new administration came an imposition under sanction of a 'head court' – a contribution from the city of £200 10s 9d sterling towards supplying the new army. From Aberdeen they marched on to Castletown of Braemar to join the Earl of Mar, who on 3 September proclaimed James VIII, raising his standard three days later.

A series of delays then occur, as the army assembled and the Keiths returned to Aberdeen on the 26 September, where the Depute Sheriff read out a manifesto and declared the Stuart Pretender King. On 1 October the Keiths and their men left Aberdeen accompanied by the magistrates and council, who probably only went with them as far as the city outskirts. The destination was now Perth, a prearranged rendezvous with Mar and all the other rebels emptying out of the hills and glens and crossing to the mainland from the isles.

Now that the speeches and proclamations were at an end, the brothers realised that Meston, their old friend and trusty tutor, had little place in what was to follow and they left him as governor of Dunnottar to hold it in the name of James VIII. Meston received his appointment as Professor of Philosophy at Marischal College later that year.)

The Keith section of the Jacobite army would have taken the coastal route southwards, collecting recruits from all the towns and hamlets on their way, before they then swung inland towards Perth, where they were to join up with Mar and the rest of the Jacobites.

Over the years since Sheriffmuir there have been numerous accounts of what took place before and after the battle: the present writer's source is the report of one who actually took part in the battle and its aftermath. Although only nineteen at the time, James Keith left a fragment of memoir recording what happened. It explains how and why the Jacobite cause was lost at Sheriffmuir and how the ancient Keith family lost its lands and what little there was left of its fortune.

While the Keith brothers had been proclaiming the Pretender in Aberdeen and north-east Scotland, others had also been busy. Tullibardine had done the same at Dunkeld, colonels Balfour and Hay at Perth, Huntly at Castle Gordon, Panmure at Brechin, Southesk at Montrose, Graham of Duntroon proclaimed at Dundee and Macintosh of Borlum seized the town of Inverness in the name of the Pretender before marching on to join Mar at Perth. The 1715 rebellion was well alight.

Mar himself set out from his estates to march by the spittal of Glenshee and Moulin, just outside Pitlochry, through Logierait and Dunkeld to Perth. By all accounts it was an unhurried and almost leisurely march south. There were also other members of the extended Keith family en route to Perth; the Earl of Kintore with his son John rode out from Keith Hall to join the insurgents, although inexplicably late for the earlier ceremony of raising of the standard. Another of the family to arrive at Perth was Lord John Drummond, James Keith's cousin and son of the exiled Duke of Perth, who had arrived from France with instructions and the Pretender's assurance that he would soon be joining the rebels.

Bobbing John, as Mar was known to his contemporaries,[†] was ill suited to the role he had cast for himself. He was hesitant, lacked

---

[†] 'Bobbing John' was a tribute to his ability to 'duck and dive' as circumstances dictated. He went with the flow until he saw a better deal or, for some other pragmatic reason, it became prudent for him to jump ship.

confidence and any decision came only after a tedious debate with all around him. His main claim to the leadership of the Scottish Jacobites came from the close liaison existing between himself and the leading English Jacobite conspirators, Bolingbroke and the Duke of Ormonde, who had persuaded Mar to run the Scottish end of the rebellion. According to James Keith, Mar had been given £7000 sterling and a promise that as soon as the rebellion began in Scotland, English Jacobites would simultaneously launch their own campaign. What was to follow, with Mar unsure of himself and dithering as he awaited news of a huge and popular uprising in England, must have had the Keiths pacing about in frustration.

Perhaps the only quick decision taken by Mar was forced on him by the necessity to secure the Perth rendezvous – this was easily accomplished by Colonel Hay, son of the Earl of Kinnoul, who was despatched on this mission with only 200 horsemen.

In October 1715, James Keith, his brother and their men, joined Mar and the assembling Jacobite army at Perth. Numbers vary and a contemporary journal credits the Keith contribution to the Jacobite army as being 300 horse and 500 foot. The acerbic Master of Sinclair, a relation of the Keiths by marriage quoted earlier, tells it differently, scornfully commenting: 'Marischal brought not fourscore of horsemen to joyne us, and they very badly mounted on Galloway cobs.' Just as Mar needed the credibility of the Keith name and Marischal's recent military expertise, it might also be the case that Marischal needed handouts from the army war chest on a regular basis.

After reaching Perth, the Earl Marischal quickly realised that if he was to have any influence on events and weight in the councils of war then he needed far more men under his command than he had brought with him from Buchan. According to Sinclair, Marischal set about adding to his command by telling the MacFiersons that they were part of the old Clan Chattan, his kinsmen, and he their 'live chief'.

Be that as it may, Marischal remained one of Mar's favourites and, apart from getting his army pay, he also received various sums of money from Mar – as much as £500 on one occasion. Sinclair further relates that Mar, in order to dig Marischal out of the embarrassment of his too-few forces, gave him two squadrons of horse from among those assembled 'for he did not like his own by no means, their horses were not so good as those of the southern counties.' He went on: 'Marischal was so modest as not to say one word, as I think he had reason.'

How the nineteen-year-old James Keith filled his days can only be a matter for speculation; his memoirs give no personal details. He very probably took up an adjutant's role at his brother's side and, of course, the Jacobite army was camped quite close to Castle Drummond and his mother's family estates. It must have been an exciting experience to be at Perth and watch the daily arrival of fighting men from all the corners of Scotland. At this time it was a high-spirited army, caught up in a sense of adventure, while Perth itself was a scene of preparation, with skirling bagpipes sounding above voices shouting in Gaelic or Doric to each other. As the Jacobites began fortifying Perth, another Keith contribution to the cause in the shape of fourteen pieces of cannon from Dunnottar were built into the defences. From all reports, the integration of the arriving forces into one army at Perth was a colourful if sometimes chaotic business. There were country gentlemen in laced attire, armed with sword and pistol and accompanied by their serving men – also on horseback – who had come from Aberdeenshire, Kincardine and Angus. From the Highlands and Islands came clan chiefs and gentlemen in even more colourful outfits, accompanied by their plaid-clothed clansmen, who wore only two thin vests under the plaid. These clansmen were not only to experience the rigours of battle but the survivors were afterwards to face the extremely bitter winter of 1715–16. Amid howls of laughter and hoots of derision came two squadrons of little ponies mounted by large Highland men with small bonnets jammed on their heads – with neither boots nor pistols. It took this comic cavalry two hours to dismount and join the camp.

The Highlanders' lack of proper winter clothing was to be a disaster. As James Keith explains:

one must know the habit of the Highlanders and their manner of fighting; their cloaths are composed of two short vests, the one above reaching only to their waste, the other about six inches longer, short stockings which reaches not quite to their knee, and no breeches; but above all they have another piece of the same stuff, of about six yards long, which they tye about them in such a manner that it cover their thighs and all their body when they please, but commonly it's fixed on

46

their left shoulder and leaves their right arm free. This kind of mantell they throw away when they are ready to engage, to be lighter and less encumber'd, and if they are beat it remains on the field.[†]

Shortly after Mar's departure from London to raise the Pretender's army, the Duke of Argyle also took the road north to Scotland where he assembled forces loyal to the House of Hanover. Argyle's forces, although better equipped and disciplined, were only 1400 strong by 25 September and the odds were increasingly stacked against them as Jacobites descended daily upon Perth. Mar himself had arrived at Perth on 28 September and, instead of pressing on to meet up with Argyle and give battle, he chose to act the part of military governor by issuing edicts and reviewing troops. He lost weeks which could have been better employed in capturing the whole of Scotland and at the same time dealing with Argyle's smaller forces.

Despite his war chest, Mar seems to have been desperately short of money, arms and ammunition. That cynic, the Master of Sinclair, says that:

'While everyone was building castles in the air, and making themselves great men, most of our arms were good for nothing; there was no method fallen on, nor was the least care taken to repair those old rusty broken pieces, which, it seems, were to be carried about more for ornament than use, though the gunsmiths were not wanting; but this was either because he who took upon him the command expected no powder from the beginning, or because what was everybody's business was nobody's.'[‡]

We have here a picture not so much of an army command structure, but of a disorganised leadership who, even making allowances for Sinclair's increasing cynicism and biting wit, could not possibly have inspired anyone in the Jacobite ranks who was able and willing to recognise the task that lay ahead. Whatever else, the Master of Sinclair was a realist and prepared to translate his words into action when an opportunity presented itself. To make good the shortage of arms in the Jacobite army he set off

---

[†] *Memoir of Field Marshal Keith.*
[‡] See Christopher Sinclair Stevenson, *Inglorious Rebellion: The Jacobite Risings of 1708, 1715 and 1719.*

with eighty men to raid an ammunition ship anchored in the Forth. Although he did not get all the arms he had expected, his highly successful escapade was a source of inspiration to the Fife Jacobites and brought still more men to the cause.

By this time the Jacobite army had swollen to around 7000 men and problems caused by boredom and inaction began to manifest themselves. A lack of quarters, pay and discipline further aggravated the situation until mutiny became a distinct possibility. Perhaps to relieve some of the pressure, Mar despatched General Alexander Gordon with some of his troops on a mission into Campbell country, possibly as a diversionary thrust to distract Argyle's attention or maybe even hoping to draw him away from his key strategic position, holding the Stirling gateway to the south. Shortly after Gordon's departure he sent old Macintosh of Borlum off with another 2000 men to bypass Stirling by making a Forth crossing during the first week of October. With a flotilla of small boats this force left the harbours of Crail, Elie and Pittenweem for Leith.

Although the Macintosh task force captured Leith, it went on to bypass Edinburgh and march on down into England where it hoped to join up and give encouragement to English Jacobites. In doing so it missed out on the main chance – to circle round behind Argyle and link up with General Gordon's forces which were to the west of Stirling. Defying his instructions from Mar and enticed by the prospect of the easy conquest of unprotected English territory, Macintosh of Borlum departed from Scotland and the coming battle.

As Macintosh disappeared into England, General Gordon reappeared from his foray in the west, bringing Mar's strength up to 12 000 men. It was now time for swift action and there must have been considerable pressure on Mar to get on with it – not least from Marischal. After a council of war on 9 November a plan was finally decided: the Jacobites would leave three battalions to hold Perth while the rest of the army marched to Dunblane. The idea was to detach some forces to keep Argyle pinned down while the rest marched on to take Edinburgh before following Borlum into England.

As always, the Jacobite plans were quickly 'leaked' to Argyle's intelligence people and with only 3000 troops Argyle marched out to meet the Jacobite army at Kippendavie, just outside Dunblane. On 10 November Mar's army left Perth and by nightfall were at Auchterarder where, during the night, the Frasers with 200 others crept off into the darkness. The Jacobites then marched to Ardoch and Kinbuck where they they spent the night of 12 November, before spreading out into the five-mile corridor of Sheriffmuir, formed between the Ochils and the River Allan.

The Jacobite army faced Dunblane with the Ochils on their left and the Allan wending its way on their right. Between them and Argyle's army lay an undulating terrain of small hills and rough ground which obscured the disposition and numbers of the opposing armies from each other. The Jacobite army should have drawn up in two lines of battle – that was the plan – although Sinclair tells us bitingly that he doubted 'since the invention of powder were so many troops packed in one small place. It cannot properly be said we had a front or rear any more than has a barrel of herrings.'

By Sunday 13 November, some kind of Jacobite order of battle had formed, with ten battalions of Highland foot soldiers forming the Jacobite front line and a second line made up of six battalions with the Perthshire and Angus squadrons of cavalry on the Ochil flank. James Keith and his brother were on the right, River Allan flank, with their squadrons of horse. Facing the Jacobites were Argyle's six frontline battalions backed by a second line of two battalions to strengthen the loyalist army's centre, and all three squadrons of the loyalist horse dragoons were concentrated on the Ochil flank.

In the near farce that followed, it was Argyle who made the first move, having spotted only part of the Jacobite army from his observation point near Dunblane. One can only speculate, of course, but had Argyle seen the whole extent of the Jacobite army that Sunday – an army which outnumbered his own by three to one – he might have decided to retreat, with his army falling back on Stirling. Whatever was going through Argyle's mind, he ordered his dragoons forwards to attack Mar's left flank, having seen what appeared to be an opportunity to inflict damage upon the still assembling Jacobites.

Meanwhile, Mar had spotted some of Argyle's troops on a rising piece of ground in front and ordered Marischal to take his squadrons of horse forward, both to clear the enemy troops and to cover the right flank of his front-line's advance.

Marischal with James Keith took their squadrons of horse forward accompanied by Sir Donald Mcdonald's foot and, on reaching the top of the rising ground, discovered the whole of Argyle's army marching along in front of them preparatory to forming into battle lines.

James Keith tells us what happened:

> On our approach, the enemy horse retired; and we no sooner gained the top of the hill than we discover'd their wholle body, marching without the beat of drum, about two musket shot from us.
>
> It was now too late to retrait; we therfor form'd on the top of the hill and the Earl Marischal sent an aide-de-camp to advertise the Earl Marr that he was fall'n in with the enemies army, that it was impossible for him to bring off the foot, and therfor desired he wou'd march up to his assistance as quick as possible, which he did even in too much haste; for the army, which marched in four columns, arrived in such confusion that it was impossible to form them according to the line of battle projected, everyone posted himself as he found ground, and one columne of foot inclined to the right and another to the left of the Earl Marischal's squadron of horse, that regiment which shou'd have been on the right, found itself in the center, separated from the rest of the horse, and opposed to the enemies foot; our foot formed all on one line, except on the left, where a bog hinder'd them from extending themselves, and increased the confusion.

Confusion was also apparent among the assembling enemy troops of whom James Keith and his brother had a clear view. Despite the pervading shambles in the Jacobite ranks, a chance too good to miss had presented itself and needed only a brave decision to carry the day. Lieutenant General Gordon seized the opportunity and ordered a Jacobite charge on the exposed left flank of Argyle's army.

A Highland charge was an awesome spectacle and took some stopping once it got under way, carrying all along in its path. The practice was to run up to within musketshot, then loose off the shot before dropping to the ground, just as the smoke from enemy lines signalled their returning fire. They then discarded their six yards of plaid and with sword in hand sped over the intervening ground to hurl themselves at the enemy.

Various reports of the Battle of Sheriffmuir have accused the Earl Marischal's squadron of riding down Jacobite foot but it seems quite clear that this 1715 equivalent of 'friendly fire' was unavoidable given the chaotic start to the battle. The Jacobite charge was immediately effective and within ten minutes, James Keith tells us, 'six regiments of foot and five squadrons of dragoons, which composed more than half of the Duke's army was entirely defeated.' On the other side of the battlefield Argyle's right wing had taken similar advantage of Mar's left flank, and James Keith says that 'Both parties pursued the troops they had broken, not knowing what had happen'd on the other side, till at length the Earl of Mar, having had the fatal news of the loss we had received, order'd the troops to give over the pursuit, and having rallied them returned to the field of battle, from whence we discover'd the enemy posted at the foot of the hill amongst mud walls, on the same ground where we had layen the night before.'

What James Keith does not tell us is that during that first charge on the enemy or, at some other time during the battle, he was shot in the shoulder and the musketball carried some of his clothing before it into the wound. The night of 13 November was spent at Castle Drummond in agony and in the care of his relatives.[†]

Having lost control of events from the beginning, Mar now let a further initiative slip through his fingers. Instead of returning at once to the attack by launching his army downhill on to Argyle's now depleted forces, Mar held yet another field conference. On the basis of an inaccurate report that both armies were of equal strength and, considering that his Highlanders had had nothing to eat for two days, he let his chance, and the enemy, slip away unmolested. At nightfall the Jacobite army returned to the previous night's village quarters some way off the battlefield. Mar had made a colossal blunder in being too ready to believe the officer reporting on Argyle's strength. The officer had based his estimate on the number of colours in evidence – rather than on the amount of ground occupied by the enemy. Keith goes on to tell us of yet

---

[†] 'James Keith, riding in his brother's squadrons, got the first of his many wounds . . . The ball, which had penetrated his shoulder, had embedded the shirt in the flesh, and he passed the night of the battle in torture at Drummond Castle.' Robert Anderson, *Memoir of Marshal Keith*.

another blunder, when Mar ordered all his horse from the left flank to go to the right, leaving the poor infantry on the left flank without the cover of their own horse and exposed to that first charge by Argyle's dragoons.

Mar awoke on 14 November, to commit yet another blunder. When his left flank had fled before Argyle's dragoons, they had quite vanished and by Monday not yet returned to him. This prompted Mar to put still more distance between himself and Argyle by marching back to Perth. Argyle had similarly seen enough of battle and began to prepare his retreat to Stirling – but not before returning to the Sheriffmuir battlefield where he picked up all the discarded arms lying about and, crucially, the Highlanders' plaids which were their main protection against the November cold. As a consequence, those of the Jacobite army without clothes were sent home to the mountains and glens to get themselves new garments and bring back with them those clansmen who had fled earlier.[†]

As the Jacobite army licked its wounds at Perth bad news reached them from England. They learned that while they had been fighting at Sheriffmuir, Macintosh of Borlum and what few English Jacobites had joined him, had been penned up in Preston by superior forces and soon surrendered. Not only was Borlum and the prospects of an English uprising gone, but the Dutch had made good their promise to support the Protestant succession. Even then some 6000 Dutch regular troops were rapidly moving up to Stirling to be put into action against the Jacobites.

[†] A contemporary ballad-maker was to give his account of the Sheriffmuir affair thus:

There's some say that we wan,
And some say that they wan,
And some say that nane wan at a' man.
But ae thing I'm sure,
That at Sheriffmuir,
A battle there was that I saw man,
An' we ran an' they ran,
An' they ran an' we ran,
An' we ran and they ran awa' man.

It was now starkly apparent to all that the English part of the uprising, which had been thought to be the principal part, had totally collapsed. From the very beginning, even before Mar left London, they had been talking bigger than their numbers warranted; James Keith estimated their strength as never more than 800 men. If there had been doubts before about the prospects of success, there were now no hopes at all and a deep depression settled on the Perth camp. Some of the Jacobite leaders quietly put out feelers to discover what terms could be expected if they surrendered.

The Marquesses of Huntly and Seaforth declared that their own lands and properties were now at risk from the Earl of Sutherland and departed with their men, promising to return in the spring. For the Keith brothers there was nothing to retreat to, so they stayed at Perth with Mar, his 4000 foot soldiers and 500 horse, to await an enemy reinforced by Dutch troops that promised to be about 12 000 strong. They hastily began to add to their fortifications at Perth, hoping that the combination of a hard winter and strong defensive positions would buy them time until their own reinforcements arrived with the spring.

With no hope of supporting troops being sent by the French, the outlook could not have been more bleak – but another player in this drama was already on his way from France. James Francis Edward Stuart, the Pretender, had left Dunkirk aboard a small, well-armed vessel laden with a cargo of brandy which was to land him and his five companions at Peterhead on 22 December 1715. It was a Christmas present the Jacobites could well have done without. The group stayed one night in Peterhead and then moved on to Fetteresso where they were met by Mar, Marischal and, almost certainly, James Keith.

One of the group around the Pretender deserves further mention because of the part he was later to play in securing positions in foreign service for James Keith. This was the Marquess of Tinmouth, son of the Duke of Berwick and later, as the Duke of Liria, the Spanish ambassador to the Russian court. Born at St Germain in 1696 he was, like James Keith, just nineteen and had been his father's adjutant in Spain in 1710. He distinguished himself at the Siege of Gerona and in 1714 received the Golden

Fleece in recognition of his services to Spain. Subsequently, he went into Flanders where he joined the Pretender on his voyage across to Peterhead and the Jacobite rebellion. Exactly the same age as Keith, and of a very similar upbringing, it would indeed have been strange if the two nineteen-year-olds had not found more in common with each other than with the elderly nobles around them. The Duke of Liria conscientiously kept a diary of his daily life and this may explain James Keith's own (less than successful) imitation that resulted only in an interrupted fragment of a memoir.

From Fetteresso the Jacobite leadership and the Pretender began to make their way back to Perth and a waiting army. Their route took them through Dundee and they entered the town with Mar riding at the Pretender's right hand and Marischal at his left. By the beginning of January 1716, they had arrived at Perth, where orders were issued to those who had meantime taken their leave to return with haste. But a shortage of money, deep snow in the Highlands and a growing lack of confidence in the main participants of the rebellion, ensured that the Jacobite army continued to diminish even after the Pretender's arrival at Perth.

Argyle had meanwhile been joined by generals Cadogan and van der Beck at Stirling, bringing with them Dutch regular troops, two regiments of English dragoons and a train of artillery. The Duke of Argyle's commission had by this time expired and was not being renewed, perhaps because his masters thought he had not pursued his mission with sufficient vigour. Overall command was now transferred to Cadogan, who was undeterred by the harsh winter weather and took his Hanoverian army out of Stirling to march on Perth. Cadogan's preparations for the march on Perth had not gone altogether unnoticed by the Jacobites and they burned all the villages and hamlets between Stirling and Dunblane. What purpose this was supposed to serve cannot even be imagined because by this time the reality of Perth's poor defences and haemorrhaging Jacobite forces had already made the evacuation of Perth an obvious necessity.

At midnight on 30 January 1716, the Jacobite army left Perth in two columns, one taking the coastal route by Dundee and the other taking an inland route which was to rendezvous at some point northwards. James Keith and his brother the Earl Marischal, along with Mar, the Pretender and other main players, took their places with the column on the coastal route, arriving at Dundee on the following night. They passed through Arbroath the next day and arrived at Montrose on the third day out from Perth. The coastal column pulled up at Montrose to learn that the inland column had almost simultaneously arrived at Brechin, six miles away. The plan up to this juncture had been to pick up reinforcements along the route of the retreat before turning around for a decisive battle somewhere around Inverness. However, Cadogan was in hot pursuit and had given his army only a day's rest after their march from Perth to Stirling; he was even now hard on the Jacobite heels. By now the Jacobite army had shrunk to only 3000 well-armed men, with 1000 barely armed at all and between 700 and 800 horsemen – all without enough ammunition for even one day's action.

Another Jacobite conference took place and Mar advised the Pretender to return to France. With the total collapse of the rebellion in England and only bleak prospects of gaining any more recruits, Mar knew that defeat was staring them in the face and it was not a matter of if, but when. Besides, the logic of Mar's argument went on, if the Pretender left for France, and it became known to the pursuing Hanoverian army, they would slacken their march and allow time for the Jacobite army also to escape. To negotiate terms and disperse was the only possible finale for the rebellion. At best they could but hope that what was left of the Jacobite army would make it to the mountains and await help from France.

The Pretender dithered, or seemed to, before asking Marischal for his advice which he was hesitant to give, owing to his lack of years and experience, asking that he be allowed to first talk it over with Mar. When together, Mar repeated to him all the positive reasons for getting the Pretender away on a ship to France, probably thinking of quite a few good reasons why he should also be on that same ship himself.

James Keith tells us what followed in his brother's discussions with Mar: we can only assume he was standing at Marischal's elbow to hear it all. Marischal said:

tho we were in a bad situation he did not think the case was so desperate as he [Mar] represented; that the troops we had in the north wou'd amount to about 7000 foot and 400 horse, which wou'd make us very near equal to the enemy; that it was true we had very little ammunition but we cou'd get as much out of Aberdeen and the places we past as wou'd serve to try the fate of a day, and even if we lost it, we wou'd be no worse than we wou'd be in taking the present course; that for the King's person, he did not apprehend it cou'd be in danger, because by sending ships away to the west of Scotland, where there was so many harbors for them to lye in, he cou'd make his escape from thence with even less danger than even the port they were at, the mouth of which was blocked up by two enemies of war; and to conclude all, he did not think it for the King's honour, nor for that of the nation, to give up the game without putting it to a tryall.

Mar listened to the impassioned speech from the young Earl Marischal but he had already made up his mind. The last thing he wanted now was a debate; for a ship had been ready and waiting since the evening of 4 February to take the Jacobite leadership and the Pretender to France. Mar heard Marischal out and told him that he would advise the King not to go, even as preparations for boarding the *Maria Teresa of St Malo* were actually taking place. Along with the Pretender went the Dukes of Mar and Melfort, Lord John Drummond, Lieutenant General Sheldon and a few servants. They set sail leaving Lieutenant General Gordon to command the army – and two letters: one to the clan chiefs explaining this hurried departure, the other to the Marquess of Tinmouth (later Duke of Liria) advising him and some others to board another waiting ship and make his escape.

This other ship had also fled, however, and it was now too late for anyone else hoping to leave for France that night. As it happens, the Keith brothers had also been given orders to make their way on board this second ship but scorned to obey the order, preferring instead to share the fate of their countrymen. No sooner had the Pretender and his companions set sail than orders were given to the Jacobite army to resume their march northwards, the cavalry being already six miles up the road ahead. To pacify the troops it was given out that the leadership had only gone on to Aberdeen where they would all meet up again and, as

morning came in, the Brechin column rejoined them at Stonehaven, where Meston was still holding Dunnottar Castle.

News of the Pretender's flight inevitably leaked out to the
Jacobite army and despair fell upon their ranks. By this time any
thoughts of a strengthened force turning around to give battle
must have been fast disappearing from the minds of James and
George Keith. Sill hard on the Jacobite heels, the Hanoverian
army were now at Montrose, where they were greeted by the news
that the birds had flown. They gratefully accepted this as good and
sufficient reason to stop and catch their breath.

While Cadogan and this troops rested, the Jacobites pushed on
to Aberdeen where a council of war was held in Marischal College.
The council debated whether the original plan for a 'last stand' at
Inverness was still an option worthy of consideration or whether it
would not be in everybody's best interests just to reach the
Highlands and disperse into the safety of the mountains. Unanimously, the hard core of rebels left decided to march on Inverness
but along the way to call on the Marquess of Huntly, who had left
Perth before the retreat began, and ask if he would again assemble
his men and join with them.

General Gordon sent the Earl Marischal to speak with Huntly
and as James Keith tells us, 'he easily perceived by his answer that
there was nothing to be expected from him, and that we must be
reduced to our last shift of gaining the mountains.' Within two
days what was left of the Jacobite army had reached Ruthven in
Badenoch where it was judged it would now be best to dismiss the
troops. James Keith goes on: 'From thence every one took the road
that pleased him best.'

The Keith brothers took the company of Sir Donald MacDonald
of Sleat, who had been with them at the opening Jacobite charge
at Sheriffmuir, joining with Clanranald's regiments who were
going home to the Western Isles. James Keith arrived in the Isles
about the middle of March 1716, after a long and tiring journey
during which he witnessed the loss of nearly a company of men in
a capsizing boat. He was to wait there with his brother for about a
month, since none of the ships they had sent for dared to run the
gauntlet of enemy men-of-war vessels cruising around the coast. As
if this were not bad enough, intelligence was reaching them daily

about two battalions of enemy troops who were waiting to embark on three frigates sent to Skye for their transportation out to the Isles. At last, on 20 April, old style, the Keith brothers along with another 100 officers had themselves a ship to get to France and James Keith says that 'after a very pleasant passage arrived the 12 of May, new style, at St Paul de Leon in Brittany.'†

There is a version of the retreat to Ruthven in Badenoch which says that the Keiths broke off from the main body of the army to visit Inverugie Castle and their mother. Apart from giving their mother advice on what she could expect, the other objective of the visit was to remove things of value from the raiding Hanoverian soldiery and dismiss servants while warning them to seek a place of safety. The Keith family plate was supposed to have been conveyed to a small hut in a field on what is now called Mountpleasant to be hidden: this hut would have been about a mile from the castle. While this tale certainly adds a touching human aside to the retreat, it may well have happened, for some 400 gentlemen broke off from the Jacobite march to take a ship from Peterhead to Wick in Caithness. The Jacobite retreat left Aberdeen for Inverugie and Oldmeldrum before going on to Huntly and the town of Keith itself. It would have made sound common sense for the Keith brothers to have broken off at Oldmeldrum with 400 gentlemen making their way to Peterhead, so that they had this security before catching up again with the main retreating body.

What subsequently befell Lady Mary, the Countess Marischal, left alone to face the wrath of an angry Hanoverian King and government in her Inverugie Castle home? As a punishment, the Keith estates were forfeited by the Crown and put up for sale at auction. They were bought by the York Building Company, a company which had diversified from its original business of supplying water from the Thames to the City of London. The York

† The introduction of the Gregorian calendar (made law in Britain and its colonies in 1752, though in use in Roman Catholic countries from 1582) endows the precise dating of events at this time with a certain cavalier charm.

Field Marshal James Francis Edward Keith by Antoine Pesne
(National Galleries of Scotland)

Keith's father, William Keith, 9th Earl Marischal, attrib. William Aikman
(in the collection of the Grimsthorpe and Drummond Castle Trust)

Keith's mother, Lady Mary Drummond by John Alexander
(in the collection of the Grimsthorpe and Drummond Castle Trust)

Keith's brother, George Keith, 10th Earl Marischal
(in the collection of the Paxton Trust)

Keith's elder sister, Lady Mary Keith
(National Galleries of Scotland)

Frederick the Great with Field–Marshal James Keith

George Keith's house at Sanssouci Palace, Potsdam

James Keith's memorial tablet inside the church at Hochkirch

Kaiser Wilhelm I's gift to the people of Peterhead: statue of Field Marshal James Keith

Building Company had scented quick and easy profits from the purchase and swift resale of sequestrated Jacobite property – but they should have stuck with what they knew best. Poor management and their venture into the unknown sector of property dealing led to the company's bankruptcy.

When the Keith property and other forfeited estates came on the market there was little interest and, not surprisingly, great difficulty in finding buyers. So great were the York Building Company's problems with resale that it had to let out its new acquisitions to former Jacobite owners, their friends and relatives. In a few cases, forfeited families were able to repurchase their own property at bargain prices. For these reasons – but more likely because Lady Keith had residual rights, as widow of the late Earl Marischal – she was allowed to stay on at Inverugie Castle. When Hanoverian troops arrived at Peterhead in the wake of the departing Jacobites they were to loot and sack the little castle on Keith Inch, although Inverugie Castle itself was left unmolested. Untouched by Hanoverian hands, lack of money for repairs to the castle meant that it was going to fall into ruin anyway.

Even in a catastrophic financial state, with her sons fugitives, her servants all gone and her daughters married off into distant parts of Scotland, Lady Mary Keith remained an unrepentant, committed Jacobite. Folklore has it that a servant maid, who had left service at the castle on her marriage prior to the rebellion, called at Inverugie Castle to pay her respects. While speaking with Lady Keith she mentioned how sad she was and how much she regretted the loss of the family's fortunes as a result of the Keith brothers' adherence to the Stuart cause. It was the wrong thing to say, for the Countess Marischal is said to have risen from her chair, making no attempt to hide her displeasure and with a scornful look told her visitor: 'Woman, if my sons had not done what they did, and what I bade them do, I would have gone out myself with my spindle and my rock.'†

A few years later another visitor came to the castle: William Meston. The sometime fugitive was now free to come out of hiding

† William Boyd FRSE 'Old Inverugie'. A lecture to Peterhead Mutual Improvement Society 1885. p. 24.

as an Act of Indemnity passed by Parliament forgave his earlier active Jacobite support. At Inverugie Castle he was given a welcome, a home and Lady Mary's protection, which was to continue for the next twelve years. Such was the Keith loyalty, pride and generosity, that she would probably have gone without herself to make sure that Meston ate. Although her roof may have leaked and money been somewhat tight, Lady Mary had well-heeled connections and both her daughters were married to earls by this time. It seems that Meston made a contribution to his board and lodging by publishing poetry and, of course, he had his entertainment value when Jacobite friends or family called.

The eldest Keith daughter, Mary, died in 1721 and Anne, the youngest of the family in 1728, while the Countess herself died in Edinburgh on 7 March 1729. By that time Inverugie Castle was already in a ruinous state and, immediately it became known that the Countess had died, roving bands of thieves from St Fergus and Peterhead began to strip the castle of its furniture and whatever else took their fancy.

Meston found himself a new benefactor in the person of the Countess of Errol, whose help enabled him and his brother to establish a flourishing academy at Turriff. Violence was very much a part of the times and it followed Meston around, even at Turriff Academy: one day his pupils were fooling around in a field when one of them pulled out a knife and stabbed a companion; the lad with the knife was one James Grant of Dunlugas. Incredibly, this James Grant went on to become a Major General in the Prussian army under Field Marshal James Keith and was Governor of Neisse in Silesia when he died in 1764. Meston himself died in the spring of 1745, just as a tragic replay of the 1715 rebellion was about to begin. His death took place 'in the straits of poverty' somewhere in either Peterhead's Longate or Wine Well (Jamaica) Street.

There is no way of knowing now whether Meston gave a guiding hand to Lady Keith's own poetic efforts during the sad and lonely years between the 1715 rebellion and her death in 1729, but there is a poem attributed to her which has come down through the centuries telling not only of her inner grief but of a still defiant woman.

When the King comes ower the Water

I may sit in my wee croo hoose
At my rock and the reel to toil fu' drearie;
I may think on the day that's gane,
And sigh and sab till I grow wearie.
I ne'er could brook, I ne'er could brook
A foreign loon, to own or flatter
But I will sing a rantin sang
The Day our King comes ower the Water.

O gin I live to see the day
That I hae begged and begged frae Heaven,
I'll fling my rock and reel away,
And dance and sing frae morn till even!
For there is ane I winna name
Wha comes the bingin byke to scatter;
And I'll put on my bridal goon
That day our King comes ower the Water.

I ha'e seen the gude auld day,
The day o' pride and chieftain glory,
When Royal Stuarts bare their sway,
And ne'er heard tell o' Whig or Tory.
Though lyart be my locks and grey,
And eild has crooked me doun – what matter?
I'll dance and singe another day
That day our King comes ower the Water.

A curse on dull and drawling Whig,
The whining, ranting, low deceiver,
Wi' heart sae black and look sae big,
And canting tongue o' clishmaclaver!
My father was a good lord's son
Mi mither was an earl's daughter,
And I'll be Lady Keith again
That day our King comes ower the Water.

In a Scottish Record Society Publication of 1900[†] we learn that the Countess Marischal was buried at Holyrood on 14 March 1729 'on the south side of Lady Blair.' she had found her last resting place

---

[†] The Register of Burials in the Chapel Royal Holyrood House 1706–1900.

in a Catholic burial ground – there is no record of where her husband lies, but it is most probably in the Keith mausoleum in Dunnottar kirkyard.

As Inverugie Castle and Jacobites in the north-east of Scotland braced themselves for the Hanoverian revenge, Parliament was busying itself in pushing a Bill of Attainder through the House. On the very day that George, the Earl Marischal, James Keith and all their comrades were setting sail from Uist to France, the Keith family was being stripped of its rank, honours, lands and property. If caught, Marischal was condemned to lose his head at the hands of the public executioner for treason. The conspicuous part James Keith had played in the rebellion had not gone unnoticed but, surprisingly, when the revenge lists were being drawn up by the Crown they seem to have overlooked his ownership of some land. Not that it mattered in any case, for in later years he was to put it at his brother's disposal, to do with as he wished.

For those who did not find a ship to France or a safe hiding among the mountains and glens of north-west Scotland the penalties were severe. Among the most harshly treated were the English Jacobites captured at Preston, some of whom were shot out of hand while the rest were shipped off to slavery in America. A sorry column of about 300 chained men were marched down to London and through its streets, lined with jeering, shouting onlookers, to await their trial and for some their execution. In the post-rebellion atmosphere there was an air of expectancy, a grim certainty about how the trials would finish. Both government and populace were demanding blood, and blood is mostly what they got.

However resolute and dignified the Jacobite prisoners, however calmly the condemned might have faced their accusers, the ferocity of the sentences when read out must have stopped the hearts of even the very brave. They were warned that they 'would be drawn to a place of execution; when you come there, you must be hanged by the neck, but not till you be dead; for you must be cut down alive, then your bowels must be taken out and burnt before your faces; then your heads must be severed from your bodies, and your bodies divided each into four quarters; and these must be at the King's disposal. And may God Almighty be merciful to your souls.'

For some of the Jacobite prisoners the axe fell. Others were to be released from their prisons a year later under the Act of Grace legislation: some actually escaped from the Tower of London by ingenious means and ruses. Lord Nithsdale's determined wife engineered his escape and the two of them fled to Rome, where they spent their remaining years together. The Earl of Wintoun cut through the bars of his prison window before his execution could take place and also escaped to Rome. Together with his son, Brigadier Macintosh of Borlum took part in a mass breakout – both of them got away safely to France.

It was a brutal end for many and, for many more, a brutal existence as slaves in America. The scale of retribution by the Hanoverian government was not as great as might have been expected, however, and the death toll by execution fell far short of what it could have been. As if wanting to put all the bloodshed behind it and quickly get Britain back to normal, the government passed an Act of Indemnity in 1717, which offered pardon and forgiveness to the rebels.

5

.

The Exile Begins: Paris

.

THE SHIP FROM UIST carrying the Jacobite soldiers arrived in the Breton port of St Paul de Leon on 12 May 1716, where the new exiles disembarked and promptly divided into two groups. One group made for Avignon – papal territory – to where James Stuart had decamped because of political pressure and where he now held his little court. The second group – including the Keith brothers – took the road to Paris, where more bad news was to meet them: James Drummond, Duke of Perth and the Keiths' maternal grandfather, who had spent the last twenty-three years at St Germain, had died that very day.

During the days of retreat to the mountains of Scotland that followed Mar and the Pretender's departure at Montrose, the Earl Marischal became an increasingly bitter man as he realised how badly Mar had bungled the Jacobite enterprise. His criticism of Mar was loud and long. Even on the ship to Brittany he continued to blame Mar for the Jacobite failure, but both Mar and Marischal knew that a post-mortem examination of the rebellion would take place and no doubt both of them were rehearsing arguments and excuses to sustain their own positions and deflect any blame elsewhere.

James Keith was on the fringe of all the bickering and in due course, after meeting relatives long exiled in Paris, he made his way to see the Queen Mother Maria Beatrix (the Pretender's mother) still living in the old chateau at St Germain, to kiss her hand. There seems to have been an instant liking between the old·

lady and James Keith, who tells us she 'received me very gra-
ciously; told me she had already heard how I had behaved myself
in her son's service, and assured me that neither of them shou'd
ever forget it; in a word, had I conquer'd a kingdome for her she
cou'd not have said more. I ask'd her permission to go to the King,
but she told me I must stay in Paris; that I was young, and that she
wou'd put me to the [Military] Academy to learn my exercises.'

But it was to take about a month for the old lady to get around
to making good her promise and during that time James Keith
lived by selling his horse tack and anything else which would help
him to make ends meet. He was too embarrassed to ask his new-
found relatives for help, which they could well have afforded and
gladly given, while his other friends and relatives in Scotland did
not yet know where he had gone or have an address to which to
send money.

A month passed after his audience with the Queen Mother; then
it all began to come together again when the old lady sent James
1000 livres and orders to enrol at the Academy. At the same time a
Parisian banker called on him to say that he had orders from
Scotland to supply him with money and that the 'King' had
ordered payment to him of 200 crowns per annum.

So there he was, a young war hero of nearly twenty, from one of
Scotland's most ancient and noble families, who had seen battle in
his King's service and been wounded in action. From various
descriptions of the time Keith was above (the then) average
height, probably about five foot nine or ten, and of squarish build.[†]

[†] The following description of the Field Marshal's personal appearance
[many years later] is given by Mr Dixon in Temple Bar: 'It was in
September, 1747, that Keith came to Potsdam. You may see him, as he
appeared to the Berliners of these days, in Metzel's striking woodcut, a
weatherbeaten, rugged soldier of some fifty summers. Rather above the
middle height, strongly but perfectly proportioned, he is shown wrapped
in his military cloak, his fur trimmed hat pressed firmly over his brows,
grasping his field glass in the fingers of his right hand. The nose is
slightly aquiline, the complexion bronzed, the chin square and massive,
the mouth straight and determined yet drooping at the corners into a
faint indication of quiet humour. A face expressive of unfailing honesty

His colouring was fairly dark and tanned, inherited from the Drummond side of the family, although the rigours of army life accentuated it until he appeared positively weatherbeaten. A portrait by Antoine Pesne dated 1753 shows a man aged about thirty-eight rather than the true fifty-seven one can deduce from the date of the paintings – Pesne was in the habit of stripping away years to flatter his sitters. James Keith always wore a wig but the eyebrows give an indication that his hair was dark and beneath them twinkled a pair of light blue eyes. Whatever his problems through life may have been, a lack of food does not appear to have been one of them, leading to an early double chin and a bit of a paunch. He had natural good manners and a charm that women of all ages found agreeable. Life in Paris must have been fairly sweet for the now-affluent young James Keith as he passed the rest of 1716 at the Military Academy.

At the beginning of 1717 Keith received a commission as a Colonel of Horse and orders to prepare to return to Scotland, since the King of Sweden was expected to send an invading force. In his memoir, James tells us that the King of Sweden's plans were discovered and prevented – what James Keith could not know was that this invasion that never happened was a diplomatic hoax 'sold' to the Jacobites and bought by them along with many other power brokers in the Europe of 1717.

Throughout most of the seventeenth century Sweden was a military superpower in the north of Europe whose highly motivated and disciplined army regularly defeated numerically superior

and sagacity, dignified by a look "of such intense goodness" that, declared one who knew him, it won the heart at first sight.' (From Robert Anderson, *Memoir of Marhsal Keith.*)

In a letter of 17 July 1781 Frederick the Great wrote to Taesart the sculptor: 'As the attached sketch is not the likeness of Field Marshal Keith, who was taller and more heavily built, it will be necessary to obtain a portrait which resembles him: and as he wore a wig, his statue should be without a hat, with a breastplate and sword. To this the sculptor Tasaert should not fail to conform: and let him be advised incidentally that the payment for the statue of General von Seydlitz will be made in the course of the coming month.' *Neue Deutsche Biographie*, Duncker & Humblot, Berlin.

enemies. The Swedish army also had proven battlefield tactics and a highly mobile cannon firepower, moving it around battlefields with a horrifying efficiency which cut down opposing forces. Sweden had once controlled almost the whole Baltic coast but came to grief when its king – Charles XII – whose whole life story was one of an ongoing war, clashed with Peter the Great of Russia. Years of war drained Sweden of all her resources, culminating in an invasion of Russia which saw Swedish armies caught in the deadly Russian winter, a precedent and disastrous example which both Napoleon and Hitler chose to ignore in succeeding centuries.

By 1717 Sweden was drained both of money and manpower[†] and its industries, such as fishing and farming, were on the verge of bankruptcy. A blockade of hostile foreign ships had all but stopped trade and her merchant fleet reduced from 775 ships in 1697 to only 209 in 1718. To all intents and purposes, Sweden was ruined. However, Charles XII found himself a brilliant diplomat and schemer in the person of Baron von Goertz, who was given complete control over Sweden's finances and all the main departments of state: he had a free hand to play the game of politics over the whole of Europe.

Only a few options were available to near-bankrupt Sweden, simultaneously at war with Russia on one front and on another facing an alliance of Denmark, Prussia and Hanover. A peace had to be brokered with one of Sweden's enemies so that the other could be dealt with. Goertz decided that to enable him to launch an attack which could win him back Pomerania, Bremen and Verden, possibly adding Norway and Mecklenburg as well, he had no option but to make peace with Russia. He bought this peace at a huge cost of ceded territory and conquered states. Goertz, in the course of his diplomatic offensive, had found that all of Russia's allies were worried about its growing strength and that the Achilles' heel of the alliance still facing Sweden lay in the personal antagonism between George I, King of England and Elector of

---

[†] 'A Dutch traveller in Sweden in 1719 found himself driven only by gray-haired men, women, or boys under twelve. "In the whole of Sweden, I have not seen a man between twenty and forty" he said.' Robert K. Massie, *Peter the Great*, pp. 712–719.

Hanover, and Peter the Great of Russia. Goertz played one off against the other in a succession of meetings.

With a Russian peace treaty in his pocket, which also held out a promise to put 20 000 men and eight men-of-war at Sweden's disposal, Charles XII was in a position to launch an attack across the Baltic. The Jacobites watched these diplomatic moves attentively, praying for an attack on Hanover by Sweden, a consequence of which would have seen Britain pouring her troops across the sea to help Hanover, leaving Britain weakened at home and vulnerable to a new Jacobite offensive – possibly with Swedish troops. To the Jacobites it must have seemed a heaven-sent opportunity and they were to subscribe over £30 000 to Sweden's ministers in Paris and London.

In the event, Charles XII was shot through the head on the evening of 30 November 1718, while on campaign against Norway. His death ended any hopes that the Jacobites might have entertained of Swedish help with their own struggle, which had played a major part in their calculations at the time.

James Keith remained at the Academy in 1717 until, in the month of June, Peter the Great arrived in Paris. James quickly made up his mind to try to get into the Tsar's service since, as he explains, 'having now nothing to trust to but my sword, I thought it high time (being about twenty years old) to quitte the Academy and endeavour to establish myself somewhere, where I might again begin my fortune.' Something went badly wrong in this attempt to join Peter the Great's army, however, and so James continued at the Academy much as before until the beginning of 1718.

Things then became a bit complicated. Just as a war was beginning between Spain and Austria, with an invasion of Sicily looming large, he found himself hopelessly in love. Friends and advisers urged him to get a recommendation from James Edward Stuart to the Court of Spain, and he did take some positive steps in that direction but did it oh so very slowly. James tells us that 'had not my mistress and I quarrel'd, and other affairs come to concern me more than the conquest of Sicily did, it's probable I had lost many years of my time to very little purpose, so much was I taken up with my passion.' What can he have meant: did his girlfriend impart the sort of news that most young men in James Keith's position dread to hear?

While James Keith was sorting out his personal life, Cardinal Alberoni of Spain had sent his fleet into Sicilian waters. When the British Admiral Byng requested the Spanish fleet to withdraw and failed to get the desired response, Byng proceeded to sink the Spaniards off Cape Pessaro.

The fat was now well and truly in the fire and as Cardinal Alberoni began preparations for his retribution against England, there was plenty of room for the Jacobites to be included in his general scheme of things. Alberoni wrote to the Duke of Ormonde in Paris, inviting Ormonde to come and see him in Madrid. Following Ormonde's visit to Spain and some string-pulling by him, the Earl Marischal and James Keith also received a letter of invitation from Madrid which they both acted on immediately. It was December 1718 and, although still recovering from a bout of ill health, James Keith set off for Madrid, quite recovering from the illness before his arrival at Marseilles. It might be that his recurring asthma could be cured with a change of air and environment; yet again, maybe a lessening of stress had a restorative effect.

James Keith and his brother the Marischal left a wintry Marseilles at the beginning of 1719 but because of bad weather their ship was forced ashore at Palamos on the coast of Catalonia. No sooner had the ship berthed than they were escorted to the commandant of Palamos who asked them to identify themselves. Of course, they had no papers and were such terrible liars that they tried to disguise their mission by saying they were 'English officers' journeying to Madrid for employment in the Spanish army. Naturally, the Commandant did not think much of their story, not least because of their lack of papers and entry from an enemy country. Unwilling to take any chances, he told the Keiths he was sending them under an armed escort to see Dr Tiberio Caraffa, Governor of Gironne.

Fortunately for the Keith brothers, an Irish regiment commanded by the Duke of Liria – a grandson of James II – was lying near to Gironne where they were sent the next morning, escorted by an armed soldier. Liria, of course, was also the Marquess of Tinmouth and a recent visitor to Scotland with the Pretender – he was that other nineteen-year-old who had met James Keith among the 1715 Jacobite leadership after Sheriffmuir.

That evening they were delivered to the Governor of Gironne's quarters along with a covering letter from Caraffa, doubtless protesting that the Duke of Liria would vouch for them. The Governor of Gironne must have realised they really were well connected, for he wasted no time before sending the Keiths on to the Duke of Liria who immediately smoothed out their difficulties for them. This was perhaps the first good deed James Keith had done for him by the Duke of Liria – but it was certainly not to be the last.

For whatever reason, the Keiths persisted in keeping their identities secret and soon found out that the Duke of Liria was in ignorance of Alberoni's projected action against England. Just how they managed to disguise broad Scottish accents to fit in with their assumed identity as 'English officers' is a mystery but perhaps they adjusted or added to their story. A bit put out by the Duke of Liria's lack of knowledge and also not a little apprehensive as to the reasons for their own admission into Spanish service, they decided to slow their rate of progress to Madrid.

Instead of post horses they hired chairs, reaching Barcelona two days later. This time they had a letter of safe conduct in their possession from the Duke of Liria, which allowed them to ask Prince Pio of Savoy, Captain General of the Province, to grant them an entry to the city without having to undergo a rigorous examination at the ports. Within the hour a coach in the Prince's livery, drawn by six mules and bearing the Prince's doctor inside, arrived to collect them. Their transport came with so much bowing and scraping that the two young Jacobites were amazed by their new, undeserved celebrity status.

The truth was that it had all been a dreadful mistake: the Prince had been told in correspondence from Alberoni to expect King James and a companion travelling incognito. The Keiths had by now given up on their assumed identities and, when they told an embarrassed Prince who they were, he advised them to just get on with their journey, making no effort to hide how sorry he was for all the trouble he had taken in arranging their transport.

Next morning they accompanied the Prince, now in a better humour, on a tour around a new citadel he was building before leaving for Madrid. Fifteen days later they reached Madrid in the evening, sending word to Alberoni that they had at last arrived.

Alberoni met them next day, somewhat frostily reminding them that business was pressing and enquiring just where they had been during the eight days between arriving at Barcelona and coming on to Madrid. He went on to tell them that the Duke of Ormonde was about to take a ship for England at the Groine and that he also wanted the Earl Marischal to go to Scotland. Alberoni wanted to know what plans the Marischal had made, and what he needed for an expeditionary force. Marischal replied that he would have to liaise with Ormonde.

After this the Earl Marischal went off to Valladolid to speak with Ormonde, promising Alberoni he would be back within four days, while James Keith was left in the Cardinal's company to give advice if so requested. Five days later Marischal returned from Benevente: his joint plan with Ormonde prompted him to ask for 4000 arms and 10 000 pistols as he revealed all to Alberoni. What he got in response was half of what he had asked for, along with six companies of foot soldiers to cover his landing while the clans were being raised for another rebellion. Even though preparations for this latest Jacobite rebellion were now in hand, the Pretender still knew nothing about it and word had to be got to him about what was afoot. The messenger chosen for the job was James Keith.

With a brief little note saying 'Pray have confidence on the bearer' and signed Ormonde, James Keith was dispatched on 19 February 1719 with 18 000 crowns in his pocket, to explain all to the other exiled Jacobites. Three days later he arrived at St Sebastian, where he paid 12 000 crowns to Prince Campo Florido for the equipping of a frigate to carry this new Jacobite landing. With some misgivings he then slipped into France, hoping not to be caught and weighing the advantages of time gained against a short time in prison if all went wrong. In the event James Keith was lucky: he made it to Bordeaux by the end of February where he had a meeting with General Gordon and Brigadier Campbell. At that meeting James Keith told them what was happening while handing over money with which to hire ships to take themselves and others over to Scotland. In the event, Brigadier Campbell was to go St Sebastian to embark.

Inter-factional problems then began to surface among the Jacobites, forcing James Keith into a series of manoeuvres. First he had to get a horse without attracting the attention of the Duke of Berwick, who belonged to a group rivalling that of his brother. By using the Marquess of Tullibardine as his cover for the acquisition of a horse he managed to get to Paris. James Keith's arrival in Paris quickly brought the Marquess of Seaforth, who was a brother of Lord Duffus and Campbell of Glenderuel, to his Paris lodgings, where he told them of his mission and offered them Ormonde's note as proof. Glenderuel smiled at Keith and told him his note would have no weight with them: had not the Earl of Mar already advised them to obey whatever orders Ormonde sent?

James Keith notes sadly: 'This plainly let me see that we had two factions amongst us, and which proved the occasion of our speedy ruin when we landed in Scotland.'

But Seaforth and Glenderuel did agree to obey orders and the next day set off for Rouen; within another ten days he had a ship fitted out and ready to leave at Havre de Grace. When Glenderuel and the others arrived to board ship, he asked James Keith whether he had seen General Dillon, to which he replied he had not. Even at this late stage, Keith had to be careful about what he said and to whom. The Jacobite party still leaked like a sieve and the Earl of Stair, then ambassador to France, had the most acute hearing which enabled him to pick up the merest whisper of a plot.

Jockeying for power among members of the Jacobite expeditionary force began immediately. The Pretender had assigned supreme command of his forces in Scotland to the easygoing Marquess of Tullibardine, in a commission dated to coincide with the expected Swedish offensive of 1717. Tullibardine was more suited to fit into the pockets of the Earl of Mar's faction, rather than that belonging to Marischal, who would anyway have done the better job. As this latest Jacobite invasion of Scotland got under way, it did so without anyone in the leadership disclosing commissions or promoting their claim to lead the expeditionary force – that was to come later.

On 19 March 1719, in a small barque of about 25 tons, James Keith set out from the mouth of the Seine on a course which would take his ship between Calais and Dover, then round the Orkneys to the Isle of Lewis to meet up with the others. The weather was playing up, however, and an easterly wind took the barque along the south coast towards St George's Channel. During the evening, two days later, the little barque found itself slipping through a fleet of much bigger ships, seven of which were darkened and the rest with no light at all. Optimists that they were, they mistook this fleet for the Duke of Ormonde's invasion fleet and did not bother to stop, because the wind was so very favourable to them. Just as well – for the darkened fleet had been a squadron of English men-of-war transporting troops from Ireland to meet the expected invasion by Ormonde. The rest of the voyage passed without incident and on 4 April they dropped anchor at Lewis, in the Outer Isles, where a few days later word was brought to them that the other Jacobite ships had also arrived and were at Stornoway on the far side of the island.

James Keith and others crossed Lewis to row out and meet his brother. Once on board he proceeded to tell Marischal of all that had transpired – the success of his French mission and, not least, the attitudes and possible commissions of those he had brought with him. Marischal immediately gave James Keith a commission as a Colonel, with blank commissions for two battalions which he was to raise in the King of Spain's name. They spoke to each other about who was likely to be in overall command of this new rebellion and Marischal admitted to James that if anyone present had a higher commission than his own, one of Major General in both the Spanish and English service, then he would just have to take whatever orders were handed out.

A council of war was scheduled to take place the next day but it was preceded by a near-poker game – everybody asked each other to show what commissions they held. Tullibardine was very quiet, so quiet that Marischal took it to mean that Tullibardine's late commission of 1717 had been deliberately kept from the council of war and that Tullibardine himself was agreeable to Marischal taking command. There then followed a dispute about whether they should all stay on board, awaiting news of Ormonde's invasion of England before taking action, or disembark there and then to launch an assault on Inverness. It was reckoned that they would only have to meet and deal with a maximum of 300 troops garrisoned at Inverness. After further debate, it was also concluded that a very real danger existed that the small, shipbound

Jacobite force would be blockaded in the harbour where they lay. This ensured that the plans agreed between Marischal and Alberoni in Spain would go ahead – it was to be a march on Inverness. But next morning dawned and the poker players picked up on the previous night's game – Tullibardine now produced a commission of Lieutenant General and, James Keith says, delivered 'a sort of speech nobody understood but himself'. It must all have been a sickening blow for Marischal and James Keith but Marischal then relinquished his shortlived command of the army while retaining command of the ships for which he had direct orders from Alberoni.

Tullibardine and Glenderuel tried once more to stop the rebel invaders from landing ashore, but against a general protest were forced to give in. In adverse weather conditions the Jacobite ships then set sail for the mainland and, after some delay, unloaded their troops and ammunition supplies. Marischal and Brigadier Campbell were quick to propose marching straight to Inverness, accompanied by the Spaniards and 500 Highlanders from the Seaforth clan but yet again Jacobite rivalries surfaced: this time in the shape of a letter.

A letter from the Pretender had been circulated to the clans prior to the invasion, which gave no indication as to who would be in command of the Jacobite army and giving the Pretender's instructions that no one was to make a move until Spanish troops landed in England. This was all that Tullibardine needed and he declared that since he had heard nothing of Ormonde's landing, he was going to stay where he was. Tullibardine went even further – he proposed that they should all get back on board the vessels and sail for Spain. It took a lot of persuasion to make him change his mind.

To pre-empt any further discussion along these lines Marischal then sent the ships away, ostensibly to save them from being blocked in or destroyed. It was as well he did, for within a week of the frigates' departure, three English men-of-war arrived. The old castle of Eilean Donan had meanwhile been transformed into an ammunition dump and left under the guard of forty-five Spaniards; it was now battered into submission by the ship's cannon and the Spaniards taken prisoner.

Tullibardine had dithered too long and now lost any initiative he might have had; the time elapsed had allowed British and Dutch troops to assemble in opposition and, of course, any thoughts of escape to sea were best forgotten. The Jacobites could only stay and fight it out. If Tullibardine himself was less than enthusiastic about what lay ahead, then the circular letter to the clans from the Pretender gave all the faint-hearted just the excuse they were needing to hold off from joining the Jacobite army. Just when it seemed that things couldn't get any worse, they did. News now arrived in the Jacobite camp that Ormonde's invasion fleet had been dispersed in a storm and that it might be the following spring before an invasion of England could take place. Tullibardine must have completely lost the place, or found courage from somewhere, for the Jacobite leaders ordered all the supporting chieftains nearest to them to assemble their vassals – only to find just about 1000 none-too-happy men arriving to join them.

Unknown to the Jacobites, the British army were only three days' march away with almost five regiments of foot and 150 dragoons. Although their advance had been held up by a lack of provisions the Battle of Glenshiel was not to be long delayed.

6

·

The Battle of Glenshiel – and Spain

·

T HEIR ESCAPE ROUTE BY sea now gone, the Jacobite landing force and those who had only lately joined it were now gathered in Glenshiel, a long glen running eastwards from Loch Duich to Loch Cluanie, with the 3500-foot Scour Ouran section of the mountain wall towering above and to the north of them. Jacobite numbers had risen with the addition of a small force from Perthshire commanded by Lord George Murray, and Argyle with one of his sons had appeared along with another eighty men. Lochiel brought 150 of his clansmen and Seaforth a further 500, while Rob Roy McGregor with one of his sons joined the camp with his men from Stirlingshire and Argyle. Add to these the 300 Spaniards from the Galicia regiment, commanded by Don Nicolas Bolano – who had been sent along to cover the landing – and the Jacobites totalled 1640 men.

Jacobite estimates of British troops at Inverness were hopelessly wrong. British army forces, with which the Jacobite council of war had decided to seek battle, were 1100 strong and had already marched out of Inverness under the command of General Wightman, an old adversary from Sheriffmuir. By 10 June, Wightman and his soldiers had appeared at the foot of the mountain slope occupied by the Jacobites.

The Jacobite positions could best be described as almost impregnable: they faced downhill over ground that was impossibly rugged and steep. Their left flank was covered by a ravine while their right was covered by a little stream flowing through equally difficult ground and it was there that they posted a detachment under Lord George Murray. What then followed in the battle reflected little glory on the Jacobites, who had been given an excellent chance to grab an early victory and bolster sagging morale.

Wightman, after only briefly reconnoitering the Jacobite position, launched an attack on Murray's position on the left flank, whereupon Murray pulled back as no reinforcements had been sent up to him. This might have been because the Jacobites were distracted by a simultaneous skirmishing attack begun on the Jacobite centre, which lasted three hours and left both sides with about 100 men killed, or wounded, (including the Jacobite Marquess of Seaforth). The main fighting involved the Seaforth contingent, which included Marischal and, no doubt, James Keith. As the evening sky darkened into night the Jacobites retreated further up Scour Ouran, where a combination of darkness and an uphill pursuit was enough to make the English forces call off the battle.

When the English ships destroyed the Jacobite Eilean Donan Castle and another, smaller lochside ammunition dump and supplies store, they deprived the Jacobites of what they now most needed: there was no ammunition left and very few provisions. As for the Jacobites themselves, most had been half-hearted from the very beginning and they were now a sorry bunch, inspiring little confidence that morning that would bring an enthusiastic and renewed offensive downhill on to the English troops. Alone among those present and offering to renew the attack was Don Nicolas Bolano, the professional Spanish soldier.

But enough was enough – Don Bolano was persuaded to surrender on condition that the Spaniards were allowed to keep their baggage. By morning, as the Spaniards negotiated their surrender, the Jacobites were climbing their way out over the mountains and dispersing into the Highland wilderness just as they had after Sheriffmuir, each taking the road he liked the best.

For the Keith brothers it was to be yet another wait for a ship to take them to safety. During this time James Keith was taken ill with fever as both brothers sought safe hiding places among the mountains and glens, both still on the 'wanted list' for their part in the 1715 rebellion. When the Act of Indemnity was passed in 1717 offers of pardon had been sent to Marischal and Southesk at the

Court of Avignon. Predictably, Marischal rejected his offer of pardon out of hand and 'with contempt'. Just as predictably, James Keith – who had found his feet in Paris and was then at the Military Academy – joined his brother in rejecting his offer of pardon 'with contempt'. They were both fugitives with lengthy records, who had just made a second attempt to subvert the state and if caught they must surely have faced the worst punishment a British court could have handed out to them.

From their mountain safety a ship was organised to take them from Peterhead and away to the Continent, and it was now up to James Keith and Marischal to get there. We have no record, nor does James tell us, that he visited his mother and Meston in Inverugie Castle before joining his ship in the port of Peterhead. Be that as it may, it would be very strange indeed if the brothers had not appeared even briefly at the castle and, indeed, may well have stayed in hiding at Inverugie until it was time to sail.

The Keiths boarded their ship at the beginning of September 1719 and only four days later berthed at Texel in Holland. From Texel they went to The Hague to speak with the Marquess Beretti Landi, the King of Spain's minister at the court of The Hague, where they asked for further orders and Landi's advice. They were told to go back to Spain with all haste and with these instructions set out next day for Liège, thus avoiding the imperial Netherlands and entering France by Sedan. They were both without passports or papers and once more had the misfortune to meet up with officialdom in the shape of the town mayor. He did not bother to find out who they were and saw to it that they both went off to prison. Luckily for the brothers they were not searched: if they had been their commissions from the King of Spain would have been discovered – and Spain was now at war with France. When they were finally locked up in prison James pretended that he had to use the toilet and, taking both commissions with him, threw them in a place which was never, ever going to be searched.

After a time the mayor remembered that he had forgotten to ask his captives their names and now, fortunately for the brothers, Marischal was able to pull a letter out of his pocket, written in French and addressed to him by the Princess of Conti. This subtle form of name-dropping was all that it took to get them out of jail and set them on the road again to Paris. Once in Paris they took a month to rest and recover from their ordeal before again starting out for Spain and Montpellier, where they hoped to cross the border. Still without papers, they found that getting into Spain was more difficult than they had imagined, so they decided to part and each try different routes. Marischal went off to find access to Spain through the Pyrenees and James started off for Marseilles. This proved to be a hopeless choice and November 1719 saw him trying his luck at Toulouse. He awoke one morning to have Marischal walk into his room and tell him of his misadventures; he had been in jail again. After being apprehended and spending six weeks in custody, Marischal had then been released on a special order signed by the King of France and given a passport to Italy along with orders to get out of France immediately.

This passport was a godsend and in January 1720 the pair set off for Genoa but, being so near to Rome and the Pretender's court, they decided to pay him a visit. The galley which was on its way to collect them had been delayed and because of this Marischal wanted to use the time to visit Alberoni – as a result of his failed politics and failed venture with Ormonde and the Keiths, he now lived at Cestri de Levante in deep disgrace, and the visit was not a good idea. Alberoni had had enough of power politics and was only just interested in what the Keiths had been up to. Next day they boarded their galley but because of bad seamanship found themselves windbound at Leghorn for another ten days. For James Keith, who generally seemed to enjoy being at sea, it was all too much and he resolved never to go aboard a Genoese galley again.

The rest of their journey must have been pleasant enough – through beautiful little Leghorn, Pisa, Florence and Sienna to Rome, where they stayed another six weeks with the Pretender before taking their leave. There might just have been another reason for visiting the Pretender, for he was to notice that they had no money and he tried without success to get an advance of 1000 Roman crowns on his own papal pension to give them. The Pope pleaded his own personal poverty and the Pretender went on to borrow the money from a banker. James Keith included this tale in his memoir only to highlight 'the genius of Clement XI' and also to show 'how little regard churchmen have for those who have abandoned all for religion.'

From Leghorn their journey took them to Genoa, where they stayed six weeks, upsetting local officialdom by sparking off a diplomatic incident. The British ambassador at Genoa, egged on by the French, demanded that the two 'rebels to the King his master' be deported from Genoa before the Keiths' presence brought down a bombardment on the city. Frantic officials called the brothers to a meeting at which they begged them to go, only to have the Keiths point to a British frigate cruising around the port and hindering them in their journey.

The brothers had to go and go soon so, taking Genoese advice, they boarded a fourteen-oar *felouque* which lay into the shore each night for safety. Twenty-nine days later, in July 1720, they arrived in Valencia and took the road to Madrid.

James's army commission from Alberoni now lay at the bottom of a toilet pit in France and he needed to get a substitute. Unfortunately, when he went to pick these papers up, he found that Alberoni had given him his original commission papers out of blanks he had to hand – without ever telling the Minister of War. Alberoni had not wanted anyone to know of his plans and probably wanted the Scottish expedition, which finished with Glenshiel, to be kept secret for as long as possible. It was to take several months before this matter could be straightened out and James was again a paid colonel in the Spanish service, though still not placed with a regiment: a situation which was to continue for the rest of the year, much to his frustration.

He tells us: 'The campagne of the year before, and the journeys I had made since, had entirely exhausted what money I had; and the Cardinal Alberoni being no more in Spain, I was, as the French say, *au pie de la lettre sur le pave*, I knew nobody, and was known to none' fortunately for him, he was to meet up with a Rear Admiral Cammock, whom he had known in Paris, and who now offered him lodgings at his house in Madrid. It seems that James Keith had a way about him, something that endeared him to others and which won him instant and lasting friendships.

Although he went on to build himself a circle of friends in Madrid, his employment limbo was getting him down and, utterly fed up, he resolved to obtain a passport for Italy and to seek his fortune there. Arriving at Barcelona he was pleasantly surprised to find that a Jesuit friend of his had used his influence with the King of Spain's confessor and managed to get him a new commission. This still was not good enough, or what was wanted, so James demanded and was given a copy of his original commission of 1719. His temper now cooled, he returned to Madrid where he sat out the rest of 1721.

During 1721, Mary – the eldest Keith sister – died. She had become John, Earl of Wigton's second wife in 1711 and her death, alongside James's continuing ill health and dangerous, fugitive lifestyle, persuaded the Countess Marischal to try and get her youngest son to return home and join her in Scotland. With this in mind she consulted the very best English lawyers and found they were unanimously of the opinion that James Keith could safely return and further advised that until he personally appeared it would be impossible for him to recover his patrimony. It appears that James Keith's inherited property had been lumped in and lost when his brother's estates were sequestrated, although he had not personally been named in the attainder action taken against the rebels. Not only his mother in Scotland thought he should return home – even his circle of friends in Spain thought this would be his best option since his Spanish military career was stalled for the foreseeable future by his blunt refusal to convert to Catholicism.

James Keith now decided to verify his position with the British government by consulting a Mr Stanhope, British ambassador to the court of Madrid, which came as something of a surprise to the ambassador. Stanhope told him he could not have chosen a worse time to seek forgiveness because the British government was aware that some new plot was being hatched on the international scene against them and, of course, had known of his recent involvement with the Jacobites in the Glenshiel affair. Stanhope also said that James's arrival in England would be wide open to another interpretation – that he might only be in England to further this latest Jacobite plot. From what we know, it is clear that Marischal was heavily involved during this period with Lords North and Gray, and Atterbury, Bishop of Rochester. Marischal was politically hyperactive among the rest of the Jacobite rebels at Avignon and it is thought that he may actually have slipped into England at this time to help move this latest Jacobite plot along.

It was strange that Marischal had not found some way to tell James Keith what was going on but, like all Jacobite plots, this one was also discovered and quashed. For James there was nothing he could do but accept Stanhope's advice. In October he set out from Madrid for Paris in the company of his friend the Duke of Liria and during the course of their journey the young men discussed the affairs of Scotland, culminating in the Sheriffmuir debâcle of 1715. They ended by agreeing that the failures had all been a consequence of the Earl of Mar's shortcomings and responsibility for the disaster could justifiably be laid at his door. James and Liria appear to have shared the same sense of humour, which led to the Duke of Liria promising, half in jest, to seduce Mar's wife, of whom Mar was extremely jealous, as an act of revenge for them both. Liria was as good as his word but, as James later wrote, Liria's malice cost him dear in that he fell so deeply in love with Mar's wife that in the end he loved the wife to the same degree as he hated her husband.[†]

A tumour had developed in Keith's shoulder and we can only speculate that it was a consequence of some botched surgery after Sheriffmuir, the result of a failure to thoroughly clean the bullet wound he had received. Meanwhile, all his affairs in Scotland had been satisfactorily concluded and money owed to him by the British government was safely in his account. With resources behind him and back in the young man's happy hunting ground of Paris, among his relatives, he suddenly lost any inclination to return to Spain. By this time he had found himself another girlfriend who was pleading with him to join the French army, although he personally had no real inclination to do so. This girlfriend must have been a pushy sort, for he was to find himself trying to join the French service through another female acquaintance with military friends in high places. To James's great relief nothing came of this manoeuvering and he says that 'under the pretence of a cure, I remained at Paris all the year 1723–24.'

At the beginning of 1725 a surgeon carried out a considerable operation on his arm. It must have been a very serious operation for his mother came to Paris to nurse him back to health. During

---

[†] The object of Liria's designs must have been Mar's young second wife, who was widely regarded by her contemporaries as being unbalanced, though she may actually have suffered from chronic PMT.

the time of Keith's convalescence, the Jacobite plot was discovered, resulting in most of the conspirators being thrown into the Tower of London and Atterbury himself being banished. The Duke of Bourbon also broke off the proposed marriage between the King of France and the Infanta of Spain, which left the Spanish nation boiling with rage at the insult. This resulted in the recall of the Infanta and all serving Spanish officers to Spain, and James Keith was one of these officers. His arm scarcely healed, Keith set out some time after the Infanta had left France and caught up with her and her entourage at Bayonne, where he joined in the ceremonious return to Spain.

Her nursing mission finished, Keith's mother stayed on in Paris with relatives until 1726, when she journeyed back to Scotland. The Countess Marischal found no difficulty in getting in or out of Britain because she had kept herself out of the plotting and political limelight and was now going home to stay with her youngest daughter Anne, who had married the Earl of Galloway. The banished Bishop Atterbury wrote to James Keith saying that although he was a martyr to gout, he had put aside water to drink the Keith family's health during a meal with the Countess in the summer of 1725. Another letter arrived from the Pretender in Rome dated 17 March 1725, to say: 'I was the more pleased to receive yours of 19 February that it was new proof to me of your recovery, tho' I wanted no new one to convince me of your zeal and attachment, of which I have received so many [proofs] both from yourself and your family. I have the satisfaction of hearing sometimes from your brother, on whom I place a particular value, and not less one on Lady Marschall, who I am sure will have shared with me in a particular manner the joy I have on the birth of a second son. Pray make her my kindest complements, and ever be assured, both of you, of my singular esteem and friendship – James R.'

Keith's mother seems to have spent most of her remaining years in Edinburgh, although we can assume she also spent time with her youngest daughter until Anne died in 1728. By this time Inverugie Castle must have been in a sorry state of repair. She was not to see her sons again and, perhaps trying to compensate for her loss, she took a young orphan of seventeen under her wing and saw to his education and upbringing until her own death in 1729. This young lad was later to become the last Lord Oliphant.

As the Infanta returned to Spain in a massive display of pomp and ceremony, calculated to boost the morale of a nation seething with the affront of having its princess rejected, Spain was looking for a means of expressing that rage. However, war was not to break out that year and James Keith retired to Valencia, where his pay cheque was to be encashed, to await developments with his brother.

By June 1726 he was still in Valencia when news came that a war between Spain and Britain was now inevitable: a part of the British fleet had sailed for the West Indies to intercept Spain's trading galleons while another fleet had sailed into the Bay of Biscay with three regiments of infantry on board, to attempt burning the men-of-war which were being constructed at St Andero. This Biscay fleet duly arrived to begin hostilities but had to think the better of it, since the port's defences had been massively increased after the French burnt six ships at St Andero in 1719.

Spanish war preparations continued with 20 000 men ordered to march to Andalusia under the pretext of building a new fort at Algeciras, across the water from Gibraltar. With war looming, there at last seemed a prospect of some action and the Keith brothers, volunteering along with other Jacobites, set off for the Spanish camp, where they arrived a month later. They joined an international force from seven nations under the command of Count de las Torres which in the early days could have taken Gibraltar at any moment, owing to the easy access allowed by the Gibraltarian authorities who had a poorly and negligently manned fortress. Having a soldier's eye for the possibilities and terrain, James Keith tells us that the Gibraltar authorities allowed access to the fortress without searching for hidden arms. He goes on to point out that there were sand dunes within striking distance where 1000 men might have been concealed. With only some 200 soldiers and 40–50 officers manning the defences at any one time, it all began to look like missed opportunities to James Keith. With dry humour he says 'this was not the design of the Count de las Torres, our General, who said that wou'd the Englis give him the toun, he wou'd not take it but by the breach.'

The Spanish pretext ended when 120 cannon arrived and the real mission of the 20 000 men was seen to have nothing whatsoever to do with building. Despite British protests, the Spanish cannon began their bombardment on their day of arrival and fired from the very entrenchments which had ostensibly been dug for new fortifications. Return fire from Gibraltar was poor but British warships soon appeared within a cable's length of the Spanish onshore positions and delivered a pounding on them. Soon, on 1 May, the seventy-gun *Prince Frederick* arrived from Britain, bringing with her a convoy carrying reinforcements for the Gibraltar garrison. For the following two weeks the Spanish artillery delivered a hail of fire at the constant rate of 700 rounds per hour from ninety-two guns and seventy-two mortars which crashed against the Gibraltar defences.

This bombardment ended only because of sheer exhaustion and lack of ammunition: the Spaniards had thrown everything they had at Gibraltar. But British supplies had now reached Gibraltar, and all the gunfire was now going in the opposite direction, in a complete reversal, as the defenders unleashed their own bombardment on the Spanish aggressors. While Gibraltar's defenders had lost only 361 men, the Spaniards suffered 2000 killed and wounded: nearly 900 had deserted and 5000 were disabled through sickness. This sickness among the Spanish troops was probably a product, in large part, of a winter of incessant rain.

If James Keith had seen bungling and military ineptitude with Mar and the Jacobite army, it was nothing to what he was now witnessing at the Siege of Gibraltar. The Spanish cannon were barely within shot of their target, to say nothing of the engineers' mistake which allowed the Spanish trenches to be fired into from the Rock. So badly had the siege been thought through that British ships could comfortably sail into the deep water a cable's length behind the trenches and also deliver fire into them. Demoralised and unwilling to take any more of the British fire in their exposed trenches, some of the Spanish forward troops had tried to make their way back out under cover of darkness. They marched straight into friendly fire from the Corsican regiment who supposed them to be a British skirmishing party out on a foray. The humiliation didn't end there; the Corsican regiment, seeing their comrades still coming on, threw down their arms and ran away. It was a shambles that even the Jacobites would have been hard put to match.

At last orders came from the court at Madrid to cease the hostilities which had by now gone on for about five months with no real effect. As Keith ruefully remarked: 'All we gained was the knowledge that the place was impregnable by land.'

Hostilities at an end and no doubt disgusted by the shambles, Keith decided to test the water again by asking for command of the first Irish regiment to become vacant. He was again to be disappointed when told that just as soon as he converted to the Catholic faith he would not only get what he wanted but that things would improve even beyond that. It was the last straw – Madrid's reply was all that it took for Keith to go straight there to seek the King's recommendation to the Empress of Russia. Keith complained that he found his religion an 'invincible obstacle' to his continuing in service to the King of Spain. Perhaps the King himself was more than a little fed up with Keith's intransigence where his religion was concerned, for he now ordered the Marquess of Castellar to write to James Keith's friend, the Duke of Liria – presently ambassador at the Russian court – to forward the Spanish court's recommendation of Keith to the Russians.

By the beginning of 1727 it was clear that the Duke of Liria had done an excellent job, for James was accepted into the service of Tsar Peter II as a Major General. Shortly afterwards Prince Schterbatov, the Russian ambassador to Madrid, called on him and asked him to inform the King of Spain of his new appointment and handed him passports for his journey to Russia. James set out a few weeks later with a parting gratification of 1000 crowns from the King of Spain in his pocket: this was at the beginning of 1728.

Something more has to be said of the Duke of Liria, seducer of Mar's wife, Keith's Jacobite comrade after Sheriffmuir and his very good friend. The thirty-two-year-old Duke enjoyed a place of superior influence at the Russian court. At Peter II's coronation Liria gave banquets and firework displays which put all the other celebratory efforts into the shade and could only have endeared him to the hard-drinking Russian nobility.

7
.
Russia
.

WEEKS AFTER BEING GIVEN his appointment in the Russian army James Keith left Spain to find himself a ship for the voyage up the Baltic, but he did so without any apparent hurry.

He did not take the quickest or most direct route to a Baltic port but tells us that he went first to Paris, staying there for about six weeks, before resuming his journey. He does not say whether the six-week visit to Paris was to say goodbye to relatives, friends or a girlfriend. From Paris his intention had been to go by Flanders and Holland then on through Germany to Lubeck but, on rethinking that route, he remembered it went through the Electorate of Hanover which might mean the possibility of his arrest, so instead he went to Amsterdam. At Amsterdam he found a ship of twenty-six guns ready to sail for St Petersburg and booked himself a passage. It then took twenty-six days' sailing up the Baltic and into the Gulf of Finland, before he at last landed at Kronstadt, a Russian island seaport which was St Petersburg's commercial harbour as well as an island arsenal fortress, being ice-free for six months of every year.

Once more on dry land, Keith wrote to the Duke of Liria, whose immediate response was to tell him to get a move on and hasten to Moscow. But the sea trip had taken its toll, perhaps bringing on an illness, so that he stayed on in Kronstadt for another three weeks before setting out for Moscow in October 1728. On his arrival in Moscow he found that the young Tsar Peter II was away on one of his regular hunting expeditions, which often stretched to three weeks' duration. During that time he was taken on a series of social rounds by the Duke of Liria, who introduced him to all the generals and principal ministers surrounding the imperial court.

What James Keith found on arrival in Moscow must have been an impressive sight. Moscow was then roughly the size of London but there the similarity ended, for it was almost entirely constructed from wooden logs. Even the streets were carpeted with logs, to allow for some mobility after the autumn rain and spring thaws had turned the streets into rivers of deep mud. At these times of rain and thaw the logged streets were virtually afloat, making passage for the normal horse-drawn traffic impossible and leaving Muscovites praying for either winter frosts or an early hot, dry summer to make mobility possible again and life more bearable.

Moscow wasn't all wooden buildings however, for above the normal housing rose dazzling, cross-carrying onion-domed roofs growing out of the top of white walls. Hundreds of these Russian Orthodox churches were spread across the city and at the centre of Moscow stood the Kremlin citadel itself, enclosing within its walls another three huge cathedrals. The Kremlin fortress, bounded by its huge walls, moat and river defences, was where Russian power was concentrated.[†] The Tsar ruled the state from his palaces within the Kremlin while nearby the Orthodox patriarch took care of the day-to-day affairs of the church. In a never-ending succession around the squares of the Kremlin were the offices of government, the courts, bakeries, laundries and stables. Crucially, for the protection of the Tsar and the government against a coup, there were also the barracks of the Royal Guards regiments.

The vast sprawling mass of Moscow had wide roads as a protection against fire, although this was a daily occurrence. Firefighters could be seen at any time, desperately trying to put out a fire and to stop it spreading, sometimes only accomplishing this by tearing down adjacent buildings to make a firebreak. In the searing heat of a Russian summer the wood dried out to a tinder dryness and it took very little to set it alight, while in the sub-zero winters the urgent need for stoves and fires to ensure survival increased the chances of buildings being set alight. Between 1571

[†] Peter K. Massie, *Peter the Great*. pp. 3–8.

and 1671 there had been four huge fires in Moscow which left large parts of the city in ashes. The only comfort for those who lost their homes was that they could be replaced very quickly because Moscow had many large stockpiles of logs. Not only that, but replacement houses were readily available in something akin to today's 'kit' houses, ready for instant assembly on the burnt-out site. Wood, even in the form of logs, was an every-ready commodity always in demand for a variety of uses. The wider logs were cut to length, hollowed out and given a board lid to make a coffin when required.

Moscow was an economic powerhouse of small traders and bustling humanity. A colourful mix of all sorts jammed the streets: black-robed priests of the Orthodox faith and soldiers in their bright uniforms mixed with the less attractive beggars and ragged holy men. Not unlike today's cities, there were buskers, jugglers, acrobats and musicians, as well as people prodding bears and dogs into performing tricks for those with time to stop and watch.

The Russian capacity for alcohol was very much in evidence. Men who had been so desperate for the price of a drink that they had sold every stitch they stood up in could be seen lying dead drunk and naked in the street. On feast days and on occasions when universal celebration was called for the body count of drunks lying about the streets would rise dramatically.

Red Square was also covered in logs, bearing no resemblance at all to the stark flat expanse which in recent years has carried huge parades of Russian armoured might on May Days. Red Square then was one big, open-air marketplace, where stalls, shops, small chapels and houses leaned against the Kremlin walls. On offer at these stalls were brocades, silks, brass, bronze, copper and iron goods, tooled leather and pottery. A vast array of fruit and vegetables was carried in from the surrounding countryside for the supply of Moscow tables. Pie-sellers and peddlers of all sorts plied their trade among the crowd with trays hanging around their necks. Most needs were catered for and these traders worked the crowds all the way down to the river, where the equivalent of today's car boot sales were taking place. Moscow women used the river itself to wash clothes and, according to European travellers, they provided other personal services after nightfall. At noon Moscow came to a halt for an extended lunchbreak and a nap.

When day was done and darkness fell on the city, people made their way back to the security of their homes while shops closed down and heavy wooden shutters were swung tight shut against thieves. After dark Moscow was a very dangerous place to be: for those who ventured out at night there was always an excellent chance of being one of the night's casualties, just one more dead body among others found in Moscow's streets with the morning light. Those murdered were routinely collected by the police and taken to a central field in Moscow, where they awaited formal identification by relatives who had missed the victim and gone to seek them. There was such a quick accumulation of bodies at this open-air mortuary that they could not be allowed to wait too long for identification and, when there was pressure on space, the bodies were simply tipped into a common grave with no ceremony.

On arrival in Moscow, James Keith would not have been allowed to stay in the city itself but been directed to find accommodation in what was known as the German Suburb, where he could either rent or buy until a piece of ground was allocated to him – of a size commensurate with his position – so that he might build a place of his own if he so desired. The German Suburb was built of two- and three-storey houses, in the European style, with large windows fronting on to wide, tree-lined streets. These houses were occupied by foreigners – mercenary soldiers, artisans, engineers and other immigrants who had the skills and knowledge Russia needed but did not have among her own population. The Suburb was built on the banks of the Yauza River and located some three miles from the centre of Moscow – it had been built at this location to keep the foreigners from spreading a spiritual contamination to the indigenous population and polluting the Russian Orthodox faith. Most of those who made their way to Russia and found themselves in the German Suburb, had done so because of a desire to advance themselves, or because their own countries had become too dangerous for them. Although the Catholic faith was frowned upon and forbidden from building a church in the Suburb, the Lutheran and Calvinist faiths were well tolerated and their churches sprang up. Even though he claimed to be of the Protestant faith, James Keith never mentions his religious beliefs or convictions.

In the German Suburb, a ghetto for Europeans, people were able to maintain a European way of life: importing books, speaking their own languages and smoking and drinking in their own way. Although the German Suburb retained its own European culture, it is almost impossible to believe that the hard drinking and other excesses of Russian hosts and friends did not spill over and affect lifestyles within it. When Russian hosts began a night's drinking everyone was expected to join in and the night usually ended when everything liquid had been consumed, or when everyone had fallen into a drunken sleep. Russian socialising had no point unless everyone got falling-down-drunk and it seems to have been expected, if not demanded, that all guests actively participate in a party and demonstrate their enjoyment by matching drink for drink with their hosts. It might just be that an ability to keep pace with the drinks alongside the Russians was a prerequisite to gaining promotion.

Would James Keith have matched the mood and colour around him at these marathon drinking sessions? His brother regularly sent him large quantities of brandy and wines from Spain; his very nature would have ensured a quick and wide circle of friends among Russians and Europeans alike which would have led to regular social invitations. We can only guess – but his later gout affliction seems to indicate that he consumed his drink alongside the best of them. Besides that, Sir William Keith, James's father, was described as a 'hard drinker' and there may have been a tendency to drink among Keith men.

Peter the Great, the late Tsar, had spent his entire life and his energies in dragging his reluctant and backward nation out of its isolationism; he had realised that if his country was ever to catch up with the rest of Europe skills and expertise would have to be brought in. With a ruthless dedication he set about building himself a new capital city, St Petersburg, a navy and an expanded army, which he then used to beat his neighbouring states and enemies – Turkey, Poland and Sweden – into a sullen submission. In the negotiations aimed at a cessation of hostilities and treaties of peace, Peter bargained for and won new territories. This greatly added to Russian prestige and made her a growing military power: being something of a joke in the early part of the seventeenth century, Russia was now a force to be reckoned with and had ambassadorial representation at most of the European courts.

James Keith had failed to join the service of Peter the Great during the Tsar's visit to Paris in June 1717 and since that first attempt there had been others sitting on the Russian throne. Peter the Great had died at 6 a.m. on the morning of 28 January 1725, but before doing so he had commanded his admiral, Apraxin, and other ministers of state that in the event of his death all foreigners should be protected – Peter had enjoyed the company of his mercenaries, engineers and other talented foreigners in the German Suburb, drinking and roistering with them in preference to Russian company. He was succeeded by his wife Catherine, propelled on to the throne by Menshikev, Yaguzhinsky and Tolstoy after the Guards regiments were first summoned to the palace to be immediately paid and then reminded of how Catherine and her husband had accompanied them on military campaigns and that they now owed her their allegiance. The Guards had long been devoted to their late Tsar and Catherine was popular with them – their support was hers for the asking.

At this time there was, however, another claimant to the throne. He was the nine-year-old Peter, grandson of Peter the Great. In the power struggle which swirled around the succession, this young boy was the choice of two powerful noble families, the Dolgorukis and the Golitsyns. Their ambitions were to control the young Peter and to use this power to reverse Peter the Great's many reforms.

Catherine's rule was brief: in his position as head of the Supreme Privy Council Menshikev attended to the governance of Russia while Catherine herself went on to spend what little time remained to her on drink, fineries and dalliance. In November 1726 the flooding River Neva forced Catherine to flee from her palace in St Petersburg clad only in a nightdress. A few weeks later, on 21 January 1727, her duties called for her to take part in the Blessing of the Waters ceremony on the ice of a frozen River Neva. She remained out in the bitter winter air for many hours as she reviewed some 20 000 of her troops and after that terrible ordeal took to her bed with a fever and continuous nosebleed which led to her death a few months later.

The scheming, devious Menshikev had already calculated before her death that instead of supporting Catherine's nominated successor – the Grand Duke Alexeivich – he would be likely to do far better by supporting the eleven-year-old grandchild as Peter II.

Assisted by Osterman, he persuaded the dying Catherine to change her mind and make the young boy Peter her new choice. Thinking well ahead, Menshikev had previously asked for and obtained Catherine's permission for Peter to marry his own sixteen-year-old daughter Maria. It was all to be a ghastly misjudgement with terrible consequences for Menshikev and his daughter.

On gaining the throne the eleven-year-old Tsar began to exercise his powers. His Foreign Minister and tutor Osterman was soon told that while Peter liked him and appreciated the job he was doing, he, Osterman, was not to interfere in his sports and pastimes. Menshikev was the next to be put in his place when, during the summer of 1727 and recovering from an illness, he made an appearance at court only to have the boy Tsar ostentatiously turn his back on him. It was not a good sign and relations further deteriorated over the next months until in September 1727 Menshikev was arrested, stripped of his high office and exiled to the Ukraine with his daughter Maria.

The power behind the throne passed to the Dolgorukis, with the nineteen-year-old Prince Ivan Dolgoruki now the young Tsar's closest friend and confidant. Prince Ivan's father, Prince Alexis Dolgoruki, and Prince Vasily Dolgoruki, were appointed to the Supreme Privy Council and before the year's end it was announced that the eleven-year-old would marry the sixteen-year-old-daughter of Prince Alexis. Meanwhile Menshikev was found guilty on further charges and given an even worse place of exile in Siberia, where he died shortly afterwards – his daughter Maria died only weeks later.

When James Keith arrived in Moscow he found that Peter II had gone off on a hunting trip with the Dolgorukis which was to stretch through the whole of the summer until harvest. Keith and the Duke of Liria used this period to socialise and, on the Tsar's return, Keith immediately sought out Osterman to beg a formal introduction to the Tsar. This was granted and within days Keith received orders to take command of two infantry regiments, part of a division belonging to Field Marshal Prince Dolgoruki and quartered near Moscow.

Not yet quite knowledgeable as to how the Russian army functioned and as yet without any words of Russian, Keith requested and was given three months' leave to learn something of the language and military procedures. He was further helped at this time by the Duke of Liria, who explained how the Russian court worked, pointing out those who had influence and could pull strings and make things happen. On Liria's advice and on the evidence of his own eyes, James Keith marked out Prince Ivan Dolgoruki as someone to seek out for friendship and – by making friends with Count Mantuov, Ivan Dolgoruki's best friend – Keith began to make his way to an inner circle and centre of power. But, as luck would have it, Liria and Mantuov fell out with each other and Keith was caught in the middle of a squabble which did him no good at all. He left this acrimonious dispute to join his regiments, hoping that it would all have blown over by the time he returned.

On Keith's return to court he found the Tsar's friend, Prince Ivan Dolgoruki, even more in favour and perceived a coldness at the court directed at himself. Like most of Russia, he was aghast to hear the announcement of the marriage between the boy Tsar and Catherine Dolgoruki. Keith comments in his memoir that the Tsar would be 'govern'd by one much fitter to direct a pack of hounds (which had been his study the greater part of his life) than such a vast empire.'

The marriage between Peter II and Catherine Dolgoruki was declared towards the end of November 1729, while the actual ceremony was scheduled for early the following year. Some of the Dolgorukis were pressing for the marriage to be consummated immediately while others, in the majority, preferred to wait so that a ceremony of rich imperial pomp could take place. Courtiers were despatched to Paris for Catherine's wedding clothes and she was escorted everywhere by Horse Guards. With a hint of bitterness Keith says she was treated as though the marriage had already taken place and she had been given the title of Empress by foreign diplomats trying to ingratiate themselves.

As Keith brooded over his career and future prospects in Russia, fate took yet another twist which was to turn things around for him. At the beginning of 1730 Peter II carried out a review of his troops on the frozen Moscow river in a ceremony similar to the Blessing of the Waters that had carried off his stepmother and predecessor Catherine. Like Catherine he sat in the freezing cold until he felt very ill. At the ceremony's end he complained to Prince Alexis Dolgoruki that he was feeling unwell, only to have his complaints brushed aside and to be taken off hunting. When Peter returned from his hunting trip in the evening his condition had worsened and he was obviously in the grip of a fever; in a day or two, it became known that the young Tsar had smallpox.

As he lay ill the Tsar had only his doctors and the Dolgorukis around him. The Dolgorukis put up a show of indifference and behaved normally to hide the seriousness and true nature of the young man's illness from all outwith the palace's inner circle, leading everyone to imagine that recovery was just a matter of time. On the night of 18 January Peter II died and Moscow awoke next day to startling and unlooked for news – Peter had died on the very day he had expected to be married.

As news of the Tsar's death spread throughout the city, all the ministers, generals and people of distinction were given orders to assemble at the Senate House, where Chancellor Golofskin made a formal announcement. The Supreme Privy Council had, however, already taken some decisions – first it was going to decide the succession on its own authority and second, it was going to break with the existing autocratic system and replace it with a limited constitutional monarchy. Back in the Senate House Prince Demetrius Michailovich Galitzin rose and addressed the assembly in a speech which ended with the declaration that Anna, Duchess of Courland, was to succeed to the Russian throne. This declaration was greeted with universal approbation and joy.

Anna, Duchess of Courland – James Keith's new employer – was a niece of Peter the Great. She was a tall, stout brunette with no social graces, a gruff waspish harridan who, despite being uneducated, had an innate shrewdness. In a continual state of boredom and lazy with it, she diverted herself with banqueting and other festivities. While she sat on the throne court expenditure rose to three times the levels spent when Peter the Great was Tsar. Given the tortuous intrigue and power politics that were characteristic of the imperial court, Anna felt the need to protect herself, and did so by surrounding herself with Germans. Osterman took charge of the Cabinet and foreign policy while Munnich took over the army with the rank of Field Marshal. This was just the beginning of a German takeover on a grand scale – German soon became the language of the court. Russian nobility were forced out of positions of power and influence they had enjoyed and, because Anna had no interest in government, her appointees were given every freedom to interpret their jobs.

The future must have suddenly seemed much brighter for James Keith and it was to become brighter still when a fourth Guards Regiment, called the Ismailovsky, was raised in September 1730. This was a regiment of footguards consisting of 2000 gentlemen, mostly Livonians, and it was so called after the late Tsar's favourite summer palace, the Ismailovo near Moscow. This new regiment gave great offence to the two original Guards regiments, the Preobrazhensky and Semonovsky, each of which had 7000 men – almost entirely Russians. Two months later, the Swede Rheinholde Lowenwolde was made Colonel of the Ismailovsky.

Although the scheming Dolgorukis were now sidelined, they had no intention of letting themselves be completely swept away by events. They had made their own plans to seize power while still using Anna as a front to cover themselves. But the Dolgorukis had left it all too late and power had by now irrevocably slipped from their hands; some of them were exiled to Siberia and others banished from the court and confined to their estates. Only a few – including Keith's military commander Field Marshal Dolgoruki – kept their positions. As the new broom swept clean and all the reorganisation took place James Keith could only watch and hope that in due course, after some years of faithful service, his turn to climb the ladder would also come. At this time he had only been in Russia for about a year.

Count Lowenwolde, already Anna's General Adjutant, duly took up his position as Colonel of the Ismailovsky Guards. It came as a complete surprise to James Keith when Lowenwolde, through General le Fort, sent a note asking that he make himself available next day at court. All night long Keith tossed and turned, wondering what offence he had given or unwitting sin he had committed, even fearing that an enemy at court had made trouble for him. Next morning, full of apprehension, Keith sought an audience with General le Fort, whom he at last found in the company of his old friend, the Duke of Liria, and le Fort's cousin the Polish envoy. Keith quickly got to the point, asking if they were aware of what he was supposed to have done wrong, and who was unhappy with him? They reassured him but the Duke of Liria, recognising what was bothering his friend, hinted that James might be in line for the post of Lieutenant Colonel of the new Guards regiment. Caught unawares, James Keith said that he found that a most improbable suggestion, since the position would most certainly be filled by a much more senior officer.

The little group, who already knew what was going on, agreed with Keith that it was perhaps something else; enjoying their secret and knowing the happiness his promotion would bring. As James himself had said, such a promotion was very unlikely and could only have been pushed along by someone of influence, such as the Duke of Liria. Still hugely embarrassed Keith reported to Count Lowenwolde's office whereupon the Count paid him a compliment and offered him the post of Lieutenant Colonel of his regiment – with twenty-four hours to make upon his mind. There was no thinking to be done: James Keith accepted this great honour immediately and two days later found himself in the presence of the Empress Anna, who formally declared him Lieutenant Colonel of her Guards. As James Keith himself explains:

'All Mosco was as surprised as I was myself: and as the emploiement is looked on as one of the greatest trust in the Empire, and that the officers of the guards are regarded as domesticks of the Souvraign, I received hundreds of visits from people I had never seen or heard of in my life, and who imagined that certainly I must be in great favour at court, in which they were prodigiously deceived.'

When Anna was first offered the Russian throne there had been strings attached: she was not to marry, and not to appoint a successor, as Peter the Great had done. She coyly accepted these conditions, until the throne and the power that went with it were hers. She then tore up her agreement with the Supreme Privy Council and abolished it. From then on all power came back into her own hands; she was helped to exercise it by the German officials who swarmed into Russia from Courland and Livonia. Among these immigrant officials was Ernst Buhren, her favourite and first minister in Courland, who now became a Russian count and Great Chamberlain.

As the Germans moved into positions of power so the screws began to tighten. The Dolgorukis and Golitsyns were perhaps the first but not the last to feel the full brunt of Anna's distrust of

Russians and the apparatus of an eighteenth-century police state was established everywhere. There was no room for dissent, a contrary view or even mild criticism; tens of thousands were sent to Siberia for momentary indiscretions and, given the Russian character, we can assume that most of these indiscretions would have happened while the offender was under the influence of drink. Empress Anna re-established the Secret Chancery, which behaved much as the KGB was to do in Russia 200 years later.

When Anna decided to reinstate the law in force when Peter the Great died, thus allowing her to nominate her successor, she rightly assumed the Russians would be none too happy. On the day before Anna's proposals on the succession were due to be published, James Keith received orders to station his Guards under arms around the Kremlin. The day broke and Moscow found large numbers of armed troops stationed at key points throughout the city. Anna had already ordered all her senators, privy councillors, generals and others to come to the palace. On their arrival she delivered a speech and at its conclusion they were all handed the text of an oath – the very same oath they had taken for Peter the Great, which would allow her to choose her own successor. Since she also wanted her whole army to similarly take the oath, James Keith saw that the oath was administered to his Guards and that all the other regiments around Moscow did the same.

This was to be the last straw for Field Marshal Dolgoruki, until recently Keith's divisional commander. He was less than careful in his criticism, and those to whom he made it; this led to his arrest and a sentence of death. This sentence was later commuted to imprisonment and he was taken off to the citadel of Schlüsselburg. In his memoir Keith describes Field Marshal Dolgoruki's fate with a certain sadness, for the Field Marshal had liked Keith so much he wanted him to marry one of his relatives.

Keith was now in charge of day-to-day security around the Empress and her court: this made him a part of the apparatus which protected the hated and alien German administration ruling Russia. It is difficult to see how he could have been comfortable in his new role, although he probably took the pragmatic view that someone had to do it and it might just as well be him. His official duties took him to the heart of the court and he was in a first-class position to note all the comings and goings. He tells us that ambassadors shortly arrived from Persia, China and Turkey, joining the European representatives already there. With his own natural good manners and social graces, Keith was well suited for the job and the Duke of Liria had found just the slot for him.

Even as early as 1730, a life of drink and dissolution were taking their toll on the Empress Anna. She was so afflicted with gout that even making her way around the palace was a painful exercise, and access to some parts of the palace was almost impossible. Anna's remedy was to build herself a new wooden palace in Moscow which took only three weeks to erect.

Remaining in favour – or even just on the right side of Anna – must have been a difficult business, because of her distrustful and dominating nature, exaggerated by alcohol. Keith wrote:

'Count Osterman managed all the affairs, which were now so well regulated that the Court employed most of the time in amusements fit for the season. While the Carnival lasted, there was twice-a-week balls in mask at the palace, the other days, Italien comedies, musick, or play; and as Peter the Great lov'd neither regularity nor magnificence in his equipage and familly, so the change appeared newer to the Russe nation; for tho' the Empress Catherine had a numerous Court, and certainly the present Empresse cannot enough be commended for the alteration she has made; for the reputation of a nation is what is to be almost as much regarded as its real strength, nothing was more necessary that the changes which might the soonest efface the notions which most of Europe has of the barbarity of the Russian nation; and as strangers form an idea of a wholle country by what they see at Court, and of this we have already the experience, since it's said everywhere that in five years the present Empress has done more to the civilising the nation than Peter the First did in all his reign.'

The year 1731 drew to a close and the Empress decided to uplift her court and move it lock, stock and barrel back to St Petersburg. One possible reason for this is that she wanted to underline to Europe that Russia had taken control of the former Swedish territories on a permanent basis; St Petersburg was in a better position to co-ordinate a response if Sweden were to mobilise again. The other reason might simply have been that she wanted to be nearer her old Courland home.

At first the Empress moved into a house left to the state by Admiral Apraxin, it being somewhat more comfortable than the palace used by Peter the Great. Peter had never spent money on palaces or personal comfort and didn't care where he laid his head at night, just as long as he could waken in the morning and see part of his navy riding at anchor from the window.

As 1732 began, James Keith was moved to another military appointment. Commanding the Empress's Guards must have been a tedious occupation with all the superficiality, grovelling and intrigue which were an everyday part of court life. For someone of Keith's character, his education and deep desire to be a career soldier, the effects of endless socialising could only have been mind-numbing. He had now spent long enough at court to know all the powerful people he had to lobby for a change of post – to have more of a real soldier's life as he climbed the promotional ladder.

In Spain, meanwhile, the Earl Marischal's enthusiasm for plotting and scheming was beginning to wane. Although he still had contact with the Jacobites and met them at councils, the firebrand activist had of late become more cautious and thoughtful. Despite a continuous flow of letters from Marischal's Valencia home to James Keith in Moscow, it is rather obvious that more letters left Valencia for Moscow than the other way round. Marischal was missing his younger brother, with whom he had shared all the dangers of battle and who had been an unquestioning and supportive companion during their time as fugitives together.

As Marischal struggled along on one or two minor sources of income in Valencia, James Keith must surely have been drawing quite a salary from his prestigious appointment as a Guards officer. If we can draw any conclusions, these have to be that James was a big spender, generous to friends and had huge overheads and expenses in keeping servants to help him entertain and return the lavish hospitality expected from someone in his elevated position.

When the loneliness of separation from his brother struck him, or in one of his regular bouts of homesickness, Marischal was fond of taking out maps of Scotland and showing visitors the extent of what had been his estates, his castles and lesser houses. Alone in Valencia, he must have drifted into memories of his childhood at Inverugie before his thoughts returned to his brother, facing the rigours of Russian winters and handicapped by his ever-present asthma.

In a letter dated 12 July 1730 from Valencia, the Earl Marischal wrote to James Keith :

I'm very uneasy about your health, and beg you will take all possible care of your breast, not only when you find it pains you, but also when you are well; all my comfort in this world is to know that you are so, and the hopes I have to see you, for in two years laying by for that journey my rent viagere, I shall be in a condition to make it, and the arrears pay'd me since the time 10 per cent, was stopt of my pension has pay'd my small debts, furnished me a little equipage, and near 200 pistoles in advance, my current pay is sufficient for my expence here, so that in two years I shall have 500 pistoles beforehand, and I am firmly persuaded that the King's goodness to me will not refuse me the consolation to be payed absent for a couple of years to go and see you; I think I cannot fail of bringing it about. If I count right I have 200 pistoles also beforehand in Arbuthnot's. I have wrote to him several times to send me my account, which I have not received, a sure sign that I am not in his debt. There was 300 pound ster: remitted from Scotland long ago by our mother to me; Arbuthnot at that time wrote that you owed him (if I well remember) 150 p. Ster: I told him that out of that 400 he shou'd be payed; let me know if it was. I think I wrote to you at that time, of this. I know you will be glad of the hopes of seeing me and therfore write this long account of my riches present or to come, and also that you may not make ceremony of demanding from hence what this country furnishes; for the money I propose to lay by for my journey, if any share of it shou'd go to your commissions, I count I have it before me in Russia with you, therfor make no ceremony in calling for a 100 pistoles at any time. This war which is like to break out, I think cannot last long, none are in a condition for it; two years I believe will again bring peace.

There is making for us long haired velvet, which imitates well tigre's skin; its much broader than the comon; 6 barres is a full sufficient to line a double breasted coat, the price 1/2 a gold pistole. Send me your measure and I will send you a sute of velvet cloaths; its very cheap, 3 crowns a bar, and a gold pistole is 5 crowns.

I told you in a former letter that I have a good damask bed with its covering which reaches doun to the ground, it costs hardly 12 gold pistoles, I can send you, your bed, your cloathes, and your lining, in a little trunk, as what you had allready used and left behind you in Spain. Let me known how to addresse it, and brandy and wine, and oil if you will. Let me have a speedy answer to all this.

I grumble at the price of charges from Spain to Amsterdam of 2 casks of red wine, 2 casks oil, 2 casks brandy, 130 guilders, but when I consider that the prime cost is allmost nothing and that surely the liquors are excellent if they arrive safe, we will find that its better to send from hence than to buy what the merchants pleases and at their price; one barrel of Rancio is worth 4 bourdeaux. The above liquors were ship'd from Amsterdam to Petersburg Aprile 21, 1730, to Mariotti for the Great Duke. I believe the fraught to Petersburg is also included, but I am not sure, for I don't well understand the heathen language of the merchants. You shall have brandy also this year, and wine, if you like the wine. Adieu

I have two Indian bows with which I shot an arow with only a wooden point thro' a door, and another arrow without any witter fix'd so in the wood that two men could not pull it out; I was forced to open the hole with a gemlet to get out the arrow; if you have any tartar friend you may have them to make a present. The bows are very long, and are not carried bended to shoot with, the string lies slack, so that when you shoot, there is no need of a brace to safe the arm from the stoke of the string.

I have sent you to Petersburg 2 seritores of Indian wood made in London; call for them from Sr H. Sterling, to whom Thraipland sent them; he sais they are very fine.

Adieu; write to me without fail once a month and send me your addresse, now that our friend the Duke leaves you.

Being hard up was, after all, only relative to the standards and lifestyle to which the Keith brothers had been accustomed all their lives. Whatever the decline might have been, it was still very comfortable alongside the grim conditions of the ordinary folk of that time.

8

·

Poland on Fire

·

IN THE NEW YEAR of 1732 the Russian government published an outline of intended reforms, among them a shake-up in the structure of the army. The Moscow proclamation declared that the army was to have an Inspector General with three inspectors under him, one of whom was to be James Keith. His new job gave him responsibility for ensuring that the army in his designated section was efficient and ready for action. In his case the section covered an area along the rivers Volga and Don and also included a part of the Polish frontier around Smolensk.

After the Empress Anna left for St Petersburg, Keith was left in command of all the troops around Moscow, so it was June before he could set out on his first tour of inspection. By that time the morass left by the spring thaw would have dried out, allowing him to make better time in covering the ground. It was a journey that was to take him the rest of the year.

Over the next six months he travelled 4500 miles, or 750 miles a month, reviewing all the thirty-two regiments in his area of responsibility. Travelling 750 miles a month alone in the roadless Russia of 1732 speaks volumes for the dedication Keith brought to his job: such dedication made him a valuable asset to the army. By January 1732 his tour of inspection was complete and he went to St Petersburg to report his findings directly to the Empress and her cabinet.

He arrived at St Petersburg to find that news of the King of Poland's death had preceded him. The court itself was buzzing with excitement as they wound themselves up over the Polish succession. The real question, of course, was who would be best from the Russian point of view. A fierce bout of international lobbying began as all the European ambassadors tried to pull Russia on to their side, each soliciting support for the Polish contender favoured by their own individual governments. Russia meanwhile had its own interests and treaties with Poland to consider.

Russia had been a signatory to the Treaty of Grodno and, as one of the guarantors, stood firmly behind a part of the treaty which expressly excluded one of the contenders already vying for Poland's vacant throne – Stanislav. Russia's main objection to Stanislav was that his election would perpetuate a single line in the succession which would ultimately lead to a strengthening of the Polish crown and therefore become a threat to Poland's neighbours in the long term.

Count Lowenwolde had also just returned to St Petersburg from an ambassadorial posting in Vienna. He was now ordered to turn around and set off to Warsaw to discover if there was a Polish candidate whom Russia could back – and who could command enough support to win an election. If such a candidate were to be found, ran Lowenwolde's explicit instructions, he was to offer him Russia's support. The Russians' fallback position appeared to be support for the Elector of Saxony, if he alone seemed capable of defeating Stanislav.

Unfortunately for Lowenwolde, he was to discover that the strength of support for Stanislav among the other European states cancelled all his options and left him with his back to the wall in diplomatic terms. He made Russia's uncompromising opposition clear to Stanislav, who had been branded a traitor to his country during the discussions of the Diet of Grodno in 1717, which further banned Stanislav from holding lands or position in Poland.

Several of Poland's greatest families, who had probably been canvassed earlier, now approached Russia expressing their opposition to Stanislav and begging the Russians to intervene. Nothing appealed more to the Russians than to enter a power struggle which could so thoroughly destabilise Poland. The scene had been set for war and some 30 000 men were mobilised at Riga into an army commanded by General Peter Lacy, governor of that city, while 16 000 more were moved up to Smolensk under General

Sagraskoi. James Keith was also on the move with 6000 infantry, marching through the Ukraine to await orders to enter Volhynia (western Poland) if required.

Understandably perturbed by these preparations, the Poles enlisted the aid of the Primate of Pototski who pleaded for more time for Poland to resolve her own differences internally, and a delay to Russian intervention. It was never going to be a sustainable strategy and Poland's bluff was soon called when the dissident Polish nobility cried for help at the end of July 1733. Only weeks later General Peter Lacy was marching on Warsaw to forestall any election that would put Stanislav on the throne with the support of the Polish people behind him.

Something should be said about General Peter Lacy, Keith's friend and comrade in arms.[†] Lacy was a popular officer among those he commanded; born at Killedly, County Limerick, in 1678, he opted for the army as a profession when just a lad and had his first taste of action at the Siege of Limerick. After Limerick's fall he fled to France where he learned more of his trade under Catinet during the Piedmont campaigns, brilliantly distinguishing himself at the Battle of Marsiglia in 1693. He had been in the Polish army before the Russian and was involved in all of the five campaigns following the Siege of Riga, which earned him the rank of Lieutenant General. Lacy had a quick temper and was prone to take offence at trivial things, although this was counterbalanced by both his bravery and generosity. He was incapable of committing a mean action and, like Keith, he kept himself out of political intrigue as best he could.

The dissident Polish nobles, together with their supporters, left Warsaw, gathering so much armed support at their camp near Prague that they became confident of beating back any attack.

But autumn had arrived, the weather had broken and Lacy was delayed as rain turned what passed for roads into a muddy morass, making his arrival in Warsaw unlikely before the end of September. Despite this delay, obvious to all, the mere threat of Russian invasion was enough to make Stanislav move his forces and, with most of Poland's nobles, he retreated to Danzig, thereby abandoning Warsaw and all of his preparations to seize the Polish crown.

[†] R. Nisbet Bain, *The Pupils of Peter the Great* (Field Marshal Peter Lacy).

Stanislav was not without support – around 20 000 men had joined him, although these men were dispersed in smaller units over a wide area, thus obliging the Russians also to split their forces. Lacy swung his army round to blockade Stanislav in Danzig, while other elements of the Russian forces moved into action, and James Keith was ordered to march into Volhynia. He crossed the frozen River Dnieper in the middle of December with six battalions of infantry, 600 dragoons and 4000 Cossacks, marching for ten days without encountering the enemy. Meanwhile his intelligence sources were telling him that Polish recruitment had boosted their numbers so that he could now expect to find himself opposed by an army of 12 000, outnumbering his own by two to one.

The Russian court decided that Keith had insufficient men to do the job; as a result Lieutenant General Prince Schahofskoi was ordered to take command and to march up with 2000 additional dragoons, joining Keith at Nemirof on 5 January 1734.

A lack of supplies forced Schahofskoi to delay the forward movement of his troops by nearly a month, and in order to keep occupied he set about destroying all the surrounding estates. On 11 January Schahofskoi gave Keith 3000 horsemen for a burning and looting expedition but Keith, not thinking this an honourable employment, tried to get himself excused from taking part – only to be firmly ordered to do so.

During the pillaging expedition he collected thousands of cattle and hundreds of poor quality horses which were sent back to the Russian lines. Along with the animals he sent a report that all the civilian population were leaving their villages and escaping into Moldavia. He pointedly complained that if he was to continue as at present, the whole surrounding country would be reduced to a desert and the Russian troops would starve.

Schahofskoi finally recalled Keith to continue the march. They reached Vinnitz on the River Bug where they found themselves opposed by 10 000 men. The Russians advanced further and when they next stopped the following day, they found the enemy just twelve miles away, camped on a plain with a forest barrier separating both forces. The enemy's plan was to wait for the Russians to come tumbling through the forest in confusion before unleashing their attack. Information about the enemy's troop strengths and disposition was offered to the Russians by a Polish informer, one whose information on a previous occasion had proved false – the informer was told to go and, should he ever return, he could expect to end his days hanging from the end of a rope.

Before moving off Keith advised Schahofskoi to change the battle order and put the grenadiers with a battalion of infantry and two cannon forward to spearhead their way through the trees and push the waiting Poles away from the rest of the advancing Russian army. This would have allowed the army and the Cossacks time to form up into battle order. Schahofskoi wasn't going to be lectured or advised in any way and sent the quartermasters on ahead. When Keith and the rest of the army were about halfway through the woods they heard the sound of gunfire as the quartermasters reached the clearing beyond the trees. Fortunately for Schahofskoi the wood was not quite so dense at his army's exit point and enough dragoons and Cossacks got through to rout the 2000 waiting Poles, driving them back another twelve miles.

The Poles retreated and by next morning they were thirty-six miles away. Orders arrived that Schahofskoi was to hand command over to Keith and return to the Ukraine. Taking no chances, Schahofskoi took 1200 horsemen as an escort, leaving Keith's corps weakened by their departure.

Keith's men resumed their march towards a town called Medziboz and its heavily fortified castle. His march was halted when the governor intercepted the advancing Russians with an offer of capitulation, which was accepted. Everything had been made ready for Keith's victorious entry into Medziboz and he was probably looking forward to a proper lodging and a decent bed for the night in the castle; Keith therefore told his major general to billet the army away from the castle and nearer to the town. With only twenty-four dragoons Keith went towards the castle – it had a good ditch, a drawbridge leading to a covered way into a courtyard – but it was only when Keith was in the castle and met by 200 Poles that he realised his mistake. Luckily no one else appeared to notice the potential trap into which he had blundered: Keith ordered his adjutant to bring up the equipment wagons and include 150 grenadiers with the transport – 'and come with all haste' he added. Keith wryly tells us that had the Poles shut the castle gates his army only had a few three-pound cannons with which to take the place against the castle's fourteen cannons which were supplied with an abundance of ammunition; he would certainly have remained a prisoner.

While Keith sweated it out, wondering if anyone else was alive to the situation, the wagons and grenadiers trundled up into the castle. With his troops now behind him Keith advised the governor that he was taking over the castle and that the governor and his garrison must seek lodging in the town. The boot was firmly on the other foot and it took only one reminder from Keith – that he had the men to enforce his will – to send a still-protesting governor and his men marching out of the castle.

Next day, at his headquarters, Keith consulted with his senior officers on whether to march out after the enemy or to wait for the return of the 1200 horse, taken as escort by Schahofskoi. They decided to wait, thinking that they might lose the returning escort in an action with elements of the 9000-strong Polish army if they further stretched the distance between them. The escort returned, bringing with them news that Baron Wedell along with 600 dragoons and a similar number of Cossacks was coming up to join them at Medziboz and could be expected in two days and that the Baron was carrying orders for Keith from General Wiesbach.

When Wedell arrived he duly handed over orders to halt the advance and quarter the troops on the Dniester. The reason for this was that the Chan of Tartary had just marched out of the Crimea with 120 000 men and was suspected of planning to enter Moldavia to join up with the Poles. Keith immediately split his army into three parts to cover all possible eventualities arising from this new development.

A month of waiting followed and Wiesbach sent a further message, that twelve companies of Polish Crown Guards had been garrisoned along with some other troops in the town of Brodi. The best intelligence available suggested that these troops might just about change sides, being less than devoted to Stanislav and thus leaving Brodi wide open for Keith to occupy. Wiesbach's orders specified that Wedell should take only 2000 dragoons as that was enough to do the job. Ever conscious of his men, Keith remonstrated with Wiesbach, telling him that to get to Brodi, Wedell would first have to get through 5000 enemy troops. Instead, Keith proposed to take his whole corps on a march to Brodi, after taking them out of their winter quarters, since the grass was now long enough for the horses' forage.

On 6 April, after a march of three days, Keith drew up his army to find out what lay ahead of them. Three prisoners were taken and their information was that the Palatinate of Volhynia was about six Polish leagues distant with 5000 men, and the Starost of Radom four leagues away with 1000 regular troops.

Keith ordered only half his horse and those carrying stores for his foot soldiers to forage; he needed the rest available in case the enemy saw their opportunity to launch a surprise attack on him. The Cossacks were somewhat undisciplined and none too careful with their foraging, which always made them vulnerable to just such a surprise attack. Against that eventuality Keith had Baron Wedell advance with 700 horse to cover the Cossacks but it was too late, for the Cossacks had already been caught at their foraging and shut up in a town by the Polish vanguard. The situation was even worse than that, however, for the Palatin of Volhynia with his whole army of 110 troops of cavalry were even now in full march against the trapped Cossacks.

Wedell was given orders to take his horse to the rescue of the Cossacks immediately, as Keith gathered the rest of his own cavalry together to follow up behind him as soon as possible. Major Heidenreich was told to march the three regiments of foot up to join the rest of the army at his best possible speed.

When he arrived Keith was relieved to find his Cossacks had been sprung from their trap by Wedell's horse, but the enemy, who were now about 5000 strong, faced them from about 1000 yards away, across a plain and with a wood to their rear.

Keith's own forces were 1700 dragoons and 1000 Cossacks: his infantry had not yet come up. He gave the order to charge and the Poles were soon driven into the wood behind them by the dragoons, where they were dispersed among the tree cover. The Poles lost 300 men with thirty-eight taken prisoner, while the Keith corps lost ninety men, mostly before Wedell arrived with his relief force.

Keith stopped his men in order to give them a day's rest before setting out in pursuit of the Poles, only to be given a letter informing him that his command had been given to the Prince of

Hesse Homburg by the Empress. Keith sent an escort of 200 dragoons to bring in his successor.

Short of provisions, Keith's – or rather Hesse Homburg's – army had to find food. They found large quantities of grain abandoned when its owners fled into Moldavia and they were to spend the next three weeks in making biscuit sufficient to feed the army for another month. By May 1734 they were marching on Brodi, bypassing a little fort in their way because it was not worth the effort involved in subduing it. On 1 June, Brodi lay just nine miles in front of them and Baron Wedell was sent to demand its surrender, whereupon he found that the information about disloyal Crown Guards had been thoroughly misleading and his demand for surrender was rejected.

The next night 2000 men went to attack the town, only to find that it had been abandoned – both troops and citizenry were now inside the citadel. This citadel contained twelve companies of Crown Guards, amounting to about 800 men, 200 other infantry and 100 dragoons. The real obstacles, however, were the thirty-two cannons, three mortars and plentiful ammunition ready for a prolonged siege.

Although the Prince of Hesse had asked General Wiesbach to send him some large cannons from Kiev, their transport over the fifty Polish leagues to Brodi was calculated to take up to three weeks. The Poles were not to know this, of course, and the Russians made a pretence of raising batteries behind some empty houses standing on an esplanade in front of the citadel. After eight days the apprehensive Poles sought a parley and after hostages were exchanged, James Keith went forward to carry out negotiations with the citadel.

The offer Keith was to get from the Poles was one of a conditional withdrawal from the citadel, carrying off as much of their weaponry as possible, while what was left was not to be used by Keith's army. Never one to pussyfoot when he held the aces, his reply was an uncompromising demand that the Poles 'surrender prisoners of war, with a promise that they would be sent no farther into Russia than the toun [sic] of Kiev, to be kept till they were either relieved or the war at an end.'

As the parley dragged on, with offer and counter-offer being played back and forth across the negotiating table, word was brought to Keith that the Poles were presently engaged in opening two new embrasures in the parapet which would allow them an increased intensity of fire on the Russians if negotiations failed and battle were to commence. Keith quickly got up and sent an officer with a drummer along to the citadel, to order the enemy to stop what they were doing at once, otherwise negotiations would be broken off and orders given for his own batteries to open up – the non-existent batteries which he pretended were only awaiting the order to fire. The parleying came to a temporary halt while an answer to Keith's ultimatum was awaited. However, it was to be the citadel's messenger who arrived first, bringing orders to the citadel's negotiators to wind up the talks and capitulate. From then on it took only two hours to agree the fine details of the surrender. The gates of the citadel were to be given over that evening and in the morning the enemy was to march out, colours flying, drums beating, to make their way to Keith's camp to be disarmed and marched off as prisoners to Kiev. Everything of any use was to be delivered up to the Russians.

It was only the Polish soldiers who were taken to Kiev: the civilian populace, who had carried everything they owned with them into the refuge of the citadel, were given freedom to take their goods and to go wherever they pleased. The blockade of Brodi citadel had taken just ten days and cost the Russians the lives of only ten men while, forty miles away, a superior army of enemy troops had waited, refusing to seek battle.

Keith's Russian army consisted of only six battalions of foot soldiers and was considerably under strength for the task it had been given. Keith proposed to his commanding officer that the citadel be blown up, rather than further reduce their strength by leaving some of their men behind to garrison it. The Prince of Hesse Homburg doubted that this line of action would go down too well with a watching Empress and her court. Instead of taking Keith's advice, he ordered that 500 men, among whom were dismounted dragoons, were to be left to hold the fortress. The rest of the army – about 9000 men – were just about to march away when orders arrived from General Wiesbach telling them to stay where they were.

Wiesbach couldn't have known it but the horses had eaten all the grass around Brodi, forcing a move on the Russians anyway. By this time the prospect of being marched off to Kiev and an uncertain fate as prisoners of war had given the Polish Crown Guards pause for thought. They were persuaded to swear allegiance to King Augustus, the Russian candidate for the Polish throne, and given back their weapons before marching out with their new Russian comrades. The Russians and Crown Guards had barely started to move when a further 1000 Moldavian horsemen joined them on the road – these horsemen had allowed themselves to be surprised by the Palatin of Volhynia only the day before and left 300 of their number dead behind them.

The army's new objective was an enemy fort at Zabarage and it was there that Keith's Russians next drew up to a halt, about 1000 yards short of the fort. A call for surrender was rejected and Keith was given 400 workmen and 600 troops to get on with a siege. It was not the first time that the fort at Zabarage had come under attack: eighty years earlier, the fort had been besieged by Cossacks, who had used covered approaches in their attempt. Using these same routes to the fort, James moved his men and equipment up to within half a musketshot of the fort under cover of darkness.

As daylight came, Keith's cannon and muskets opened up on the fort – until then it had had no inkling he was anywhere near them. Recovering from their initial surprise the fort engaged in a brisk return of fire but this was only to last until noon, when they too gave up and surrendered as prisoners of war. In all the fire exchanged between the two sides Keith lost only two men, with two casualties. When Keith entered the fort he found it manned by 200 men and armed with fourteen cannons, two mortars and an abundance of ammunition which would have allowed for a much more extended defence.

General Wiesbach's orders restricted any further scope for a move from where they were and, to profitably use their time, corn was harvested from the surrounding fields to supply food for both the fort at Zabarage and Brodi behind them. As grain was being taken from the fields they were joined by General Major Spiegel and two regiments of foot, two of dragoons and 1000 more Cossacks, bringing the corps strength up to 18 000 men. James Keith reckoned that had permission been granted, they could have driven the confederate Polish army to the other side of the River

Vistula. Instead they stayed where they were until October, with nothing very much heard or seen of the Poles, apart from some skirmishing which cost the Russians forty men and two officers.

Winter was fast approaching and the first flakes of snow began to fall. Keith's army went into various winter quarters which protected their extended lines of communication stretching all the way back to Kiev. James Keith, Prince Hesse Homburg and General Heidenbach took quarters at Sokal until 30 December 1734, only to learn that the enemy had moved even further away, allowing them to move up all the Russian troops quartered on the River Bug. They went on to take control of most of Volhynia, comprising the east side of Poland from the Sanne to the Dnieper. But winter had really arrived by now and the Russian army was to stay where it was until the spring of 1735 allowed them to pick up their campaign again.

James Keith's own account of 1734 manifests a view of life softened by a quiet good humour, occasionally soured by a hurt cynicism. There seemed to be no malice in him, as evidenced by his obvious anxiety to spare civilians in war zones and his own troops from unnecessary exposure to danger. His words and actions suggest, unusually for that time, a humane side to his character.

In the spring of 1735, Keith's army moved out of their winter quarters to strike further into Volhynia. As they pushed forwards all opposition faded away before them until there was nothing to stop Keith's troops from making a rendezvous with General Peter Lacy who was at this time still laying siege to Danzig: King Stanislav was now looking out at a huge Russian army from within his fortress city.

The Empress and her court at St Petersburg wanted a quick end to this war, not least because things were again looking ominous on Russia's southern borders with Turkey – even during Peter the Great's time there had only ever been periods of grudging peace between Russia and Turkey before hostilities broke out again. Perhaps because it was thought Lacy had taken too long over the Siege of Danzig, or perhaps because Munnich appeared to promise a quicker result: whatever the reason, Field Marshal Munnich replaced Lacy as supreme commander and Keith was appointed second in command.[†]

Munnich had joined the Hesse Darmstadt army with a commission in 1701 and had served under Prince Eugene; he fought in the War of the Spanish Succession, took part in both the Siege of Landau and the invasion of Provence, was present at the Battle of Oudenarde, made a colonel for his valour at Malplaquet and left for dead on the bloody field of Denain where he was then captured by the French. His French captors so impressed him with their culture that he affected French manners and etiquette for the rest of his life. This Francophilia gave his employer Peter the Great noticeable misgivings.

Munnich joined the Russian service after successfully submitting plans for the fortification of Peter the Great's newly acquired Baltic provinces and was subsequently given the post of Lieutenant General of Engineers, making his debut at St Petersburg in 1721. Munnich had an extremely juvenile appearance and so disgusted his rough and ready Tsar with his *esprit* and *finesse* that Peter largely ignored him.

But Munich's star really rose when Anna came to the throne and he was successively War Minister, Field Marshal, Governor of St Petersburg and Chief of the Corps of Cadets.

General Lacy's job at Danzig was never going to be easy. After he had garrisoned Warsaw, Thorn and the other places he had captured, Lacy found that he only had 12 000 men left to conduct the siege. These troops were spread over twelve miles and exposed to attacks by an estimated 50 000 guerrillas.[‡]

On 17 March 1734 Lacy was relieved of his command by Munnich who arrived with reinforcements. Two days later a strongly fortified redoubt named 'Scotland' was to fall to the

---

[†] Field Marshal Burkhard Christoph Munnich came from a line of Oldenberg squires who had long been producing talented engineers. His father and grandfather had both been officers in the Danish service and contributed towards the elaborate dyke system in the Delmenhorst district between the Weser and North Sea. R. Nisbet Bain, *The Pupils of Peter the Great* (Field Marshal Burkhard Christoph Munnich).

[‡] Thomas Carlyle: *Frederick the Great* vol. 1. p. 320.

Russians in a night attack during a driving gale. As the siege went on the ill-equipped Russian troops were being lost to the cold through their lack of boots and sheepskins. There was no forage for the horse and the Polish guerrillas were a constant harassment. Nothing ever happened fast enough for Munnich and even though he did not have the requisite artillery that was not to stop him from launching another succession of assaults which were doomed to failure from the beginning. In one single night, he lost between 2000 and 4000 men on an assault against a strongly defended position called the Hagelberg, for which he was roundly condemned by his military colleagues.

Some mortars eventually arrived for Munnich and by 6–7 May, Fort Sommerschantz had fallen, cutting Danzig off from its port at the mouth of the Vistula. On 10 June the Russian fleet under Admiral Gordon brought Munnich eighteen large mortars and forty-eight battering cannons which ranged in calibre from eighteen to thirty-six pounders. He now had all he needed to bring Danzig to its knees.

Munnich first turned his attention to the French contingent on the Isle La Platte and trained his fire on them. The French surrendered and were then taken on board the Russian fleet as prisoners bound for St Petersburg. Perhaps it was Munnich remembering French kindnesses during his own days as a prisoner, but when the French arrived at St Petersburg each prisoner was given a great coat lined with sheepskin, while the officers had one lined with fine foxskin.

After the French surrender on La Platte, the fortress of Weichselmunde also surrendered and King Stanislav realised that it was time either to flee or stay and be taken prisoner. On the night of 27 June, he slipped out of Danzig disguised as a cattle dealer and escaped to Prussia. Danzig fell to the Russians on 30 June; it surrendered unconditionally after 135 days of siege that had cost the Russians 8000 men.

Although James Keith distinguished himself in the action and was promoted to Lieutenant General, he must have hated being party to this profligate use of his soldiers, when it could only have been a matter of time before hunger or negotiation opened the gates of Danzig to the Russian army. This was not to be Keith's last spell of duty with Munnich as his superior officer and he was soon to find himself involved in yet more useless bloodshed.

9

·

The Siege of Otchakov

·

DANZIG WAS NOW AN open city and Stanislav had fled. Keith and Lacy were given orders to take 20 000 men and march to Mannheim, where they were to join forces with an Austrian army commanded by Prince Eugene. After a tedious two-month march through Silesia and Thuringia they met up with their Austrian ally on the banks of the River Neckar. Hardly had they greeted each other than they learned that the fighting was over and a peace treaty had been concluded between the warring nations.

Peace in the 1700s was a fragile and short-lived flower, however. When a young James Keith had taken the decision to be a career soldier, he had at least ensured himself a lifetime of regular employment on active duty. No sooner had the War of the Polish Succession ended than yet another war broke out: this time the hostilities were between Russia and her Austrian allies, and Turkey.

From 1733 onwards, the French had been at pains to engineer a rupture between Russia and her neighbours, Sweden in the north and Turkey in the south, and France's efforts were now rewarded.

A series of affronts to Russian national pride prompted Foreign Minister Osterman to advise the Empress to go to war against the Turks. A formal declaration of war was drawn up by Osterman and despatched to the Turkish Grand Vizier on 23 July 1735. While Keith and Lacy were in Austria their less than popular superior Munnich was ordered to proceed at once from the Vistula to the Don and there to make preparations for opening the Russian campaign.

117

A more pragmatic reason for the war was, however, geographical: the estuaries of all five of Russia's great rivers flowed into Turkish waters, giving Turkey a stranglehold on Russia's commerce; it also allowed Turkey to help herself to all the area's cattle and grain. The keys to Turkish control of this huge area of commercial importance were the heavily manned fortresses of Azov and Otchakov.

Throughout 1736 Munnich prepared for war, but he was soon joined by Lacy, who had been given joint orders to wage war. It was to be an uncomfortable partnership: Lacy couldn't stand the sight of Munnich and had himself been made a Field Marshal since the siege of Danzig. This personal rivalry between the pair had been inflamed after Keith and Lacy had gone to help Austria: Lacy had stayed at the Viennese court, which also heartily detested Munnich, and the Austrians had presented him with his portrait set in diamonds together with a beautiful gold and scarlet casket containing 5000 ducats. While James Keith remained with the army in the north, Lacy now left him to join up with Munnich in the Ukraine.

Munnich and Lacy lost no time in making a bad start, both now being of equal rank and both having been led to believe that they were to be in overall command of the army. As they began to plan operations in pursuance of a war against the Turks, the situation worsened quite dramatically. Professional jealousy and personal animosity made any agreement impossible and they finally managed to agree only to keep in touch and let each other know what they were doing. Munnich then went off to invade the Crimea and Lacy marched off to lay siege to the fortress of Azov, promising to hurry his troops along to Munnich's aid in the Crimea after he had finished his chosen task.

On 20 April 1737, Munnich began his march across the steppes to Perekop at the head of 57 000 men. On his way south he was constantly attacked by Tartar tribes and, as an interesting defensive tactic, adopted the old Scottish battle formation of a schiltron. In this case, however, the schiltron was hollow and mobile with his troops on the outside perimeter and field artillery positioned at the corners. This was the first time this battle formation had been used by the Russians.

These huge squares moved on across the flat, featureless plain between the Ukraine and the Crimea, a slowly moving fortress of men, animals and baggage trains. Indeed, the necessity of the baggage trains must have been irritating for Munnich because of their slowness. He was reported never to begin a campaign with anything less than 80 000 supply wagons.

As his army rolled along, the Tartar nation was being mobilised – all the males from seventeen to seventy and hundreds of Tartar women now joined in the war. The Tartars chose their moment and launched an assault on the Russian schiltron, attacking it simultaneously on all sides in two hours of solid battle. It was all to no avail – the Tartars fled from this first exchange of fire and the Russians never even lost a man.

Munnich stormed along, capturing the fortress of Or-Kapi and the Lines of Perekop: this was a trench system, each deep trench twenty-five fathoms broad and stretching clean across the isthmus connecting the Crimea with Russia. With the fall of the Lines of Perekop the Tartars fled into the mountains taking their wives and children with them. But Munnich's Russian army was now very short of fresh food and water, while dysentery made its presence felt and horses began dying in their hundreds for want of forage.

After some more fighting Munnich rendered the Crimea a virtual desert, incapable of any defence, and returned with his army to the Ukraine.

As Munnich took the Crimea apart Lacy was no less effective at Azov, although he met with much stiffer resistance. On 18 June a Russian bomb found its way into the main magazine at Azov, blowing up 300 houses and five mosques. Eleven days later Azov surrendered and Peter Lacy sent his eldest son off with the keys of the fortress to the Empress Anna that same evening. Lacy then left Azov and marched into the Crimea to make good his promise to join Munnich, only to find that Munnich was long gone – without even bothering to tell him of his departure. It would probably be something of an understatement to say that this did not endear Munnich to Lacy.

By the time he had returned to the Ukraine, Munnich had lost 2000 men in battle but had lost a total of 30 000, or half his force, to hunger, an unhealthy climate and sheer fatigue. Munnich did not look after his men: after marching them for hours in scorching heat, his soldiers would often simply fall down dead at the roadside. For Munnich's long-suffering troops the war was still not finished – Munnich took the field at the end of April 1737 to open his second campaign, which was to prove the bloodiest of the war and involved a Russian army of 70 000 men.

For this second campaign James Keith was given orders to leave Silesia taking Lacy's army with him and to join Munnich in the Ukraine. Munnich's primary objective this time was the Turkish fortress of Otchakov, situated between the rivers Dnieper and Bug. It was by far the largest Turkish fortress and was defended by 20 000 of Turkey's best soldiers.

On 29 June the Russian army crossed the Bug; forming three huge squares it followed the river to Otchakov where it halted within a cannonshot of the fortress on 10 July. Otchakov was shaped in the form of an irregular oblong, flanked by bastions. Three sides were surrounded by a parapet and a glacis, with a twelve-foot wide ditch below, although on the sea side of the fortress town it was only protected by a low wall, poorly defended.[†] Munnich had hoped to meet up with his siege train, stores and ammunition: they had been put onto a fleet of large, flat, double sloops, built just for the purpose of conveying his supplies down the Dnieper. The sloops had been sent off in plenty of time but had fallen victim to the same misfortunes as befell Peter the Great; his boats had run aground in shallows or been lost to roaring rapids. Munnich had no supply boats, and no one could tell him when or even if they would arrive. For eight miles around Otchakov the grass had been burnt by the Turks as had all the wood; there was not a stick with which to construct siege equipment and water was also in short supply.

For the next two days Munnich occupied a few half-ruined Turkish redoubts situated in gardens around the town before starting to bomb Otchakov. Munnich blazed away with what little he had, always anticipating the hour when his sloops would appear at the mouth of the Dnieper until, in the early morning of 13 July, they saw that the wooden houses in Otchakov had caught fire and that the firefighters were not succeeding in putting the fires out.

† Thomas Carlyle: *Frederick the Great*, vol. 1. pp. 413–414

James Keith was in the centre of Munnich's line and taking the brunt of returning Turkish gunfire when Munnich's thoughts turned to him, as he contemplated a diversion whereby the firefighters might be distracted from their task, allowing the fires to burn further out of control. His plan was to launch an assault upon the fortress walls, knowing all the time that even when they got there, nothing was available to take his men over and into Otchakov. Even worse, there was not a bit of cover to shield the Russians from the Turkish defenders' fire as they advanced up to the mouths of the fortress guns.

Keith turned from watching the battle to find Munnich's adjutant behind him on horseback with orders from Munnich to 'advance within musketshot, General Keith'. To which Keith, pointing out his soldiers lying dead on the field, frostily replied: 'I have been this good while within it'. This riposte was conveyed back to Munnich but did not have the desired effect; the adjutant came back with yet another order: 'Advance within half a musket shot, General Keith, and quit any covert you have!' Keith could only acknowledge this order while at the same time sending back his respects and remonstrances about the waste of human lives.

Yet a third time the adjutant came back – 'Field Marshal Munnich is for trying a scalade; hopes General Keith will do his best to co-operate.' Keith moved his forces closer to the walls only to be met with a wet ditch twelve feet wide – and he without engineers or equipment to help him across. For two hours under murderous fire Keith did what he could to overcome this obstacle until finally his men would take no more and retreated out of range of the enemy guns. As Keith's Russians moved back under the cover they had first found in the gardens around the town, the Turks made a quick foray out to kill all the wounded as they lay helpless beneath the walls.

Munnich saw his forces retreat and, either in despair or frustration, threw his sword to the ground exclaiming 'all is lost' before going on to try and blame his defeat on Keith's excessive 'impetuosity'. Keith was furious when he heard this, having only obeyed orders which were against his own better judgement. He sent a message to Munnich, asking him to desist from saying such things about him – otherwise he would seek a court martial, when he would not fail to point out each and every blunder Munnich had committed since the siege began.

The siege at Otchakov in July 1737 lasted for three weeks. It took four assaults in all before the fortress finally fell, the fourth assault cost the lives of 3000 men. In the end the town was in flames and the main arsenal exploded, killing 6000 men. The Cossacks, alive as ever to any opportunity, saw a chance to run off with the Turkish horses corralled just outside and to the rear of Otchakov. The Turks came out to try and save their horses from capture and the Cossacks forced their way in behind them as the Turks retreated into the town.

The butchery in Otchakov was unspeakable, with no quarter asked or given from either side. The Turkish dead were estimated at 17 000 killed on the walls or in the ditches, with a further 3000 drowned as they tried to swim out to the safety of Turkish galleys anchored in the harbour. Sometime, somewhere, during all the confusion and noise of battle, Keith happened to glance downwards and find a little Turkish girl clinging desperately to his stirrup. He leaned down and scooped her up to the safety of his saddle as the battle raged around him, for his own troops would have recognised her dress and cut her down along with the Turkish soldiers. This young girl's name was Emete Tulla: her father had been a captain of the Janissaries and her rescue by Keith was an incredible piece of good fortune for her. Emete Tulla was to be given a home by the Earl Marischal and eventually became his adopted daughter.

The siege of Otchakov now over, Munnich was forced to take his army fifteen miles distant to escape the stench of decomposing bodies. The Russians had lost many men in the action with a disproportionate loss of officers, and Keith himself had not come out of it unscathed. He had been wounded in the knee.

After the battle, Keith was lying injured when Munnich paid him a visit. 'Monsieur de Keith' said Munnich, after all the niceties and mutual congratulations had been attended to: 'Methinks it is partly to you that we owe the success of this great entreprise.' 'Nay, your Excellency,' replied Keith, probably still remembering the recent slanders so lately thrown at him, 'nay I don't want to make the least merit out of the affair. What I did was done absolutely in obedience to your orders.'

Towards August Munnich returned once more to the Ukraine, leaving Keith in sole command of the occupying army. The rest of the campaign was uneventful and the army marched and counter-marched along the Bug, covering against any further attack while the Russians rebuilt what were now their own defences. Keith's musketball wound in the knee did not heal but he stubbornly refused to rest or seek better medical help. Given the limited medical expertise available to him, it was something of a miracle that he did not lose his life through gangrene or some other infection. All through the winter of 1737–38 he continued in his command, giving orders and directions to the 50 000 men in Russian-occupied forts and positions along the Ukrainian border. When he was forced to leave his bed he was transported in a hammock and, not surprisingly, his leg got worse. The wound finally forced Keith to leave his command before hostilities resumed once more in the spring of 1738.

When word of Keith's condition reached St Petersburg, the Empress Anna promoted him to General of Infantry, remarking to courtiers that 'I would sooner lose 10 000 of my best soldiers than Keith.' News of the injury also reached Valencia, where the Marischal hurriedly packed his bags and set off for Russia. The Earl Marischal had been sending casks of brandy, wine, snuff and other goods to James in Russia almost from the moment he left. In return he had requested certain other presents for himself: along with the furs and other Russian goods of interest to Marischal, James Keith had sent him two young men to be his servants, a Tartar called Ibrahim and a Kalmuk named Stepan, both of them at one time prisoners but now the devoted personal servants of the Earl Marischal. This group now left Spain for Russia, crossing through France, Germany and Warsaw to meet up with the wounded general.

Although the Russians and their Austrian ally were more than ready to sign a peace treaty, the Turks had been victorious in Hungary and were not yet ready to consider peace. As the Russian officer responsible for the conduct of war in the Crimea, James Keith felt that he had to carry on in his post for as long as he could. But when Marischal caught up with his brother, near the Black Sea, he was in an extremely poor state of health. To Marischal the wound looked serious and he was less than impressed with his brother's medical care. So concerned was he that he worked hard at persuading Keith to return to St Petersburg, in order that more expert doctors could examine his leg. Marischal prevailed and a motley group comprising James Keith, Marischal, Ibrahim, Stepan and Emete Tulla set off for St Petersburg, probably accompanied by a substantial armed escort.

After a trying and extremely painful journey they at last arrived and the Empress's personal physician was sent to examine Keith. Marischal had arrived just in the nick of time; the Empress's surgeon now proposed that there was really no alternative to amputation, and a weary Keith, suffering so much pain, agreed to let the surgeon get on and do it. Despite his brother's obvious agony Marischal wasn't prepared to hear of amputation and was faced with the daunting task of telling the Empress's surgeon that he wanted another opinion – implying that the Russian was not up to his job and risking the wrath of the Empress herself. As it happened, the surgeon himself fell ill, providing just the excuse Marischal needed to get James Keith out of Russia and off to Paris, which was a centre of excellence for medical science at that time. Marischal is reputed to have said 'I hope that James will yet have much use of his leg, and won't give it away so easily, at least, not till I have bespoke the best advice the world can give.'

The Empress Anna gave permission for her general to seek help in Paris and had them come to the palace before leaving Russia. James Keith was carried into Anna's Winter Palace for his audience, accompanied by Marischal and Buhren. Among her dogs, dwarves, bird cages and courtiers, Anna expressed sympathy for Keith and gave him 5000 roubles for his expenses. It is interesting to note that when the Keith brothers left St Petersburg they went to Paris via Berlin where they met King Frederick William of Prussia, Keith being carried into his presence on a stretcher. It is reported that the King's son (later Frederick the Great) was also present and everyone was much impressed with what they discovered of each other.

Once in Paris, it did not take long for Marischal to gather a group of surgeons around his brother's bed; they too shared the Russian opinion that the leg would have to come off. One surgeon, however, suggested that instead of hurrying to take the leg off, they should enlarge the wound for a closer examination.

This more radical surgeon got his way and there, deep in the knee, was a piece of gaiter. It only now needed the wound to be cleaned for the healing process to begin, but the months of pain and the privations of war had left James Keith a sick man. Ever anxious for his brother's welfare, Marischal took Keith away to Bareges in the Pyrenees where the spa's healing waters could work their therapy. A whole summer at Bareges with his brother looking after him helped Keith to a full recovery before journeying back to Paris, where he walked into the full glare of public attention because of the reputation generated by his military exploits.

But the storm clouds of war were again gathering, only this time it was Sweden, with French support, that was making angry noises against Russia. Keith received orders from St Petersburg to leave Paris and go to England on a diplomatic mission, taking a route by Brest for a good look at what the French fleet was up to.

Despite his previous efforts to bring down the House of Hanover in 1715 and 1719, James Keith was now an accredited envoy of the imperial court and as such had diplomatic immunity. As was to be expected, the presence of a leading Jacobite at the British court created a frisson of excitement in London. It must have been a strange experience for George II to meet with this avowed rebel, now a major player in the power politics of his time. Keith came to London in February 1740 and he was to stay there until May, fêted by an idle society whose curiosity had to be satisfied. He must have enjoyed the mixed reaction both to his notoriety as a rebel and the recent fame he had acquired as a senior Russian general – but there must too have been the added pleasure of speaking to a sophisticated London society and enjoying better conversation and manners than he could ever hope to find in Russia.

Word of Keith's arrival in London spread far and wide and soon reached Peterhead. The town was just as excited as London that their famous son was back on British soil. The magistrates of Peterhead met to discuss what public recognition they should give to James Keith's arrival in Britain and finally decided to send him a letter, which they did on 23 February 1740. However, life in London must have been hectic and enjoyable, for it took until June for Keith's reply to reach Peterhead, and by that time he was already on his way back to Russia. When Keith's letter did arrive, it was delivered by a relative of his who added a covering note telling the magistrates that Keith had the honour of drinking all the magistrates' health and expressed a regard for his native country and particularly the town of Peterhead. Keith's letter went as follows:

Gentlemen

I received with the greatest pleasure the letter you did me the honour to write me, and return you my most sincere thanks for your kind wishes and expressions in regard to myself and family; nothing could be more agreeable to me than to see that, after so long an absence, I am still remembered by my countrymen, and particularly by those whom I'm obliged to look on as nearer to me than even most of the rest. I am only sorry that my gratitude can be but expressed at present in words, but I hope you will be persuaded, that in everything that lyes in my power, nobody will be readier and willinger to serve you than,

Gentlemen,
Your most obedient and most humble servant,
James Keith
London, May 4, 1740.

Keith returned to St Petersburg, breaking his journey to visit Marischal on the way. As a parting gift Marischal gave James a negro boy called Mocho to be his personal valet. In a letter to his brother it becomes obvious that Keith servants were more like members of the family and James wrote to Marischal: 'Many compliments to Mademoiselle Emete. You never tell me anything of Ibrahim and Stepan. I should be glad to hear if they are still with you, and if they behave well. I believe I have already told you, that Mocho was not with me at the affair of Rossbach. He was ill of a fever at Leipzig. I like him very much; he is exceedingly attached to me; and as he gets older, he becomes more steady.' Mocho was to serve Keith faithfully up until his death.

10

·

Sweden and Eva Merthens

·

KEITH'S CELEBRITY IN EUROPE could scarcely have failed to be reported back to St Petersburg by Russian ambassadors. Always popular with the Empress Anna, Keith was called to the court on his return where he was presented with a gold-hilted sword (which had an estimated value of 6000 roubles or £1500 sterling) as a token of Russian gratitude for his services to the nation. The war with Turkey had ended with a peace treaty in 1739 so the presentation sword was a recognition of his contribution to the recent war effort and a mark of his increased worth to Russia. The Russo–Turkish war had dragged on long after James Keith left to get his leg attended and, by its end, Russia had suffered 100 000 casualties – some in battle but the rest in a typhus epidemic which swept through the army.

The Empress Anna died in 1740. Few of her oppressed subjects shed tears; the mercenaries and other foreign help she had recruited for Russia were almost universally disliked. Her death occurred when Keith was in the Ukraine, where he had been appointed governor. For him and all other foreigners, in the German Suburb and elsewhere, it must have been a time of acute anxiety as they anticipated the power struggles which would follow Anna's death.

Incredibly, Anna had named a two-month-old boy as her successor; Ivan VI being the son of her niece the Princess of Brunswick. Buhren, her favourite, had been hovering like a vulture over Anna's deathbed and at her demise he moved quickly to declare himself regent to the baby Tsar in the opening shots of a power struggle.

It took only three weeks for Buhren, the *éminence grise*, to fall victim to a coup engineered by Munnich and carried out at midnight. Buhren was sent into exile and the baby Ivan's mother became Regent, while Munnich slipped into the position behind the throne so recently occupied by Buhren. Scarcely a year passed before the wily old Foreign Minister, Osterman, played his hand and despatched Munnich. The two-year-old baby, innocent victim of Russia's ambitious politicians, had been Tsar for only fifteen months without even knowing it and was now to spend the next twenty-two years of his life securely locked up in Schlüsselburg prison.

The plotting and scheming came to an end in November 1741, after a final coup in which a new Russian Empress took the throne. She was to add pressure of another sort to James Keith and hasten his departure from Russia.

The Empress Elisabeth grasped the Russian throne mainly for reasons of self-preservation and to pre-empt moves by the baby Ivan's supporters which could have led to her internment in a convent. Elisabeth Petrovna was the daughter of Peter the Great and Catherine, his second wife, who had in turn become Catherine I and briefly ruled after following him on to the throne. Unlike her father – who didn't hesitate to hand out a death sentence, either by hanging, beheading or breaking on the wheel – Elisabeth swore not to sign another death warrant and in 1744 formally abolished capital punishment. Elisabeth's accession to the throne was mainly a result of the support given to her candidature by the Russian nobility, who were sick of being ruled by Germans, and not least because of her popularity with the Guards. Her support from the nobility and the Guards, together with active help from foreign ambassadors representing the governments of France and Sweden, was enough to secure the throne.

Elisabeth succeeded her sister while still in her early thirties. Fair and full figured, warmhearted and generous, she moved a British minister to report back to his government that she 'had not an ounce of nun's flesh about her'.[†] Just so; when Anna had been on the throne Elisabeth's morals were very much a matter for concern for her, not least because of her partiality for big grenadiers to help warm her bed. Completely different in character from her predecessor she had all the high spirits of a teenager, blending a warmth and exuberance which manifested themselves in her sheer enjoyment of each and every social event. All in all, she must have been a fairly pleasant person to be around while her 'common touch' endeared her to courtiers and peasantry alike, for she was as likely to be found in conversation with one as with the other. However, she also knew where her support lay; foreigners were to be slowly eased out of public office to make room for Russians, and once the Russians got into power, they soon began to make life difficult for all the foreigners beneath them whom they had long resented.

Elisabeth's spending on clothes would have broken any man's heart – she dressed in the latest fashions with the aid of a Paris dressmaker. Her expertise on the dance floor was celebrated – a skill that can only have improved with the amount of practice Elisabeth had in the round of social events she either sponsored or attended. When she wasn't at a ball, she might be found playing cards, gossiping or engaged in field sports. The darker side of her character – traits which should be remembered in relation to James Keith – were that she had a hair-trigger temper and was notorious for her over-reaction to slights or insults, real or imagined. Sensual, although not to be described as beautiful, she was fond of food and could be described as a gourmand.

When her normal good humour gave way to a vile temper, her cursing and swearing were truly awesome to all who found themselves within earshot. Educationally challenged and with no intellectual pretensions, Elisabeth had a fixed belief until the end

---

[†] 'Elisabeth brimmed with warmth, high spirits and bonhomie, was extremely sociable, and enjoyed the uninhibited company of peasants, gypsies and Cossacks as much as that of courtiers (one of her favourites, whom she married secretly, was a Ukrainian Cossack). Luxurious and pleasure seeking (not an ounce of nun's flesh about her – remarked the British minister).' A. Lentin, *Russia in the Eighteenth Century*, p. 54.

of her days that Britain was a connected part of the European landmass. She nevertheless also had her father's shrewdness of judgement which enabled her to make accurate assessments of men with whom she came in contact. Like her father, she genuinely wanted what was best for Russia but was ill-equipped to handle the complexities of government; she left the broad mass of detail to ministers while only taking a spasmodic interest in affairs of state. Indeed, her ministers not only had difficulty in getting an audience with her, she would only find time to sign papers at her own convenience and when there was nothing else to divert her attention.

Self-centred and self-indulgent, what Elisabeth wanted Elisabeth was going to have. If she wanted one of her generals – a stateless foreigner out there in the German suburb – who was moreover dependent on her for his employment, who was going to stop her?

Shortly after his return from Britain and the sword presentation ceremony at St Petersburg, Keith had taken up an appointment as governor of the Ukraine, where he was safely out of the way as the struggle for power began. Apart from taking another oath of allegiance to Elisabeth on her accession, life would have gone on much as usual. During his all too brief, one-year governorship, he carried out his duties with all his typical humanity and understanding; this made him hugely popular and loved by the people of the province. It was said of his governorship that 'he made the natives complain that he should never have been appointed, or never have been recalled.'

James Keith's stay in the Ukraine was cut short when war again broke out in August 1741 between Russia and Sweden. Keith's new appointment was as second in command to his friend Field Marshal Peter Lacy, who was assembling an army to march into Swedish-occupied Finland.

At the summer's end in 1741 the Swedes, prompted by France, decided that they should take advantage of the turbulent upheaval occasioned by the Empress Anna's death. It seemed to make sense to strike hard and first while the Russians were deeply engrossed in their own divisive power struggles.

Another factor in Sweden's calculations was the 'war-on-two fronts' scenario: they calculated that Russia might simultaneously be facing their own forces in the north and those of Turkey in the south. It didn't quite work out that way, however, because Austria withdrew from the war and Osterman was left to get the best deal he could in a peace treaty with the Turks. Osterman brought in France as an independent mediator and the French managed to negotiate away all the Russian gains in the Treaty of Belgrade. By this treaty Russia lost access for her shipping into the Black Sea and was left with just Azov, minus its defences.

The Swedish army's march on Russia came to grief at Viborg, when the Swedes met a Russian army of 50 000 men commanded by Lacy and Keith. From then on it was only a matter of time before the Swedes were forced into retreat and, in September 1741, Keith played a central role in the siege of Willemstrand which cost the Swedes 3000 men while their commanding officer, Major General Wrangel, became a Russian prisoner. James Keith appears to have become something of a specialist in sieges; his bravery and control of operations during the Willemstrand siege so impressed the imperial court that he was awarded an increase in salary. Shortly before Willemstrand fell, Lacy returned to St Petersburg from his post at Viborg leaving Keith in sole command – and he did this while intelligence sources were telling him that a relief force of Swedes, comprising every man they could muster, was marching towards them. It says much for Lacy's confidence in Keith that he should have gone off and left him at this time and Lacy's faith becomes even more marked when one considers that there were two very competent and famous Russian generals subordinated to Keith's command in this army.

Shortly after Elisabeth came to the throne Sweden and Russia held exploratory peace talks: these failed and the war resumed because Russia felt that Sweden wanted too much by way of settlement. It was a disastrous decision for Sweden, for very soon her army was in precipitate retreat, abandoning its stores as it fled across the River Kymen from superior Russian forces. Defeat followed on defeat, as Nyslot, Helsingfors and Abo, Finland's capital, each fell in turn to the Russians who had more men and a superior military expertise to that of the Swedes.

Keith's role during the westward Russian offensive along the Baltic had been to amass fleets of gunboats while at the same time attending to the huge amount of operational planning detail without which great ventures are often lost. Instead of being happy at their army's success against the Swedes, the new Russian ministers and courtiers in St Petersburg, who had taken over at Elisabeth's accession, were far from pleased – consumed, in fact, with jealousy. The success of their army meant very little to these Russians who were now desperate to get rid of the foreigners. From high positions at court they incresingly made their presence felt until the nitpicking and petty interference became so unbearable that the foreign mercenaries requested permission to retire from Russian service en masse – this included James Keith.

Horrified at the possibility of losing the majority of her best soldiers, the Empress begged Keith to stay, promising him a command against the Persians and the Order of St Andrew. He accepted the decoration but declined the Persian command and it is interesting to speculate just how much of a hand he had in organising this protest by the mercenaries. Shortly after this climbdown all the foreign soldiers decided to stay after all, reinforcing the possibility that the whole episode was contrived by Keith to flag up his own and other mercenaries' discontent at court interference.

During this time of unrest in the Russian army the Queen of Sweden died; Russia wanted to ensure that her own selected candidate now ascended the throne. James Keith was once more ordered to take an army towards Sweden backed by a fleet of ships. Using his ships for amphibious landings and also to neutralise any Swedish seaborne threat, Keith's progress towards Sweden itself was unstoppable and he went on to capture the Aland Islands. The Alands were just too close to the Swedish mainland and Stockholm to be ignored by the Swedes, who sent their own fleet to attack Keith in his forward position. The Swedish navy came up to the Alands to engage with the Russian ships only to find that they had come within range of shore-based batteries which pounded them with heavy fire. This seaborne battle continued into the night before the Swedes finally withdrew into the darkness.

Clearly the position of Sweden was now hopeless and, in the negotiations that followed, Elisabeth offered to return most of the conquered territory if the Swedes in return would elect Duke Adolphus Frederick as their king. There were no real choices available to the Swedes and a deal was done: a new hereditary king ascended the Swedish throne.

Grudgingly, the Swedish leadership had acquiesced to Russian demands but the Swedes were incensed: the choice of ordinary Swedes for king had been a Prince of Denmark, and the Swedes now demanded the heads of those who had commanded the defeated Swedish army in Finland. Only a part of their demands were met with the execution of the defeated Swedish generals. This took some of the heat and anger out of the situation, allowing the election of Duke Adolphus. Curiously enough, the Swedish peasantry soon changed from a position of uncompromising hostility to one of rapturous welcome for Adolphus, turning out into the streets of Stockholm in huge numbers to greet him at his coronation.

Not all of Sweden was overjoyed, however, and Sweden's peace and contentment were all too shortlived. Propaganda and agitation sponsored by Denmark now began to whip up anti-Adolphus fervour. This dissatisfaction finally boiled over and 20 000 Dalcarlians (malcontents from the northern Swedish province of Dalkartsa) rose in arms and marched on the capital to demand Adolphus's resignation.

Adolphus quickly found that there was absolutely nothing he could say or do to appease the insurgents and fighting soon broke out in the streets of Stockholm between the Dalcarlians and government troops. When it was all over 3000 Dalcarlian rebels were dead; the rest were taken prisoner by the king's forces.

It had been a sobering experience for Adolphus and, since there was no guarantee that the Danes would not engineer a repeat of such unrest, he called on his Russian sponsors for help. Again it was to be James Keith who was sent, this time at the head of a 10 000-strong army. His very name was now enough to strike terror into the civilian populace – he was already a living legend through his more recent military successes against the Swedes in Finland. All of Sweden knew and recognised his expertise in military organisation and was aware of how he could weld both army and navy together into a cohesive fighting force as he had demonstrated during the Aland Islands battle. They knew that if Keith was intent of invading Sweden, they would at very best only be able to delay his march before his army entered Stockholm.

Keith arrived in Sweden as supreme commander of a Russian invading army, invested with plenipotentiary powers by the Russian court. His honesty, straightforwardness and manifest dislike of double dealing quickly communicated itself to the Swedes, who found that he was quick to stamp on anything that was less than open or honest. He became popular in Sweden and as a new year gift was presented with yet another sword by a grateful King Adolphus. By 23 June 1743, his mission in Sweden was complete and he was recalled to Russia. The time had come to take his leave and he called on Adolphus: at this farewell meeting with the king of Sweden he received yet more presents – a portrait of Adolphus, £1000 sterling and yet another sword to add to a growing collection.

An anecdote from the Swedish campaign gives an insight into Keith's character. After the Russian and Swedish armies had first clashed in 1741, a Swedish trumpeter arrived under parley at Keith's camp, bearing a letter for one of the Russian officers. In circumstances unknown, the contents of the letter were quickly communicated to the Russian troops who panicked, shouting that they had been betrayed by their foreign officers. These Russians then ran about the camp dragging hapless foreign mercenaries out of quarters, intending to murder them. Hearing all the uproar, Keith ran straight from his own tent into the centre of the fracas, grabbed the ringleader by his lapels and loudly ordered that a confessor and hangman be brought for the man's immediate execution. This had the effect of a deluge of cold water on the Russians, quickly cooling the situation. Fortunately for the condemned man, Field Marshal Lacy had arrived during this episode and witnessed all that happened, astutely seeing fit to grant a pardon before the hangman could do his job. As mentioned earlier, Keith was given command of the Russian army by Lacy over two senior Russian generals, either of whom might reasonably have been expected to take over: the disclosure of the Swedish letter and subsequent mutiny by the Russian troops might just explain why Lacy left James Keith in command.

When James Keith left Sweden to return to Russia he was accompanied by a young woman named Eva Merthens. After the victorious Russians swept through Finland they went on to take

Abo, the Finnish capital, and it was in Abo that James Keith set up his army headquarters to oversee the occupation.

During his time there, possibly on a tour of inspection, Keith found a young orphan girl in a Russian camp containing civilian and military prisoners of war. Aged about fifteen or sixteen, she had come of honourable parents and a respectable background – it is not clear how she found herself in a prison camp. For Keith it was love at first sight and, in what was a characteristic action, he rescued her from her predicament and took her under his protection. Equally predictably, Keith then saw to it that Eva was given an education so that she learned to speak French and read Latin but, like Keith himself, she only ever had indifferent German. Perhaps equally predictably, Eva Merthens was later to become Keith's mistress.

There is no description of Eva as she grew into womanhood but we might reasonably expect her to have had Nordic fair hair and blue eyes. We do know that Eva had forceful eyes that struck all who met her and that she had a penchant for healthy activities, such as bathing in ice cold water. She was also very intelligent, with a beauty and charm matched by a stately figure.[†] The *Dictionary of National Biography* briefly comments that Eva was 'pretty and clever'. She wasn't, however, to be a 'stay at home' mistress; she visited Keith when he was on campaigns and often stayed on to nurse him through his bouts of asthma when he couldn't leave his army post. It is reported that James Keith showed no interest in other women and Eva, unsurprisingly, was the sole object of his affections.

In later years, after Keith had joined the Prussian army, Eva must have been a much admired asset on the social circuit. It seems that she was 'highly regarded' by Prince Henry of Prussia,

---

[†] 'In Abo, Keith met a young orphan, Eva Merthens, a child of honourable parents, one among the civilian and military prisoners. Keith fell in love with Eva, he had her educated, and most likely would have married Eva, but for the great difference in background.' Varnhagen von Ense, *The Life of Field Marshal Jacob [James] Keith* p. 82. (Von Ense was a nobleman and historian, an officer with service in Russia in 1812 and a representative at the Congress of Vienna).

the brother of Frederick the Great, who was near Eva's own age: it must be remembered that there was a huge age difference between James Keith and Eva, perhaps as much as twenty-nine years. The social chasm between them was equally wide, for Keith came from ancient nobility while Eva was of Swedish or Finnish middle-class origins. Almost certainly the class difference, more than that of age, was an unsurmountable obstacle to marriage as far as James Keith was concerned and he never did marry her. It seems also that the Earl Marischal and Eva did not get on: possibly the patrician Marischal felt that Eva was insufficiently well-born to merit a Keith's protection. Both were possibly motivated by jealousy of one sort or another, leaving James caught in the middle. Long after the relationship had produced children, Marischal was pointedly telling his brother that he should be thinking of marrying so that the Keith family line would be perpetuated; and when he mentioned marriage Marischal did not have Eva in mind. After Keith's death, Marischal made it plain in his will that he did not recognise his brother's children and his attitude was positively transparent in the years prior to James Keith's death.

James Keith's return to Russia was marked by his formal reception at court by the Empress Elisabeth. In the time that had elapsed since his wound at Otchakov there had been little opportunity for the Empress to meet with her general, and it may have been at this audience that Keith ignited passionate feelings in Elisabeth. It is most unlikely that sixteen-year-old Eva joined Keith for his audience; she was probably left behind at Liefland, a large estate owned by Keith at Rannenburg in Livonia and given to him as a gift by the Russian government. (It may have been to Liefland that tutors came to improve Eva's education and where she and Keith had some home life together during periods of army leave. The title deed to this estate can be found in the Aberdeen University archive.)

Given the way the Russian court worked it is unlikely that James Keith could have kept his mistress a secret for any length of time – gossip and intelligence of one sort or another must surely have got back to Elisabeth. Like Marischal, Elisabeth would not have seen Eva as being of any consequence and, given her own loose morals, she would have looked on Eva as just a plaything keeping her senior general happy. What Marischal and the Empress could never understand was that Keith was hopelessly in love with Eva and, being an honourable man, acted just as though he was legally married to her.

The year of 1744 seems to have been one of settled domesticity and unhurried duty for Keith, but in France the Jacobites were busy organising themselves for a rebellion planned to take place the following year. In the period leading up to the 1745 rebellion, Jacobite overtures to the Empress of Russia asking for James Keith to be freed from Russian service to help them had been ignored. Elisabeth had declined to respond: firstly because James Keith was on a mission to Poland where he was to advise the king, at that time being menaced by a new military superpower, Prussia. Secondly, Russia and Britain were enjoying a cordial relationship at this time and the Empress had nothing to gain from having Keith fighting against a friendly country for a cause in which she had no interest. Marischal had probably also come under pressure to ask for Keith's help in this latest rebellion, but we know that his head had now come to rule his heart and he advised James Keith that this uprising had no future and that he should stay well clear of it.

After two unsuccessful attempts to overthrow the Hanoverians, Keith must by this time have seen the impossibility of taking on a well-disciplined, well-fed and well-armed British army. The petty spites and jealousies of clan chieftains, unwilling to take orders from anyone, will have remained fresh in his memory. Keith, if he considered it at all, must have decided that there was no way in which he was going to be allowed to run a Jacobite campaign or have his orders obeyed by senior chieftains. A new rebellion, but with the same players, was quite clearly going to end in a very similar way to the spectacular defeats and retreats of Sheriffmuir and Glenshiel.

James Keith did not return to Scotland and neither did Marischal, but when the royal standard was raised at Glenfinnan relatives of the Keith brothers were there with the assembling clans. When the early, heady success of the Jacobites ended with a decision at Derby to abandon their campaign and return north, it must have been a bitter pill for many to swallow. For the Drummonds – Perthshire exiles returned from France to join the fray – the long weary retreat to Culloden was the end of all their hopes and dreams and they must surely have known it. Lord John Drummond, Keith's cousin, commanded the centre of the first line of the Jacobite army at Culloden. Commanding the left wing – composed entirely of MacDonald regiments – was Lord James Drummond, Keith's cousin, who styled himself Duke of Perth.

Among the clans stood the Scots Royal, a regiment recruited from among exiled Jacobite Scots and a regular French regiment raised by the Drummonds for King Louis of France. This regiment of exiles had all volunteered to fight for Prince Charles Edward and the French government had given them furlough to do it. The Scots Royal was commanded by Lord Lewis Drummond, son of the attainted Earl of Melfort, yet another domiciled Frenchman and Keith cousin. There was yet another Keith relative on that battlefield in the person of Viscount Strathallan.

When the Jacobite army turned about to face into the sleet of a late spring day, they saw a British army waiting with cannon primed and loaded with grapeshot; they looked on lines of disciplined, red-coated soldiers who were not going to flinch or run in the event of a Highland charge. On Wednesday, 16 April 1846, battle commenced and accurate fire from the British cannon tore great holes in the Jacobite army, which numbered 6400 foot soldiers and 2400 horse. They just stood there, taking it all, with no capability of their own to silence the British cannon with a return fire. This punishing hail of grapeshot became too much for Clan Chattan, which was the first to break ranks and tear away in a desperate, wild charge. Many of the clan who had survived the initial cannonfire to join the charge were to be cut down as if by firing squad by the successive volleys of musketfire from lines of soldiers firing sequentially to order. The clansman who did make it, who fought through to close with the enemy front line, was not met by the bayonet of the soldier immediately in front of him – but by the thrusting bayonet of the soldier on his right, which was directed some where beneath the clansmen's raised sword arm.

It was not a battle where bravery carried the day. The winners might easily have been called before the Battle of Culloden ever began, but the cold-blooded butchery that followed the battle would have left even a hardened James Keith standing aghast, such was the carnage and brutality of the aftermath. In the wake of the Jacobite defeat followed a killing frenzy, as Cumberland's troops scoured the fields and ditches for wounded clansmen, shooting or bayoneting them to death.

Lord John Drummond escaped to France, only to find himself in jail the following year after a roundup of Jacobites ordered by the French government. Lord James Drummond, Duke of Perth, died on a ship carrying escaping Jacobites to France and was buried at sea. During the course of the battle, Lord Strathallan had tried to hold back a torrent of British dragoons with about forty horsemen and perished, cut through the waist by a slashing sabre stroke.

While his mother's side of the family were fighting a last-ditch battle for the Stuart cause, James Keith found himself on a pinnacle of popularity with the Empress Elisabeth. He was now the commander-in-chief of all the Russian troops facing across the border to the Prussian army and he was at their head to take the salute when Elisabeth moved her entire court to Narva for a review. Despite his popularity with the Empress, and although he didn't yet know it, his career in Russia was already finished.

Lord Hyndland, British ambassador to St Petersburg, had seen his chance to make mischief for Keith by having a word in the ear of Bestuchef, Elisabeth's favourite courtier and Keith's implacable enemy. Taking Bestuchef's whispered advice, Elisabeth forbade Marischal to enter Russia; he couldn't even rejoin his baggage at Riga, where both his luggage and James Keith were waiting for him. The brothers contrived, Empress notwithstanding, to meet at Schultzenburg on the border, but for James Keith, this was a final insult.

11

·

The King's Man

·

AFTER THEIR MEETING AT Schultzenburg, Marischal bade Keith goodbye and began his journey back to Venice; first, however, he went to Berlin for a few days. Of course the Keiths already had at least one other member of their extended, exiled family living in Berlin but this visit leaves one wondering if Marischal was already putting out feelers on his brother's behalf.

By 1747 Bestuchef's intrigues were taking an increasing toll on Keith's patience. Apart from a steady flow of minor aggravations, Keith's career was fast going downhill: he was being progressively demoted in the Russian military. While his position in the army was being undermined, he also had the headache of the Empress's romantic designs on him; a headache with no possible cure and which was very likely a popular topic for court gossips. In a letter Elisabeth described James Keith as 'the only man who can bring up a future heir to the throne in my mind and in the footsteps of Peter the Great.' Keith's anxiety was heightened by Elisabeth's growing passion for him, and he wrote of his fears to Chevalier Drummond in Berlin: 'The Empress is resolved to raise me to a height which would cause my ruin as well as her own.' It appears that even the Empress could not hope to win against the forces at court who would be against her proposed match with Keith but it also seems that Keith was less than overjoyed at the prospect of Elisabeth's hand in marriage.

Matters continued to deteriorate until Keith was left with only two regiments under his command; his brother was banned from ever walking on Russian soil and the Empress's infatuation made his position ever more dangerous. The last straw for Keith came when the Prince Repnin, Keith's military junior, was given command of a Russian auxiliary corps of 30 000 men being sent to the Rhine. This was a command which Keith had coveted but which he now knew was never going to be his – by this time all the signs clearly pointed towards a quick exit.

There are different versions of what happened next: some say that he requested permission to leave Russian service, while others say that he quietly slipped out of Russia, unnoticed and without permission. His military records in Berlin, which could only have been compiled with Keith's help, tell this version: he applied for leave to depart from Russia and this was granted in July 1747. He then took passage on a British ship to Copenhagen and from there went on to Hamburg where, in a letter dated 1 September 1747, he made an application to King Frederick II offering to put his services at Prussia's disposal. The timescale seems to fit with this explanation of events.

James Keith wrote a number of letters to Marischal explaining his difficulty in leaving Russia; it seems the real truth lies somewhere between the different explanations put forward. These are Keith's own words, related to his brother:

> At the same time, one of my friends at Petersburgh wrote to me that my *congé* was ready, but that I could not receive it till I had sign'd some paper, the contents of which he did not know; and that he was well inform'd that if I refused to sign it, the resolution was taken to arrest me. You know what that signifies. Some days after, he wrote me another billet, that my discharge was sent to the feldtmarshal, with a reserve that I should never serve, directly or indirectly, against Russia; and that if I refused, that the feldtmarshal shou'd arrest me. While I was reading the billet, an adjutant came, desiring I should go to the feldtmarshal. I found the poor man in the greatest consternation possible: he had the auditor general with him, and another, as witnesses. He told me my demission was on the table, but that he had an order from the college of war not to deliver it to me, till I had sign'd another paper. I desired they might be read to me. The demission was a simple one, in the ordinary form, signed by the empress, the first of July: the order of the college of war, of the forth, to exclude me out of the army; and which was already published to the commissariate and bureau of provisions that I might receive no more pay nor forage. When they were both read, I told the feldtmarshal that I was visibly already out of the Russian service, both by the empress's demission,

and the college's order; I could not see in what pretence they could impose laws on a British subject, who might serve when and where he would: on which the feldtmarshal begg'd me to consider of it. I said it was a scandalous paper; to which he answered, that it was indeed scandalous for those who imposed it. As I had no mind to make the journey to Siberia, I desired it might be read to me. The contents were that I promised never to serve, directly nor indirectly, against Russia; and that if I fail'd, I submitted to be judged by the Russian military articles. As soon as I heard it read, I told the general auditor, that I was ready to sign it immediately; because I knew the articles too well, not to be sure that there was not any one that forbid a free Englishman, as I then was, to serve in what manner I would: on which I signed the paper, and giving it back to the auditor, I told him that if ever they took me alive serveing against Russia, I was willing they should make a new article to condemn me. I was very sorry for what I had said, and I saw the feldtmarshal was no less; for I was sure the fellow wou'd write it immediately to Apraxin, who would draw consequences from it, that might be dangerous: but as I had my demission and passport, I resolved to prevent them; and having found an English ship ready to sail, I took my passage aboard for England, being afraid to come here directly by land, for fear of being arrested in Courland.

From the contents of that letter to Marischal it is quite clear that Keith still had very highly placed friends in the Russian court who were prepared to stick their necks out and warn him of what was going on. Keith never referred to his friend at court by name, in case his letter was intercepted. He continues:

In this manner I got clear of the Russian dominions, but had a very bad passage to the Sound, nineteen days contrary wind and blowing weather; for which I was not sorry, for this gave me a pretext of quitting my Englishman at the Sound, and declaring that I would go by land thro' Holland. They were very inquisitive at Copenhagen, if my real intention was to go to England; and the duke of Sonderbourg made me overtures of entering into that service.

In another letter Keith tells what happened next:

As soon as I got on shore in Denmark I wrote a letter to the king of Prussia, offering him my service, and soon after set out for Hambourg, where I received a very gracious answer, on which I went straight to Berlin, where two days after my arrival he declared me fieldmarshal of his army. As he stay'd only one day there, I had no resolution more. Baron Mardefeldt had already told me that I was to have 8000 crowns a-year, with which I can live easier here than with twelve in Russia, where our immense equipages eat up all our income: and I find I have really more than for one; therefore, consider what a pleasure it would be to me to share it with my dearest brother, I know it would not be in the least disagreeable to the king, and even quite the contrary; but in some posts, count Rothenbourg, who is almost as impatient to see you as I am, will write to you more fully on the subject.

In his letters to Marischal, James Keith does not mention Eva Merthens at all: in fact, he gives the impression that he will be living alone in Berlin and would welcome his brother's company. As an added inducement to Marischal, Keith goes on to tell him how pleasant life is with the King:

I have now the honour, and, which is still more, the pleasure of being with the king at Potsdam, where he ordered me to come two days after he declared me fieldmarshal;[†] where I have the honour to dine and sup with him almost every day. He has more wit that I have wit to tell you; speaks solidly and knowingly on all kinds of subjects; and I am much mistaken if, with the experience of four campaigns, he is not the best officer in his army. He has several persons with whom he lives in almost the familiarity of a friend, but no favourite; and he has a natural politeness for every body who is about him. For one who has been four days about his person, you will say I pretend to know a great deal of his character; but what I will tell you, you may depend upon: with more time I shall know as much of him, as he will let me know; and all his ministry knows no more.

So no mention of Eva; but he cannot surely have left her to make her own way out of Russia, taking a risk that she would be taken hostage either for his return or future good behaviour. Keith must have taken Eva and Mocho with him and although he does not tell us from which Russian port he set sail, the odds are stacked in favour of a departure from Riga, which was close to his Liefland estate and whose governor was his friend Peter Lacy. Most perplexing and difficult to fathom is the part that the Empress

---

† 'On Russian matters Friedrich likes especially to hear him [Keith] – though they differ on the worth of Russian troops. 'Very considerable military qualities in those Russians' thinks Keith: 'imperturbably obedient, patient; of tough fibre, and are beautifully strict to your order, on the parade ground or off.' 'Pooh, mere rubbish *mon cher*,' thinks Friedrich always. To which Keith, unwilling to argue too long, will answer: 'Well, it is possible enough your majesty will have to try them, some day; if I am wrong it will be the better for us.' Thomas Carlyle, *Frederick the Great*, vol. 2. p. 376.

Elisabeth played, or did not play, in Keith's departure from Russia. Long afterwards Elisabeth was left to mourn his going and to pursue him with letters begging his return. There is no record of him ever returning her correspondence and it is likely that he did not, preferring instead to put that part of his life behind him.

James Keith's impressively slick change of employer could not 'just' have happened; we may surmise that Marischal will have been one of the players involved in smoothing Keith's road to Berlin. Another who played a part in restarting Keith's career – by drawing Frederick the Great's attention to his fame in Russia and actively lobbying for him – was Major von Winterfeld. Von Winterfeld had had a long connection with Russia, for it was there that he had first met his wife, Fraulein von Malzahn, the stepdaughter of Munnich, Keith's superior officer at Danzig and Otchakov. Von Winterfeld had been poorly educated but possessed a quick and clever mind and disguised any deficiencies with a lofty and imperious bearing. He had arrived in St Petersburg on 19 December 1740 to organise a Treaty of Alliance between Russia and Prussia, and met his future father-in-law across the negotiating table. Treaty negotiations were not concluded until 27 December, giving Keith plenty of time to make von Winterfeld's acquaintance while he, perhaps, made that of the Fraulein, for Munnich was banished in March 1741.

In the year following Keith's arrival in Berlin his health broke down yet again, perhaps because of his chronic asthma or as a result of his many campaigns. During 1747–48, Frederick wrote a great many letters to his invalid Field Marshal, expressing concern for his health and anxiety that he might lose him. Colonel von Manstein, who had also departed Russia and meantime become Frederick's adjutant, was under orders to forward regular reports on Keith's health to the King. Keith's ill health dated almost from his arrival in Prussia – a change of climate may have been responsible. Meanwhile, Frederick blamed Keith's house; advising him to give it up and find another less damp and to stay in Berlin rather than move to Potsdam.

Given his poor health, there may have seemed to James little opportunity for mending his fortunes. Although he was an expert on the Russian military machine and useful to Prussia, that had to be a time-limited usefulness. Lying in his Berlin sickbed, he must have reflected on the Jacobite failures, his lost estates in Russia and a Prussian career blighted from the start by illness. At fifty-two he did not have much time to put matters right; another mountain was waiting to be climbed.

Not until the autumn of 1752 did Keith's health improve sufficiently for him to take up his duties in the army of Frederick II, whom he had described in such glowing terms to the Marischal.[†]

Frederick, whom history has called the Great, had been born in Berlin on 24 January 1712. The fourth to be born in a family of ten, two princes had already been born and died before him. Frederick ascended the Prussian throne when his father died in 1740.

Of slender build and about five feet seven inches tall, Frederick was both intellectually and militarily gifted. Shortly after his marriage, he began to distance himself from his wife and to shun female company. Apart from his mother (to whom he always appeared with his hat in hand) and his sister, the Prussian court seems to have been without any women at all. Not that Frederick lacked sympathy for women or did not understand them; he just did not want them around. His whole life parallels that of Charles XII of Sweden, who only ever wanted to be with his troops, marching from battle to battle. Given his attitudes and preferred lifestyle, a question mark must hang over Frederick's sexuality.[‡]

His brother, Friedrich Heinrich Ludwig, born on the 18 January 1726, and his parents' ninth child, was an altogether different sort: Prince Henry was much more appreciative of the female form and

---

[†] Thomas Carlyle, *Frederick the Great* vol. 1. p. 16–26; See also vol. 2. p. 393; vol. 3. pp. 11, 168.

[‡] 'Highly respectable too, and well worth talking to, though left very dim in the Book, is Marshal Keith; who has been growing gradually with the King, and with everybody, ever since he came to these parts in 1747. A man of Scotch type; the broad accent, with its sagacities, veracities, with its sly twinkles of defensive humour, is still audible to us though the foreign wrappages. Not given to talk, unless there is something to be said; but well capable of it then.' Thomas Carlyle, *Frederick the Great*, Vol. 2. p. 376.

an accomplished soldier himself. He was about the same age as Eva Merthens, Keith's mistress, and we are told that Prince Henry 'admired' Eva.

Frederick knew how close the Keith brothers were and shortly after James came to Berlin he asked Marischal also to join his service. It was a welcome invitation to Marischal, and he lost no time in accepting the offer, leaving Venice for Berlin in January 1748. Any hoped-for intimacy, with both brothers, Eva, Emete, and the servants Mocho, Ibrahim, and Stepan all under one roof was short-lived. Whatever sparked the animosity between Eva and Marischal was not to disappear and, by 1749, the tensions and atmosphere created between the pair led to Marischal going off with his ménage to a house of his own.

James Keith regularly visited Frederick the Great. Each man was stimulated by the other's opinions and company. On 8 September 1749 Keith was made governor of Berlin for which he received a welcome £2400 boost to his salary, exclusive of other emoluments and bonuses.[†] He was also made a Knight of the High Order of the Black Eagle and given honorary membership of the Royal Academy of Sciences. Knowing Keith's financial difficulties, the extra money must have been the most welcome gift of all.

Keith's health continued to improve until he was at last able to play a greater role in events organised for the Prussian court. In August 1751 he was to be found judging a mock military competition between royal princes at a grand carnival, although all the indications are that carnivals were not Keith's chosen way of finding relaxation. It seems that away from military duties he was contented with home life, happy to devote himself to domestic chores which should really have been left to the servants.

Guests at the carnival came from allied states friendly to Prussia, mixing with Prussian nobility in a colourful crowd bent on enjoying themselves in feasting, drinking and a little debauchery

---

[†] Kurt von Priesdorff, *Soldatisches Führertum*. Hanseatische Verlagsanstalt Hamburg

as well.[†] It takes just a little effort of imagination to see Eva, a twenty-six-year old full of fun and gaiety, at the heart of this huge party and very much aware that she was winning admiring male glances from all around her. As the evening turned to morning her fifty-five-year-old lover still recovering from his illness, might well have gone home to his bed, leaving the other younger, fitter members of the party to get on with the carousing.

The circumstances surrounding Eva's disgrace and subsequent banishment from Prussia have been hidden from history and a veil discreetly pulled across whatever sins she committed at the carnival.[‡] It seems that Frederick the Great had been viewing her secret conduct with some displeasure and was completely outraged by the carnival scandal. He ordered her to leave Prussia; friendship and respect for his Field Marshal was not going to save Eva this time, whatever had happened was the last straw for Frederick, and Eva made her way into exile. Just where she went to from Berlin is far from clear but given her relationship with Keith she needed both anonymity and a powerful protector watching for her safety.

But others had been observing events and none were more watchful than Hanbury Williams, the British envoy at Berlin. He wrote to the Secretary of State as follows:

> Hitherto my labours have been in vain. But I think I have at present hit on a method which may bring the whole to light. And I will here take the liberty humbly to lay my thoughts and proposals before Y. Grace. Feldt Marshal Keith has long had a mistress who is a Livonian, and who has always had an incredible ascendant over the Feldt Marshal, for it was certainly on her account that his brother, the late Earl Marischall (alive, but attainted) quitted his house and they now

---

[†] 'For nine years after his arrival in Prussia, he enjoyed the sweets of peace to which he had been so long a stranger, and acquired honour to himself in the departments of arts and *belles lettres*. His active mind was never at rest, but always engaged on subjects often very dissimilar. He was the King's art collector – his picture buyer – and seems to have conducted this peculiar business as much to his satisfaction as he afterwards did many a battle and siege.' Robert Anderson, *Memoir of Marshal Keith*.

[‡] Thomas Carlyle, *Frederick the Great*, Vol. 2. p. 326.

live separately. About a week ago (during Feldt Marshal Keith's present illness) the King of Prussia ordered that this woman should be immediately sent out of his dominions. Upon which she quitted Berlin, and is certainly gone to Riga, which is the place of her birth. Now, as I am well persuaded that she was in all the Feldt Marshal's secrets, I would humbly submit to Your Grace whether it might not be proper for His Majesty to order his Minister at the Court of Petersburg to make instance with the Empress of Russia that this woman might be obliged to come to Petersburg, where if proper measures were taken with her, she may give much light into this, and perhaps other affairs. The reason why I would have her brought to Petersburg is that if she were examined at Riga that examination would probably be committed to the care of Feldt Marshal Laoci [sic], who commands in Chief, and constantly resided there, and I am afraid would not take quite so much pains to examine into the bottom of an affair of this nature as I would wish.

Hanbury Williams had probably hit on the exact truth where Peter Lacy was concerned; he was in an ideal position to offer shelter and protection to Eva. He was far enough from Moscow and such a powerful man that no one would have dared to question his actions or provoke his wrath; had he wanted to help his friend James Keith, then there was nobody better placed to do it.

While the British government contemplated torturing pillow secrets out of Eva, she was soon well away from it all in a place of safety. But did she go alone? Over the period of their relationship it is said that two sons, Daniel and Alexander, had been born to James and Eva. If that were so, what would have happened to the boys in these changed circumstances? Given Keith's almost fanatical attitude to education, the probability is that the boys stayed with their father in Berlin while Eva went off alone. If that is accepted, then visits to their mother in Riga or at some nearer rendezvous might also have taken place. The whole episode must have been quite shattering for Keith as he struggled to come to terms with what had happened: apart from the bitterness and loneliness he felt after losing Eva, his natural generosity would have meant him sending her all the money he could afford to make her exile as comfortable as possible. There is no doubt that Keith loved his young mistress and probably harboured some guilt about being unable to offer her the security of marriage which might just have saved her from exile. Keith had a deep understanding of human nature and weaknesses and would have well understood that his all too frequent absences on duty for long periods at a time must have contributed towards Eva's fall from grace.

Marischal, who disturbed the Keith household from the very start of his stay in Berlin, had in the meantime made himself indispensable to Frederick the Great. They both lived on the same high intellectual plateau, shared mutual interests and developed a close rapport. The question may be asked as to whether Marischal had a hand in helping Eva out of Berlin for reasons of personal jealousy; there was certainly no love lost between them – Marischal might just have mentioned it to Frederick before the opportunity arose to get rid of Eva. Marischal was now the Prussian ambassador to Paris with a pension of 2000 crowns: his appointment arose as a response to the French appointment of an Irish Jacobite to the Prussian court.

When he had any money Keith never had it for very long. It was either spent or given away. He was flat broke on a regular basis and always waiting for his next pay packet. Frederick disliked any impropriety and expected his generals to aspire to his own spartan lifestyle; any loose financial untidiness would most certainly have been viewed with grim disapproval. Knowing this, it had become Keith's habit to absent himself from court when he found himself in dire financial straits as a way of avoiding a possibly embarrassing situation. On one such occasion, when short of money, he was at home when Frederick had to see him on urgent business and called at the Keith residence. He found his Field Marshal busy in the garden, using paper cannon and pins in changing positions as he sought the best way to focus and concentrate firepower.

Frederick was delighted to join in this *Kriegsspeil* (war game); so pleased was he that when he got a frank admission of insolvency as the reason for Keith's absence from court he cheerfully paid all his debts for him. Keith went on to extend the parameters of his game invention until it became known as *Kriegsschachspiel* or 'war chess', involving thousands of small cast figures. Keith and Frederick played out many theoretical battles together.

When his army duties allowed, Keith took an interest in promoting trade between Prussia and Britain. He persuaded Prussia as to the quality of English cloth and helped Scottish merchants who were at this time trying to open up trade with the East Indies.

In view of his past generosity, one might have expected Marischal to have quietly helped James Keith with some money when he had none. The again it might not have mattered how much money James was given, it was just as likely to have slipped through his fingers as was habitually the case. Yet again, it may be the brothers had become just a little estranged after Eva's departure.

12

•

The Seven Years' War: Lobositz

•

WHEN JAMES KEITH RESUMED military duties in late 1752, it was as part of a formidable army already on a war footing. The total strength of Frederick's army now stood at about 150 000 regular soldiers; this number would increase to about 200 000 with the addition of all the supporting tradesmen and others necessarily involved in supplying and servicing such a force. Frederick had great ambitions for Prussia: his expansionist dreams were already causing consternation in Europe, as allies and enemies grouped themselves in readiness for what seemed an inevitable conflict.

The next three years passed quietly. As he had already done in Russia, Keith had to learn a new language and a new military language, too; he had to familiarise himself quickly with Prussian drill, tactics and regulations. On his return to duty he was given two adjutants – Varenne and Grant; that same Grant from Dunlugas near Turriff in Aberdeenshire who had benefited from Meston's tutorials; that same Grant who had stabbed a fellow student.

Keith's military records in Berlin reveal that he was made a Member of the Royal Academy of Sciences and had this honour bestowed upon him as a mark of appreciation for his translation of various works of English literature into German. From what we have been told of Keith's German it is safe to assume that he was in line for an honour and the translation services were just a convenient pretext. At this time he was also given a position as the King's art collector though in his life it is difficult to think of a period during which he might have acquired some expertise in this field. Antoine Pesne was the official court painter and he completed at least three known portraits of Keith. Just what James Keith brought to art in eighteenth-century Prussia isn't perhaps too clear but Pesne at least made sure that Keith's framed face looks out at us from various gallery walls. One portrait of Keith in the Peterhead Museum, dated 1753, shows a vigorous young man, perhaps in his late thirties; the portrait was actually painted when Keith was fifty-seven years old. Antoine Pesne was either very keen to keep his court appointment or Keith was giving him commissions to make sure he had plenty to eat.

Frederick's military build-up did not go unnoticed by neighbouring European states, particularly Russia and Austria, the two allies who had in recent years been joined in a war against Turkey. Tension was so heightened between these states that they were only waiting for the first one to blink before ordering their armies into action. In a provocative first move, Austria stationed an army under General Browne (an Irishman by birth) in Bohemia/Moravia in 1756. From that position the Austrians were poised for a first strike across the Elbe into Silesia and Browne only awaited the order. Saxony was allied to Austria and, although their army numbered only 18 000, they were ready reinforcements for an Austrian bridgehead once the Austrians crossed the Elbe. Less conspicuous perhaps were the Poles, with another army of about 18 000 and also ready to take the field against Prussia.

The European stage had been long prepared for this approaching war; under the pretext of taking a health cure, the Prussian General von Winterfeld had in fact been making a tour of all the areas along the route of Frederick the Great's expected offensive. Von Winterfeld meticulously took note of all the roads, forts and terrain of military interest to Berlin, making sketches and taking notes as an *aide-memoire* for his report to the Prussian high command.

The war began with an opening strategy familiar from other wars: Frederick demanded to know from Austria just what she meant by stationing Browne and 60 000 troops in Bohemia then, pretending that he did not fully understand the answer given, he asked the same question again. None of the answers were ever going to stop him or change anything: there was now no turning back.

Sealed orders were sent to the generals commanding three Prussian armies, telling them to go on the offensive along previously arranged routes towards agreed primary objectives. One column, under Duke Ferdinand (another of the King's brothers), was at Leipzig by the evening of 29 August 1756, where it took possession of the town. The column on the right was commanded by the Duke of Brunswick while the middle column was commanded by the King himself with Keith as his second in command. These three Prussian columns had about eighty miles between them and marched with discipline, had regular timed rest breaks and progressed at a speed which brought them to planned stopping places at prearranged times. The commanding Prussian officers had only to consult their maps and timepieces to know exactly where the other columns could be located.

As this formidable army advanced, so the Saxon army retreated back into its natural mountain fortress heartland, to the wild country around Pirna. By 9 September, Frederick and Keith with their centre column had entered Dresden, planning on a short stay while they collected the original Menzel documents which were in the possession of the Polish queen. These documents had no other value than that of a propaganda piece to justify Frederick's 'first strike' in the war. Some books credit Keith with having contemptuously marched into the Polish queen's palace for a virtual smash and grab of the papers but this dubious honour belongs elsewhere. It was a certain Prussian officer named Wangenheim who has been correctly identified as the one who broke into the queen's strongbox.

Frederick and Keith were now in Saxony with around 60 000 men while General Schwerin was in Silesia, poised with another 40 000 to break out through the Glatz mountains into the Bohemian plain. The big problem was the Saxon army holed up in the mountains; they were always going to pose a threat to the area of the Prussians advancing into Bohemia. The Saxons could not be left alone or simply ignored, so their mountain stronghold was ringed with Prussian troops while the main Prussian army was brought along the Elbe to swing around through the Erze mountains. This manoeuvre left the Prussians confronting Browne and his Austrians, daring him to make an attempt to free his Saxon allies imprisoned in the mountains. It took 30 000 Prussians to blockade the Saxons and James Keith was sent with another 32 000 to march on Aussig and Nollendorf where he was to keep an eye on the Austrians as the Saxon troops went on a starvation diet in the mountains to the rear. King Frederick's command post for his campaign was located at Torgau.

Orders came from Austria for Browne to break through the Prussian army and allow the Saxons to escape. He then set off from the foot of the Erze, or Metal Mountains, towards Pirna, taking his 60 000 Austrians with him. It was an unfortunate piece of timing for, no sooner had Browne's army started to move towards Pirna than Schwerin broke out of Silesia, through the Glatz mountains and into the Bohemian plain where he then attacked a much smaller Austrian force under Piccolimini. While Schwerin was engaging Piccolimini – in a difficult country of river crossings – Keith was encamped north of Browne's march on Pirna and waiting for him at Johnsdorf on the Bohemian slopes of the Metal Mountains.

Towards the end of September 1756, Browne had moved his army up to Budin, where it was then encamped making preparations to cross the River Eger where it would be within two days' march of seeking battle with Keith's army. However, Frederick must have lost patience or felt rather out of it at Torgau, for he joined Keith's army and took command, taking them down from their high commanding position overlooking the Austrians, who had by this time crossed the Eger and set up camp. The Battle of Lobositz was to begin next morning, on Friday 1 October, 1756.

Both Prussians and Austrians awoke that Friday to find that they were hidden from each other by a thick mist which limited visibility to about 100 yards. This mist did not begin to lift until later that morning, at about 11 a.m.

Frederick's vanguard was now pressing on down through the foothills and was soon spilling out through a pass between the Lobosch and Homulka hills into the plain beyond. Behind a curtain of mist, Browne's army was already assembling into battle order. On reaching the plain, the Prussians split to the right and left, forming two lines deep, while the Prussian cavalry took up a position three lines deep at the centre, in the entrance of the pass, where it took some skirmishing fire from light probing Austrian forces.

Periodically the morning mist cleared to give tantalising glimpses of what the Austrians were doing before closing in again and obscuring everything from view. The mist then rolled back for a period, allowing Frederick to see some 1500 horse manoeuvring: erroneously, he believed that he had seen the retreating rearguard of Browne's army. He ordered twenty squadrons of cavalry, led by two field pieces, forward in a charge. It was a ghastly mistake, for the cavalry charged into a curtain of grapeshot thrown at them by cannon batteries on their Lobositz (left) flank, which tore them to bits and forced a retreat. The cavalry had only just regrouped and were hurtling forward in another charge, when the mist receded to show Frederick just what a hellfire he had ordered his cavalry into – too late came his order for the cavalry to return. This time they galloped straight through the cannonfire and through a curtain of mist before finally coming to a halt after clearing a twelve-foot wide wet ditch and landing in a bog with a stream running through it.

In extricating themselves from that desperate position and getting back to their own lines the Prussian cavalry were again thoroughly shot up, suffering huge losses – when the shattered remnants straggled back, they were given the rest of the day off, to recover from their ordeal.

When the mist lifted at 11 a.m. it revealed that Frederick had not in fact set his cavalry on to the tail of Browne's retreating forces, but carried out a full frontal assault on the whole Austrian army. Now Browne had his guns loaded and was patiently waiting for the Prussians behind the bog where the Prussian cavalry had lately come to grief. The clearing mist also allowed Browne a better view and he saw that there was a weakness on his right flank from the overlooking Lobosch Hill. To make good this deficiency Browne pushed more of his troops out to cover the exposed right flank; this move changed the whole axis of the battlefield, so that Lobositz now became the focal point as both armies converged on each other.

As the first bloody battle of the Seven Years' War got under way, Keith was storming the village of Lobositz at the head of the regiments Hulsen, Manteuffel, Itzenplitz, Blankensee and Quadt. This left wing of the Prussian army forced its way through obstructing barriers of vineyards, fences and walled areas in a ferocious drive towards Lobositz; Frederick's right wing and Browne's left stood looking on as spectators. At one point Browne's left wing tried to start forward to engage with the Prussians but found itself instantly pinned down by cannonfire from Homulka Hill.

Pressing home the attack on Lobositz, Frederick ordered the second line of the left flank to join the battle in support of the first and on clearing the vineyards both lines merged to find themselves only three furlongs from Lobositz. The Austrians came on into the face of cannonfire and the full fury of the attacking Prussians. After some three hours of pitched battle, during which Prussian muskets had nearly all fired ninety cartridges and the battle was reduced to bayonet and musket-butt in hand-to-hand fighting, the Austrians were driven back into Lobositz. Unfortunately for them, Lobositz had taken a punishing with a continuous barrage of cannonfire and was now well alight; it now provided the worst sort of sanctuary for the Austrians. Their disorderly retreat continued in the face of Prussian ferocity, taking them back on to their own army's left flank.

To save his retreating right wing, Browne swung his left wing with its cavalry out and round to halt the Prussian advance, which was without any cavalry of its own: the Prussian cavalry was still recovering from its early morning mauling by the Austrian cannon. This move by Browne had the effect of blunting the Prussian advance, allowing him to move his army back a couple of miles to regroup. His tactical withdrawal was spotted by Frederick, who detached a part of his army in an attempt to cut Browne off from his stores and ammunition, forcing him into a hurried night march to reoccupy the ground he had only lately left. It was an expensive manpower decision for Frederick, for it cost him 3308 men while the Austrians lost 2984.

Next day the Battle of Lobositz resumed, raging for seven hours before Browne called his army off the field at 5 p.m. There would now be no relieving army for the besieged and starving Saxons walled up in their mountain stronghold and, while Browne was unwilling to retire, his army was unable to go forward; he pulled them back again to Budin, not too far from the battlefield. A standoff then ensued before Browne received a directive from the Austrian court telling him to get on with the job and relieve the

156

Saxons. Browne sent couriers through the Prussian lines to tell the Saxons that they were to hold on until 11 October by which time he would be with them.

Browne's strategy was to detach 8000 horse and circle wide around the Prussian army in a sixty-mile detour. The complicating factor in Browne's plan was that when the Saxons broke out of the mountains they still had to build a bridge or find some other means of crossing a river between themselves and the Austrians. Otherwise it was all quite feasible: the Saxons were to be covered by Austrian cannonfire at their river crossing near the village of Königstein. At a signal of two cannonshots, the Saxons were to launch an attack on two obstructing Prussian posts and at the same time Browne's cannon were to begin a destructive covering fire on the Prussians from behind them. The success or failure of Browne's plan hinged on the Saxons breaking through the Prussian cordon.

The Saxons had been reduced to only ten ounces of meal per day; to be told at this juncture that they were expected to hold out until 11 October further reduced morale. The long days of hunger for both men and horses slipped by until the time arrived for the Saxons to try and break out. True to his word, Browne had made all the promised preparations and by the appointed date his cavalry and cannon were concealed in wooded cover ready to strike into the rear of the watching Prussian army.

From its very beginning the Saxon breakout was handicapped by its commander, General Rutowski, who was simply not equal to the task which lay in front of him. Rutowski's planned escape route for his army involved them crossing the Elbe and, instead of acquiring the special craft which were readily available to construct pontoons, he decided to float his men and equipment across the Elbe using nearby boats. On the night of 8–9 October and in pitch darkness, Rutowski's boats set out to cross the Elbe with forty peasants pressed into taking the tow ropes. The Saxon flotilla of men and equipment managed to slip past the first Prussian battery at Pirna but their luck ran out and they were spotted by the second battery. When the Prussian cannon roared off at the boats the peasants who had been towing them quickly made themselves scarce and the drifting boats were only saved from disaster when the soldiers took the ropes themselves. Then it was the turn of the civilian helmsmen, who complained that they were not being paid to do their job under cannonfire and delivered an ultimatum that either they be allowed off the boats or they would steer them over to the Prussian side of the Elbe. The Saxon crossing of the Elbe deteriorated into an amazing shambles.

Faced with this crisis, Rutowski then belatedly remembered that copper pontoons could be had at Pirna; pontoons which he should have used at the very outset. Rutowski was now falling dangerously behind the schedule agreed with Browne and it was a frantic scramble down to Pirna to collect the pontoons. They were then to be carted only as far as Thurmsdorf, opposite Lebenstein and a mile short of the Königstein rendezvous, to be assembled. Rutowski's position was all the more desperate because he had only a few engineers who knew what they were doing when it came to stringing out a pontoon bridge.

Two days late in their schedule the Saxon pontoon bridge was close to completion when the heavens opened in a deluge which drowned all the approach roads to the bridge in a sea of mud. Wagon transport got bogged down in the mire and was abandoned while cannons became immovable, rooted obstacles in the path of those fortunate enough to be mounted.

Morning broke on 13 October; still only a trickle of Saxon troops had made it across the pontoon bridge and could just be seen as they tried to form up in driving rain and gale-force winds. Finally, some 14 000 Saxons made it across the Elbe to safety where they then cut their pontoon bridge adrift behind them – only to have it float intact downstream to the Prussians who promptly intercepted it and tethered the pontoons into place for their own river crossing.

Hungry and by now days late for their agreed meeting with the Austrians, with most of their baggage, food and weapons lost, the final devastating blow to Saxon morale arrived in a letter from Browne:

> Headquarters, Lichtenhayn,
> Wednesday October 13, 10 p.m.

Excellenz – have waited here at Lichtenhayn since Tuesday, Expecting your signal cannon; hearing nothing of it, conclude you have by misfortune not been able to get across; and the Enterprise is up. My own position being dangerous (Prussians of double my strength entrenched within a few miles of me) I turn homewards tomorrow at 9 a.m.; ready for whatever occurs till then; and sorrowfully say adieu.

For seventy-two hours after receipt of Browne's letter the starving Saxons marched onwards into the pouring rain until a realisation came that there was no direction in which they might go that would not shortly bring them face to face with Prussian troops. They did the only thing left to them and sought Prussian terms for a surrender.

Before the negotiations got under way the Prussians hid their mailed fist in a velvet glove. The tired and hungry Saxons were given all the food they could eat and then the terms of their surrender were starkly spelt out: the Saxons would surrender, become prisoners of war and then 'volunteer' to join the Prussian army. In a beggars' choice of a situation the Saxons could only accept what was offered to them; their army was shortly afterwards broken up into its various units and incorporated into Frederick's.

On 8 November 1756, Keith was based at Lobositz with his men when he was given a commission to negotiate an agreement with Browne on an exchange of prisoners of war. But winter was fast approaching and there was an urgency to get the Prussian army into its winter quarters to await the spring offensive. Not unlike today's sporting community with football in winter and cricket in summer, war in the eighteenth century also had its season. The military needed time to recruit and train new soldiers, and to plan tactics for a new season of war in the spring.

The armies of all the warring nations were now striking camp and returning home before the snows of winter made the conduct of war a virtual impossibility. Keith marched his army home to winter quarters in Gross Sedlitz, leaving only von Winterfeld with reduced forces keeping a watch against an improbable surprise attack. Once his men had been settled into quarters Keith would have made his way back to Berlin; his health was too fragile to risk it unnecessarily under canvas in the cold of a central European winter. Anyway, he had his teenage boys to go home to.

13

.

The Battle of Prague

.

WHEN JAMES KEITH WENT home to Berlin he might have expected his military duties to ease off somewhat but he was immediately given an ambassadorial role to play throughout the winter of 1756–57. During this time he was to be found renewing friendships and connections as he contacted powerful people in both Britain and Sweden, aiming to try and keep Sweden out of the hostilities expected to resume in the spring of 1757. Keith's efforts at preventing Sweden from joining all the other nations now sharpening their swords preparatory to war, were not rewarded with success, although Frederick the Great gratefully recognised his Field Marshal's diplomatic activity in a number of letters to him.

While the Prussians were hastily making preparations to meet an influx of armies from angry European neighbours, Prussia's senior military men were also playing their war games, enabling them to finalise supply logistics and timescales involved in the military options available to them. This kind of military planning was a Keith speciality, so we must assume he had some involvement in it, although his understanding of German must have seriously handicapped him in making a contribution. Carlyle asserts that it 'being then [March or April, weeks before he left Saxony] [a translator] was employed to translate the Plan of Operations into French, for Marshal Keith's use, who did not understand German . . .'

As the whole of continental Europe moved on to a war footing, alarmed by Frederick's ambition, there was just one friend left to Prussia and that was Britain. As usual Britain's priority was her own long-term self-interest and in this regard she wanted France well tied down in a European conflict so that French colonies and trade could be grabbed with the certainty of minimal interference.

The days of winter passed and the renewal of war could not be long delayed. Frederick wrote to Graf von Finck, setting out his wishes just in case his luck ran out and the Prussian armies took a beating. His instructions were that the royal gold and silver were to be melted down for coinage and he also set down a number of routes out of Prussia by which surviving members of the royal family were to make their escape to safety. His strict instructions were that in the event of his capture by the enemy, no ransom was to be paid and that the country's affairs were to go on as though nothing had happened. Despite this, it seems that he had not the slightest intention of being taken alive, for he carried a phial on his person containing five or six pills which would ensure any time spent as a prisoner would be of short duration.

The European states (principally France, Austria, Russia and Sweden) decided to carve Prussia up and apportion pieces among themselves: Sweden, for example, wanted Pomerania. The allies seemed confident that the extinction of the Prussian state would not take long: their joint armies at this time are calculated to have been 430 000 men. Against these formidable forces the Prussians, who had now regrouped, were able to put 150 000 men into the field, together with a British expeditionary force in Hanover which gave them an additional 60 000 men. Britain also poured £1 million into the Prussian war chest and sent ships to patrol the Baltic.

The daylight hours of winter 1757 lengthened and the European states were still busy oiling their war machines preparatory to marching into a Prussia lined with defensive trenches. They expected a war of attrition in which the Prussians would be quickly worn down by sheer numbers and firepower. The Austrians had again moved Browne, with a huge army, into the Bohemian plain where they had come to a halt just short of the Metal Mountains. Browne had been ordered to march into Saxony as soon as the weather would allow. All around their borders, the Prussians could see hostile armies assembling.

However fast the allies thought they were moving Frederick was moving even faster. As his enemies were to find to their cost, he was better organised and more prepared than any of them; while they were still looking for better weather and an end to winter, the Prussian armies were already on the offensive. On 20 April 1757, they lunged southwards into Bohemia in three columns with Prague as their objective, all three columns timing their march to arrive together for a decisive battle on 6 May. The Duke of Brunswick led one army column out of Lausitz, Frederick and Keith led another over the Metal Mountains and Schwerin, with von Winterfeld commanding one of his divisions, came bursting out of Silesia. All three columns headed straight for Prague in an eighteenth-century *Blitzkrieg* which left poor Browne and his Austrians standing helplessly in the way of the onslaught. The Prussians sped onwards, trying to cut off the retreating Austrians, led by Browne and Königseck, from their escape routes across the numerous bridges which led to safety, all the time collecting vast amounts of *matériel* abandoned in the Austrian flight.

The Prussian advance continued inexorably and only Königseck felt brave enough to turn on his pursuers. The Austrian chose Reichenberg for his stand because of its great defensive potential: broken undulating terrain was interspersed with woody hills and streams. On Wednesday 20 April, the Duke of Brunswick came up on Königseck to find him completely blocking his path.

Königseck's stand was to prove a hopeless gesture, for early in the morning of 21 April the Prussians struck with a force that sent the Austrians reeling. Even though the Austrians rallied twice in an attempt to throw them back, the Prussian fury was more than they could cope with. Königseck's stand left 1000 Austrians lying dead on the battlefield and another 500 taken prisoner. Meanwhile, Keith was in the King's main column of 45 000 infantry and 15 000 cavalry, hurrying on towards Prague.

The Austrian retreated had gathered a momentum of its own and could not be brought to a halt; it was to continue until Sunday 1 May, when they marched through Prague to make camp on high ground beyond the city on the Ziscaberg. The Austrians were now commanded by Prince Karl: Browne was his second in command. It seems that Prince Karl and Browne were not a temperamentally suited duo and the headlong retreat to Prague had heightened the tension between them: tempers flared on a regular basis and their noisy squabbles were overheard by the troops.

Frederick and Keith were hot on the Austrians' heels and, scarcely had the Austrians begun to dig themselves in on the Ziscaberg, than the Prussian vanguard arrived behind them to take up a position on the Weissenberg, which looked directly across Prague at the Austrians. By the evening of Monday 2 May, the whole of Frederick's column had arrived to view the garrisoned city beneath them in the setting sun and, shifting their gaze beyond Prague, they saw the Austrian army spreading itself across the Ziscaberg slopes some five miles away. Prince Karl and Browne had chosen an extremely strong defensive position and could look forward to having Marshal Daun join them with another 30 000 men in the next two days.

General Schwerin had seen his column's advance held up by difficult river crossings and he was now a day late in his march schedule. As they waited for Schwerin, the other Prussian generals went off to do some reconnaissance, leaving James Keith on the Weissenberg where he was keeping the Prague garrison occupied in watching his preparations.

Prussian supply wagons were even now arriving at Leitmoritz after being shipped up the Elbe on river boats. By 6 May and bang on time, Schwerin, von Winterfeld and King Frederick made their rendezvous on a pontoon bridge spanning the Moldau. What lay ahead was no easy task, for the Austrians had dug themselves in and were now perched 600 feet above the Prussians on the grassy slopes of the Ziscaberg. This position gave the Austrians a commanding field of fire down on an attacking enemy. At its summit the Ziscaberg flattened out into a plain where, behind all the gun emplacements, trenches had been dug and lines of infantry and cavalry were also waiting.

With Daun and his 30 000 troops expected imminently, it seemed prudent that the Prussians come to battle as soon as possible, even before nightfall. On 6 May 1757 the Battle of Prague commenced exactly on time and as Frederick and his generals had planned months before. An attack led by Schwerin and von Winterfeld on the Austrian right flank quickly got under way, leaving the disbelieving Austrians scrambling into battle order: what followed was carnage.

Von Winterfeld led the attacking spearhead of Schwerin's troops and they were soon caught in a hail of cannonfire, in which von

Winterfeld fell wounded from his horse with blood pouring from his neck. He regained consciousness moments later to find himself eighty paces from the Austrians and his own troops falling back. Schwerin's main battle group followed von Winterfeld and soon found themselves in difficulty; what they had previously thought to be green meadows were in fact semi-dried fishponds, covered in a coating of algae. Schwerin's troops could make only slow headway through the mud of the fishponds and were all the while taking a fearful punishment from Austrian cannonfire but, even as the caseshot blasted holes in the Prussian ranks, others came charging over the bodies of their fallen comrades. Eventually the Prussians closed on their enemy with bayonets and cold steel and began to take the advantage. As the battle raged both sides were sending in new regiments to plug the gaps; Browne was busy with his Austrians when a cannonball took off his foot in what was to prove a fatal wound. By this time too the seventy-three-year-old Prussian General Schwerin was dead: shot while urging on his troops at the very front of the battle.

As the infantry fought it out in a bitter hand-to-hand combat for the Ziscaberg, Zeithen and his Prussian cavalry broke through to close with the Austrian cavalry and proceeded to charge them off the battlefield. The battle was now definitely turning and Prince Karl, the Austrian general commanding, appears to have suffered a mild heart attack whereupon he was carried from the field down into Prague to join the wounded Browne. With both their leaders gone it was the end of Austrian resistance and 40 000 of them fled after Prince Karl and Browne into the safety of the city. These vast numbers of men and horses crammed into Prague should have meant an early surrender as starvation took its toll. With this in mind and to avoid being taken prisoner, some of the Austrians thought they might escape capture by leaving through the city's north gate and on up the Moldau River. Prince Karl appears to have somewhat recovered from his heart attack, for he twice opened the north gates to escape with his army only to find James Keith standing there waiting with his Prussians. The Austrians were trapped in Prague.

The war had started well for the Prussians in 1757 and the Austrians had taken a hammering in the south but in Hanover, in the north, a mixed army of predominantly British troops were facing forces from France, Russia and Sweden. Frederick now had to repeat his early success in the south and in this he was helped by the release of some of his Bohemian army and additional supplies captured during his recent offensive.

Back in Prague, the city was taking a terrible punishment from Prussian cannonfire directed from gun emplacements on both the Weissenberg and the Ziscaberg. Daun, who had been expected as the city's saviour, took fright at what had happened and halted his march but, although terrified to advance further, he continued to pick up fleeing Austrian soldiers to swell his own ranks. Three days after the Austrian army, with a mortally wounded Browne and Prince Karl, had packed themselves into Prague, heavy Prussian siege cannon and plentiful ammunition were shipped up the Elbe from Dresden. On 9 May, from vantage points on Weissenberg and Ziscaberg, these cannons opened up on Prague, firing red-hot balls on to buildings suspected of housing ammunition.

Although the city was a particular challenge offensively, either by virtue of its location, walls or armaments, the fact that 46 000 men were packed inside made it a wholly different proposition to times when only a normal garrison stood guard. During some of the intervals between cannon volleying there were surprise attacks mounted on Prague but they were always beaten back by the defenders. Morale was surprisingly high among the Austrians; siege batteries stretched for twelve miles around Prague and for four weeks those batteries poured shot into the city. James Keith had his camp on the Lorenzberg, a control and observation post for directing the fire from the Weissenberg.

After four weeks of punishing bombardment the Austrians offered to surrender but only on condition that they were permitted free withdrawal. This offer was completely unacceptable to the Prussians, who in their response demanded that the Austrians either surrender and enlist with them or give an undertaking not to take up arms against Prussia for six years.

Serious cannonfire again resumed on 19 May and on the night of 23–24 May, 10 000 Austrians handpicked for their strength and valour tried to cut their way through the encircling army. This attack was concentrated on an area under Keith's command, on the west side of the Moldau, and it took a major effort to bring it to a halt. For six hours, from somewhere between 1 a.m. and

2 a.m. until 7 a.m. the fighting raged, before the Austrians withdrew into Prague, leaving 1000 dead behind them. Food supplies were now so low that the cavalry's horses were being slaughtered to feed the hungry city. To the innocent civilians caught up in the siege it must have seemed that their tortured existence must soon end in surrender but even nature was to take a hand in events, to the advantage of Prussia. On 29 May the weather broke in a deluge which sent the swollen Moldau raging down in a flash flood that carried everything away before it. Forty-four Prussian pontoons were swept from the bridge structure they formed at Branik and only prompt action by Keith's troops, who doubled up and secured pontoons on their side of the river, stopped those from being lost as well. While nature unleashed her fury, tearing at the Prussians in their tents around Prague, in the lower parts of the city there was heavy flooding and people who had taken refuge from the shelling in their cellars were drowned. The cellars had also functioned as safe places to store food but the food was now floating about, utterly ruined.

Hardly had the storm abated and the rain ceased than a rocket exploded into the sky signalling that the Prussian batteries should commence fire again. In this latest bombardment a still-damp Prague was soon blazing, adding another 9000 casualties among the civilian population to an ever-increasing death toll. The Austrians now tried to save their diminishing food resources by forcing 12 000 citizens out through the city gates, perhaps hoping they would also become a burden on Prussian resources. But in a horrific precursor to the concept of total war, the civilians were told that they must either go back into the city, or be shot. The civilians were re-admitted to the city. One has to wonder what James Keith's feelings were at this time: was his natural humanity sublimated to the military necessity of Prague's surrender? We have to remember that Prussia was fighting for its very existence and the *Befehl ist Befehl* ('orders are orders') rule was then as now a fact of military life.

By 8 June much of Prague was a blackened, smoking ruin, with desperate people trying to take cover from cannonfire, and often buried alive as buildings collapsed on top of them. A long seige was not in the Prussians' interest for they had other problems to attend to and it seems they took advice from spies about where they might find the city magazines with their cannon to get a quicker result. They even freed a legendary burglar called Kasebier from his Stettin jail and a sentence of hard labour on his promise to infiltrate Prague and pinpoint the magazines for the army.† Kasebier was only too glad to get away from breaking stones and he was to twice slip in and out of Prague with targets for the cannon to lock on to before he vanished completely. Maybe he had decided that he had done more than enough to repay his debt to Prussian society, or perhaps his sentence of hard labour was followed by a death sentence in Prague.

While Prague was being battered to a ruin by siege cannon, the Duke of Brunswick had been keeping an eye on Marshal Daun who until then had kept well away from the city. Brunswick had just 20 000 men to Daun's 60 000 and, by 9 June, he was getting a bit edgy about being able to hold Daun off from Prague with his inferior numbers. Little did he know that Daun had been given direct orders to march to the relief of Prague and link up with Prince Karl's forces regardless of cost. With these orders from the Austrian court, Daun began his advance towards Prague on 12 June, sending messengers out in front of him to advise Prince Karl to expect him on the 20th. Almost inevitably, one or more of the messengers were intercepted and Daun's letter fell into Prussian hands.

Ten thousand Prussian troops with Frederick the Great at their head immediately hurried off to reinforce Brunswick, leaving orders for another 4000 to make haste and join them thirty-five miles away at the Brunswick camp. Frederick joined Brunswick that same evening and spent the night only three miles from where Daun was resting his head in the Austrian camp. Daylight came and as both armies were being fed the Prussians were out already looking over the land and planning battle.

---

† 'Spies being, above all, essential in this business, Friederich had bethought him of one Käsebier, a supreme of Housebreakers, whom he has, safe with a ball at his ancle, doing forced labour at Spandau (in Stettin if it mattered). Kasebier was actually sent for, pardon promised him if he could do the State a service. Kasebier smuggled himself twice, perhaps three times, into Prag; but the fourth time he did not come back.'
Thomas Carlyle, *Frederick the Great*, Vol. 3. p. 132.

The opposing armies were drawn up roughly in parallel against each other, each building natural defensive positions into their lines. Between the Prussians and Austrians lay the Vienna–Prague highway, with the small town of Kolin just twelve miles distant. Both armies were occupying ground filled with grassy knolls and little streams, a generally broken, undulating terrain with bogs and small woods at intervals.

Prussian reconnaissance confirmed that only Daun's left wing was vulnerable to attack. To spearhead this attack, Zeithen's cavalry and Hulsen's foot soldiers were detached to give battle while the main battle plan was for the whole army to march up behind Hulsen, ignoring all else, and to feed into the battle thereafter as reinforcements behind the Hulsen–Zeithen spearhead.

At 2 p.m., the Prussian army began to move eastward in two columns, only coming under spasmodic and ineffective fire from Austrian positions. First to make contact with the enemy was Zeithen, who in a repeat performance of his cavalry charge on the Zisca, smashed his way through Nadasti's opposing Austrian cavalry which had been stationed across the Prague–Vienna highway, blocking the advance. In the wake of Zeithen's horse came Hulsen's infantry, bringing cannon up to their front for an opening salvo, preparatory to a series of bayonet charges which sent the Austrians reeling back out of their positions. Having dealt with the enemy cavalry, Zeithen was now free to attend to the fleeing Austrians, driving the chaotic mass of men along before him in a headlong retreat. He was busy at this work when his cavalry forces were caught in a steady stream of cannonfire from a wood on his right; so savage was the Austrian fire that Zeithen had to halt his pursuit to allow Hulsen's infantry to go in and clear the wood. It was only when the infantry reached the wood that they found it to be packed with enemy and, worse still, behind the wood and the infantry, enemy cavalry was also massed and biding its time.

Things went seriously wrong for Hulsen, because instead of a steady flow of reinforcements coming up to join him, and feeding into the battle, there was nothing whatever; all Hulsen could do was hold on with what he had and hope for the best. The problem had been Mannstein, an impetuous man, who was unable to ignore Austrian fire to his flank on the way up to join Hulsen. The fire had so irritated him that he broke his forward march in order to detach troops to silence his tormentors, breaching the explicit orders he had been given. His disobedience was to prove disastrous, for far from being a temporary skirmish, Mannstein was drawn ever deeper into an action from which he could not disengage – he was now totally deflected from the objective he had been given. It went from bad to worse when more Prussian troops, marching up to help Hulsen, became involved in the Mannstein diversion, being deceived by all the action into thinking that they had come up to the frontline. Instead of circling around to Daun's left wing for their attack, the Prussians were now throwing themselves uphill against positions which their officers had earlier dismissed as impervious to attack, leaving Hulsen and Zeithen desperately in need of support.

After Frederick had hurried off to join Brunswick, James Keith had been in command of the left wing of the Prussian army at Prague: he was thus well out of the battle now raging. His job was still that of carrying on the siege offensive and raining cannonfire down on Prague, unaware of the shambles and disaster in the making at Kolin.

As the sheer scale of the debâcle came home to them, the Prussian command could only hope that their disciplined troops would extricate themselves from the battle in some kind of order. Hulsen could not hold his position and was soon fighting a desperate rearguard action as he was pushed downhill to merge his forces with the rest of the army retreating northwards to Nimburg.

Unwilling to accept the defeat that was staring him in the face, Frederick tried to rally some of his troops for an assault on an enemy battery which was proving impregnable. Soldiers were falling dead around him from battery fire; the situation was desperate when Lieutenant Colonel Grant (late of Dunlugas and Meston's Turriff Academy) – who was sitting on horseback beside the King – remarked 'Your Majesty and I cannot take the battery ourselves.' Frederick responded by turning round and, seeing nobody there, put his telescope once more to his eye for one last look before turning his horse and riding slowly away.

The Battle of Kolin was irretrievably lost and Brunswick and Moritz were put in charge of the Prussian retreat to Nimburg some fifteen miles away. Meanwhile, for whatever reason, Marshal Daun failed to press home his advantage and stayed put when he could have pushed on to an even greater victory. Hulsen and Zeithen's units were still intact, however, and capable of savaging any pursuers. Of their 60 000 strong army the Austrians had lost 8114 men and of the 34 000 Prussians, 13 773 were lost.

On the Sunday evening of 19 June 1757, Keith and his camp at Prague heard of the Kolin disaster; this left him and the other generals silently contemplating the scale and implications of their defeat. Keith himself did not waste any time on introspection but instantly recognised what now had to be done, for the siege equipment was then quickly dismantled, assembled and loaded on to baggage trains for shipment to Leitmoritz. By 4 p.m. on 20 June he had a highly organised and protected withdrawal underway, carrying everything of any use along with it. We are told that the withdrawal took a 'chequerwise' pattern: an innovative and skilled troop movement that could only have been accomplished by the highly drilled Prussian army.

On Tuesday 28 June the beaten Prussian army with Frederick, Brunswick and Moritz caught up with Keith across a river bridge near Leitmoritz, where the Prussian army was to spend the next four weeks resting and preparing for the next challenge. As he surveyed his tired, depleted army at Leitmoritz, Frederick was informed that his seventy-one-year-old mother had just died in Berlin.

Prussia's enemies were now closing in for the kill and, as huge Russian forces were massing along some of her borders, equally large Franco–Austrian armies were hurrying to take maximum advantage from the Kolin debâcle. Even the Swedes, numbering just 20 000, felt safe in invading Pomerania. By 3 July, Cumberland ('hero' of Culloden) was under attack and falling back from a challenging advance by forces under D'Estrees in Hanover. Cumberland (by this time obese and ill-equipped to handle the job in front of him) was constantly on the retreat through Hanover, back towards the Weser.

While events were still unfolding on Prussia's northern borders, the main Prague army, now re-equipped and regrouped, was marching home to deal with the developing crisis. As they marched home they planned to secure the mountain passes through Silesia and Saxony behind them, cutting off the pursuing Austrian army and preventing their joining their other enemies. Prince Karl's army, now freed from imprisonment in Prague, had merged with Daun's into a huge force 70 000-strong which then set out after the retreating Prussians. The Austrians soon found that the road in front of them was far from empty; a small Prussian army commanded by Prince August Wilhelm (the King's brother) had been left to fight a rearguard action behind the main Prussian force. August Wilhelm also had von Winterfeld, Zeithen and Schmettau as advisers but no matter how great the expertise at his side, the huge numbers of Austrians kept pushing this rearguard army along in front of it.

Prince August Wilhelm then embarked on an erratic and barely logical retreat, losing baggage, wagons and men to marauding bands and rough terrain as he went. This humiliating retreat eventually arrived at Zittau, where the Prussians found themselves relegated to the role of spectators, as the Austrian army subjected Zittau to the same red-hot cannonball treatment so recently dished out to Prague. Helplessly they watched, until at last Zittau fell and August Wilhelm was left with no other option but to march his dispirited troops back to Bautzen. When news of his brother's poor performance reached Frederick, he hurried from Leitmoritz to see what could be salvaged of the situation, leaving Moritz of Dessau with 10 000 men protecting the mountain passes into Saxony around Pirna while James Keith followed at an easier pace with the ammunition and supplies. As he travelled, the King continued to be given more bad news of enemy incursions into Prussia, none of which improved his already bad temper.

When Frederick arrived at Bautzen he exploded into rage at his brother, telling him that it was only his good fortune in being a member of the royal family that saved him and his generals from facing court martial and a certain death sentence. August Wilhelm was sent back to Dresden in complete disgrace and, a year later, still bitterly feeling that he had been made a scapegoat for what was sheer bad luck, died at Oranienburg.

James Keith arrived after the royal rage had subsided and August Wilhelm departed. Along with Frederick and an army of 56 000 men they started off for Bernstadt on 21 August 1757, to begin a frustrating game of hide and seek, with the Prussians looking for battle and the Austrians doing their best to avoid it.

Elsewhere, Soubise's Franco–Austrian allied army were at Erfurt, while Cumberland was still retreating in Hanover and the Swedes were intensifying their grip on Pomerania. Richelieu's French army stood pointing in the direction of Magdeburg and an 80 000-strong Russian army was poised and ready to strike into eastern Prussia. That was the position on 29 August as Frederick arrived in Dresden with a reduced army of only 23 000 troops.

The Brunswick army had been tasked with protecting the routes into Prussia from Silesia and were camped near Görlitz when the Austrians decided to try their luck. In a probing attack, they tested the Prussian defensive line at a small hill called Jakelsberg, which had no great strategic significance or military value whatsoever. Von Winterfeld was to see it very differently when he heard his grenadiers were under attack; he sprang on to his horse and galloped up to Jakelsberg where he found his men retreating. For some reason the retreat was wholly unacceptable to von Winterfeld; he rallied his men to retake the hill but was then shot in the chest, becoming one more of the day's casualties. Yet another of Frederick's generals, this time a close friend, had gone.

As von Winterfeld lay dying at Jakelsberg, Frederick was marching from Dresden to Erfurt on 30 August with just 23 000 men, incredibly hoping to meet up with Soubise and Hilderhausen's 50 000-strong army. Yet none of the assembled armies, totalling around 150 000 men, were at all keen to close in for the kill, leaving Frederick tramping all over Prussia to no purpose. For twelve days they marched on Erfurt, with Keith commanding the main body of the army and Ferdinand and Moritz leading the rest.

So bad did his situation appear to Frederick that he put out feelers for a peace treaty to the Duke of Richelieu on 7 September, advances which were derisively rejected out of hand. Meanwhile, Cumberland found that he had run out of places to retreat to: behind him lay only the sea. Embarrassed by his son's military incompetence, the British king began negotiations which led to the convention of Kloster-Zevern and the evacuation of British troops. Cumberland was never to be given a military command again.

On Tuesday 13 September, the Prussian army arrived at Erfurt to find the occupying enemy troops departing to safety. It seems that even the thought of Prussian troops in their vicinity terrified allied armies, allowing some amazing successes to follow from outrageous Prussian bluff. An example of this was given by Seidlitz who, with only 1500 men, put an army of 8000 to flight. In doing so he collected a vast amount of abandoned equipment without even losing a man.

On 14 November, the Prussian army had split into two, to cover itself against attack; they had heard that 80 000 Russian Cossack and Kalmuck troops under Apraxin were looting and committing atrocities such as appalled even these battle-hardened Prussians. It was all too much for Frederick: the Prussian General Lehwald was detached with 25 000 men to deal with the Russians before their advance brought them to Königsberg. Although he did his best, Lehwald suffered reverses in the face of overwhelming odds and firepower.

The only relief for Prussia – when the darkest storm clouds broke just for a brief moment – came when the Russians were told that Empress Elisabeth was dying of dropsy. With the expectation of Elisabeth's imminent demise and knowing that Peter, her successor, was an admirer of Prussia and Frederick the Great, Apraxin turned his army around and marched it back into Russia.

At Erfurt it was time to pack and move on again. The Prussians had learned that 4000 Austrians were marching on Berlin itself. Too late they arrived at Berlin, to find that the Austrians had come and gone, leaving only after they had extracted a ransom from the city.

14

·

Three battles: Rossbach, Leuthen and Olmutz

·

KING FREDERICK LEFT LEIPZIG with the vanguard of his army on 30 October 1757, leaving Keith and Duke Ferdinand to bring up the main army for their first stop on the march at Lutzen. Next morning, at 8 a.m., the town of Weissenfels (pop. 6000) awoke to the sound of marching Prussian boots when Frederick and half his army drew up in close proximity to the town. The other half, not very far away, was commanded by James Keith and continued its march on Merseburg. Shortly afterwards the Weissenfels garrison of 4000, reinforced by two French battalions, was on the receiving end of steady cannonfire which soon smashed buildings and gates, forcing the garrison to make a hasty exit from the town and escape across the Saale bridge, which they then burned behind them. The burning of the bridge only bought them a little time, for Prussian engineers soon constructed another bridge of sorts a mile downstream, allowing their army to get across.

In the morning light of Tuesday 1 November, Keith was gazing across the river at Merseburg where the bridge was down and Soubise waiting for him with batteries of cannon at the ready. His appraisal completed, Keith sent Duke Ferdinand off to check the situation around the Halle bridge, twelve miles away, only to have it reported that this bridge was also down – and Broglio was waiting for him on the other side.

Soubise and Broglio's positions soon had to be evacuated, however, for they were both vulnerable to an attack by Frederick's army which had poured across the new bridge made by their engineers. They soon had to withdraw their 60 000-strong army up

174

to higher ground some miles to the rear and assemble them again in battle order. As their enemy retreated, Keith and Ferdinand replaced the bridges, doing it so quickly that by 5 November all the Prussians were across on the other side. Keith's men and those with Frederick now stood very close to each other, near to the village of Mucheln where their enemy was encamped, while Frederick's left wing was spread around Rossbach.

With six other hamlets, Rossbach covered a six-mile radius loop of the River Saale. Within this plain were a couple of streams and two small risings which could hardly be described as hills. Apart from a big hollow, it was singularly featureless and devoid of any cover. Among the scattered hamlets, Rossbach occupied the highest ground and looked down on to Mucheln across the hollow.

On 5 November, at eight in the morning, Frederick poked his head out through the roof tiles of the house he was occupying to see what the French and Austrian armies were doing, only to find them on the move. The King's plan proposed a cavalry attack to slice off a part of the enemy's departing army, and to this end horsemen were soon prepared to engage the enemy on the Freiburg road.

This withdrawal was not a retreat by the French and Austrians, as had so often been the case in the past. They had looked at Frederick's position and estimated that his army only amounted to 10 000 men and was wide open to attack. The allies intended swinging their 50 000 men up behind and on to Frederick's left wing as a prelude to rolling up his flank while, to close the trap, the Austrians had gone along to tear out the makeshift bridge at Herren Muhle, sending this possible means of Prussian escape floating away downstream.

Watching eyes in the Prussian army saw the allied manoeuvre to their flank and a breathless messenger came to tell all to the King's lunch table where he sat eating with his generals. From twelve noon until 2 p.m. they just carried on eating – at 2.30 p.m. the orders were given and by 3.00 p.m. the Prussians were also on the march.

The allied army saw the Prussians move out and assumed they were seeing a panic-stricken rush for an escape over the bridge at Merseburg. This assumption was incentive enough for them to move their march up a gear and begin a slow climb up the only two hills for miles. It was 3.30 p.m. and the Prussian General Seidlitz was already in place and hidden by the top of the hill, waiting to sweep down on his enemy. Suddenly the French and Austrians looked upwards and all they could see was a solid wall of horseflesh and flashing steel thundering down on them in an avalanche of pounding hooves. Seidlitz and his cavalry sliced through the infantry three or perhaps four times again and again, until both the enemy infantry and cavalry were sent reeling from the field. In all, the action took just half an hour, before Seidlitz withdrew his cavalry into the hollow to regroup.

As Seidlitz and his men waited in the hollow, Frederick came over the top of the hill preceded by 22 cannons blazing fire down onto the allied army below. It is of interest to note that all of this hellfire came from just one small part of Frederick's left wing: it came from the five battalions under the command of James Keith in the second or reserve line. The Prussian infantry advanced towards the chaos of confused and panicking allied troops until they stopped at forty paces to empty their muskets into them in a murderous fire which continued at a rate of five rounds per minute.

As cannonfire poured death down the hill and Prussian muskets sent volley after volley crashing into the allies, Seidlitz saw another opportunity open for him and again threw his cavalry at the enemy rear. Darkness began to fall at 4.30 p.m. but by this time it was all over; a darkening night sky served only to slow up what was now a virtual turkey shoot. Soubise and Hildburghausen had lost 3000 men (killed or wounded) with 5000 taken prisoner, including eight generals and 300 other officers. Prussian losses were 165 killed and 376 wounded. Outnumbered three to one at the beginning, only half the 22 000 Prussian troops saw action that day, giving a good example of how Prussian speed of manoeuvre and efficiency could defeat much larger armies in the field – it also explains why these larger armies were slow to seek battle. The comprehensive defeat at Rossbach crippled the Austrian army. By 7 November, their French allies were fifty-five miles from Rossbach and still running, as Soubise hopelessly tried to halt their flight and regroup at Nordhausen and Heiligenstadt.

Despite the embarrassment of Cumberland's enforced withdrawal from Hanover, Britain still had an interest in these continental wars and sent 12 000 troops to help Prince Ferdinand, later increasing these forces to 20 000.

In the aftermath of Rossbach James Keith reported events to his brother:

> As I knew that Weideman had written to you, my very dear brother, the day after the battle, and that, consequently, you had been made acquainted with my health and safety, I thought you would pardon me, if I delayed a little in writing to you. We have honoured the late affair with the name of a battle, though it was really nothing but a rout. The enemies wished to attack us, but we were beforehand with them. By the rapidity of our movements we were enabled to attack them in the flank, while they were marching. Their cavalry sustained the first shock, but soon was overthrown. Their infantry did not do its duty well, but fled precipitately, after three or four discharges from our battalions on its flank. After this it was, in fact, only a flight, and a pursuit, which lasted till dark night. You may judge by this, that the loss has not been great. On our side about 100 men killed and 235 wounded. The enemy may have lost 1000 men killed but we have taken at least 4000 prisoners; and if darkness had not favoured them, their army must have been entirely destroyed; for we drove them from within a league of Mersebourg to the River Unstrutt; where there is only a single bridge, over which they defiled during the whole night, in order to place themselves in safety. We have taken more than sixty pieces of their cannon, many standards and colours; and generals, dukes, marquises and counts, in plenty. We have especially taken a great many of the Swiss, who do not seem to be such good runners as the French. Such was generally our battle. When I have read the accounts of it, which will be printed, I will erase all the falsehoods on both sides, and thus make for you a true account, which will be only for yourself and for our good chancellor; for one does not write the truth for the public. Prince Henry is wounded with a musketball in the shoulder, but as he has no bones broken there is no danger. Be assured that this family can never last, if the war continues; they expose themselves too much. The King was, the other day, in a place of greater danger than any of his generals. For this time he escaped, but the next he may not be equally fortunate; and a catastrophe may happen, the very thought of which makes me tremble. Adieu, my dear brother. My health is still good, in spite of the fatigues we undergo.

In Silesia, the Austrian Prince Karl, with Daun as his second in command, was pressing hard on Brunswick's heels as he desperately tried to fight them off. Seeing Brunswick in difficulty, Frederick left Rossbach to give him some help against Prince Karl's 60 000 men and Nadasti's 20 000.

Prince Henry was left to guard Saxony; James Keith was sent with forces to Bohemia while Frederick himself left Leipzig on 13 November with 13 000 troops to aid Brunswick and relieve Seidlitz. Keith described this march to his brother:

> I am returned this morning from my course into Bohemia. My campaign has been very short, and yet I am very well contented with it; having executed everything I had proposed to myself, both by destroying several large magazines belonging to the enemy, and also by drawing a corps of from 14 000 to 16 000 men of the enemy towards my side, by which I have delivered the King from them, and thus favoured his projects on Silesia. I can say, with truth, that this campaign has been a virgin one; for on my side there has not been a drop of blood spilt, and very little even on that of the enemy; but they were in a dreadful fright at Prague, for, from the moment I passed the Egra at Budyn, the inhabitants fled from the town. My march had also been a pretty rapid one. I set off from beyond Mersebourg on the 17th of last month. I have been within four miles of the walls of Prague, and now, here I am come back again. I can, at the same time, assure you, that the troops are not more fatigued, than if they were just come out of winter quarters.

During this period, when Keith was marching into Bohemia to draw off enemy forces, Frederick was hurrying to the aid of Brunswick and the relief of Seidlitz: but he had left it too late. Between the time of his departure from Leipzig and 14 November – twenty-four hours, in fact – Seidlitz had capitulated leaving Brunswick alone to face an Austrian army of 80 000.

In a battle which raged for fourteen hours, along eight miles of countryside, Brunswick's took heavy punishment. The battle progressed with the Prussians steadily losing ground along most of their front; only Zeithen was still able to drive the Austrians back across the River Lohe. Brunswick held a council of war with his officers and listened to proposals for a night attack but, recognising that the odds were heavily stacked against such a move, decided instead to withdraw across the Oder. By this time he had lost 8000 men killed and wounded, and eighty of his cannons were also gone. When Brunswick rode out next morning on a doubtful reconnaissance mission, only to be captured by a few Croats, whispers and a question mark were left hanging over his courage. He was taken to Vienna as a prisoner only to be released to return to Prussia, where Frederick highlighted his disgrace by giving him command of the invalid garrison at Stettin.

What was left of Brunswick's army marched off towards Glogau leaving Prince Karl to move confidently in for the capture of Breslau. The Austrians not only looked invincible but felt so. Brunswick was not the only one to have his military prowess condemned as inadequate, for his second in command was arrested and Zeithen took over the army with orders to rendezvous with Frederick. Zeithen did this on 3 December 1757, both armies meeting at Parchwitz.

On a high because of recent victories, the Austrians decided to find Frederick's army and deal with it in a once-and-for-all battle. What they couldn't know was that Frederick, even with his much smaller army, had exactly the same thing in mind and was already closing in on them with the vanguard of a Prussian army which had four columns coming up behind him. The serious fighting began at Neumarkt, when the Prussians seized the town and a commanding hill beyond it, capturing 569 Croats and killing 120 out of the 1000 men in the garrison.

Prince Karl and his army had meanwhile crossed the River Weistritz and formed a long line with the river behind them. Their position intersected the Prague–Vienna highway at right angles and had good, natural defensive features of woody hills, swamps and villages. His headquarters was located in the village of Leuthen.

For James Keith the past months had been a never-ending succession of battles against an enemy who invariably had much greater strength than the forces under his command. Being part of an army which relied on rapid deployment and quick reaction to command meant being completely alert to what was happening in battle. With Frederick up there on the front line, any officer would also have needed to keep an eye open for directions from the supreme commander. James Keith was not only fighting for the Prussian state but against his own recurring ill health and the fatigues of battle with their attendant stresses and strains. Since Prague there had scarcely been a break from war, with the Kolin aftermath, Rossbach – and soon the bloodbath of Leuthen.

When Prince Karl of Austria heard that he had lost Neumarkt he knew that he had not only lost a forward post but also his army's bakery, which had a capacity to provide bread for 8000 men. After Neumarkt's fall, the Prussians were on the move again, marching through the early morning mists and poor light until, only some eight miles along the road, they arrived at the village of Borne to find their path blocked by Nostitz and three Saxon dragoon regiments. Nostitz had been positioned there to act as an early warning system for the main Austrian army. Unfortunately for him, he did not have an early warning system for himself and failed to recognise the Prussians until they were coming at him through the misty half-light of morning. In the brief action which followed, 540 Saxons were taken prisoner and Nostitz himself was fatally wounded. Nothing now stood between the Prussian and Austrian armies and Frederick, in his vanguard, found an elevated viewpoint where he could watch and weigh up the Austrian dispositions over the three hours it took for his army to arrive.

The Prussian plan was to launch an assault on the Austrian left wing using what they called their 'oblique order' or *schräge Stellung*. It was a battle manoeuvre used by armies in ancient times, which could only work with highly disciplined and well-drilled troops. Its success lay in its precision: one battalion would lead off at a measured pace for fifty steps, then another, then another, and so on, until what seemed to be a hopelessly jumbled and confused mass of men suddenly received an order – to turn either half right or half left. In an instant the jumbled mass suddenly took a shape which simultaneously brought the maximum number of troops into battle with a cutting edge of bayonets and musketfire at an angle of 45° to the enemy lines.

This Prussian manoeuvre was choreographed by a formidable trio in the persons of Wedell, Prince Moritz and Zeithen, and directed on to the Austrian left wing commanded by Nadasti. There was absolutely nothing the Austrians could do in the face of the Prussian advance and they were given no time to react as their flank was attacked. With no respite or time to reorganise, they fell back from their positions. The retreat began as the only way to save the Austrians being rolled up and engulfed in the Prussian advance. For an hour the battle raged among the churches, steadings and orchards. Not only was Nadasti taking severe punishment on the left wing but furious fighting was taking place at Leuthen, where Austrian cannon batteries were making a stand among the buildings and nearby windmills. So close was the Prussian attack that when Prince Ferdinand opened up his cannon on a target near Radaxdorf, an emissary came hurrying up to tell him he was actually firing on his brother the King – Ferdinand almost swooned with terror on receipt of this information.

In a constant stream of cannonballs and musketfire the windmills, churches and houses sheltering the Austrian army were shot to bits; it was then time for the infantry to go in with bayonets fixed. Lucchesi, the Austrian cavalry commander, saw this and thought that since the Prussian flank seemed unprotected he would charge down with his cavalry, in decisive style, finishing the battle at a stroke. Lucchesi, however, had not seen or been aware that the whole of the Prussian left wing's horse were just waiting for that sort of move and ready to pounce. As Lucchesi and his cavalry thundered past him towards the Prussian infantry, Driesen swung his Prussian cavalry up out of a hollow to take them from behind. The Austrian cavalry were scattered to the four winds and Lucchesi paid for the mistake with his life.

The Battle of Leuthen cost the Austrians 21 000 prisoners: 3000 men died, 7000 were wounded, and 116 cannons captured. In all, it had taken just three hours for the Austrian army to be reduced to a broken ruin. Some credit has to be given to the Prussian soldiers but the battle was won by focused firepower, enabling an army of only 30 000 men to take on and totally wreck an opposing army of 80 000. For Frederick's enemies it was not just the speed of manoeuvre, the concentrated firepower or the rapidity with which they covered ground: the truly terrifying thing was the way in which the Prussians seemed to welcome each new trial of strength.

James Keith wrote to his brother describing the battle.

My dear brother,

We give battles here, as elsewhere people give operas; there have been three in the last month, of which we have lost one and gained two; but the last appears to me decisive in our favour. I can assure you, that from all accounts I have seen, the loss of the enemy has been immense. Cannons, equipages, all is taken; and in troops, either killed, taken prisoner, or deserted, they must have lost, at least, 20 000 men. There are, besides, nine battalions, and many wounded, shut up in Breslau, who it is impossible should escape from us. Lucchesi is among them, who was wounded in the first battle, lost by the Prince of Bevern; but was not very fatal on our side, as our killed and wounded did not exceed 1800 men. General Zeithen is still employed in pursuing the Austrians, and has written word to the King, that he has found the greater part of their heavy artillery near Strehlen, and taken possession of it; but we do not yet know whether it is that belonging to their army, or that which they made use of at the siege of Scheidnitz. In short, the victory is complete; and costs us, as I hear, about 4000 men.

Hardly had the smoke cleared from the battlefield at Leuthen than the Prussians were again on the march, for by the next day they were on their way to lay siege to Breslau and its 17 000-strong garrison. From the time of their arrival it took just twelve days, in the very worst sort of weather, for the gates of Breslau to swing open and let the Prussians in. Within Breslau another huge load of war booty was captured which went to feed their war machine. The Liegnitz garrison, seeing all resistance to the Prussians being battered into the ground, also decided to quit, which left only Scheidnitz to be dealt with in the following spring. It was now 26 December 1757, and the 'war season' was coming to an end as bad weather forced armies to leave the field and take to their winter quarters. Prince Karl and the exhausted remnants of his beaten army went back to Austria, where he was removed from any position of command and subsequently took up a form of retirement in the Netherlands. Frederick took his Prussians to winter in Breslau and between the campaign's end and the beginning of a new offensive in 1758, he organised a series of balls and other social functions to while away the time. As the winter's calendar of social events filled up, so also did recruitment activity get underway to replace the army's losses; the target recruitment figure was to have 145 000 under arms, of whom 53 000 were to be sent on duty to Silesia.

Empress Elisabeth of Russia had not fulfilled everyone's expectations and died of dropsy but was still very much alive when Apraxin returned from east Prussia with her army. Not only was she very much alive but so furious with her general that Apraxin was dismissed and court martialled. Apraxin was not the only one to go, for he was joined by Bestuchef, her chancellor, who had lately been Keith's tormentor in Russia and largely responsible for his departure.

The Empress wanted the east Prussian territory back in her possession and was not going to await the return of spring to send off an army. She despatched 31 000 men under the command of Fermor on 16 January 1758. As might be guessed, the only obstacle to Fermor's progress to east Prussia was the quagmire which had been the roads, but even that was not enough to stop him from eventually entering Königberg. In the tradition of Russian profligacy with troops, Elisabeth then sent another 104 000 men and 75 000 Cossacks as reinforcements, although these additional forces were not to join Fermor until June 16 1758.

Britain seems to have decided to play a diminished role in the war, although agreeing to give another subsidy of £670 000 to Prussia. She reduced her active support with a decision to send no more troops to Hanover and by refusing to provide a fleet to stop the Russians supplying Fermor by sea. The reasons for this appear to be that Britain did not want to jeopardise trade with Russia. Until the end of April 1758, the European powers carried on with their war preparations and there was only a little skirmishing as opposing armies eyed each other and waited for a first move.

War recommenced on 19 April 1758, when the Prussian army with Frederick again at their head broke out of the Grussau and Landshut region in two columns of 40 000 men. They first marched eastwards to Troppau before swinging south. The Austrian Marshal Daun, who had been watching all this movement, suddenly realised that the direction they had taken could only mean one thing – they had the town of Olmutz (pop. 10 000) as their target. Olmutz was a priority for the Prussians because it had become a vast military arsenal and storehouse; it was strategically placed to feed and arm Austrian armies marching on Prussia.

The vanguard of the army was led by Frederick while Keith commanded the second, rearguard column. Daun had been absolutely correct in his guess that the Prussian objective was Olmutz but he must have derived some comfort from knowing that Olmutz was heavily fortified and capable of withstanding siege – this would allow time to respond with an army to raise the siege. Indeed, Olmutz was so heavily fortified that it was able to withstand seven weeks of a fierce summer siege.

The march on Olmutz began from Neisse on 27 April but it was not until 12 May that Olmutz appeared ahead of the Prussians. Not only did they see a heavily defended town but they were soon to know that their extended lines of supply up to Olmutz were vulnerable to attack and posed another problem. They had to cart supplies over 120 miles of hill and valley, all of which gave ample scope for enemy ambush and, even from the very start of the campaign, they were losing men and wagons to hostile action on a daily basis.

Progress with the siege was nevertheless well advanced and it appeared that although its fall was not going to be immediate, it would, only be a matter of time. But ammunition and food were running short and this deficiency needed to be made good to fuel the final push which would take them inside. A convoy of 3000 four-horse wagons, laden with supplies, left Troppau for Olmutz under the command of Colonel Mosel, while Zeithen and his cavalry came back from Olmutz to give the wagon train cover against the enemy during its slow and laborious progress through ninety miles of hill and dale.

Marshal Daun sent two officers, Laudon and Ziscowitz, out with the Austrian cavalry to intercept Prussian supply wagons.

The wagon train trundled its weary way, shielded by Zeithen from numerous attacks, until they got through the Pass of Domstadle. On clearing the pass they almost immediately ran straight into cannonfire, which so frightened the civilian drivers that many turned about for home or simply cut the traces and galloped off, leaving their wagons behind. Even though the wagons were eventually grouped into a *Wagenburg* (wagon fortress), this still did not allow Zeithen the freedom of movement to which he was normally accustomed. As his convoy was progressively destroyed, he had to engage in a fighting retreat which took him all the way back to Troppau. Of the 3000 wagons at the outset, only 250 made it to supply the besieging army at Olmutz.

As Laudon closed the road between Troppau and Olmutz, Daun could be seen on manoeuvre in the distance: this clearly told the Prussians that their siege had run out of time, not to mention food and ammunition. By Saturday 1 July a withdrawal had been planned and its execution begun. All the Prussian guns suddenly opened up on Olmutz in a sustained barrage, lightening the load of excess ammunition for the journey homewards and under the cover of darkness at 2 a.m. on the Saturday morning, Keith was on the move with 4000 packed wagons, as the Austrians in Olmutz kept their heads down in the face of the Prussian fire. Prior to moving off, Frederick wrote to James Keith saying 'You must impress on all officers of your army that no one should show himself to be discouraged, and if an officer acts or talks as though everything were lost and does not show confidence and encourage the soldiers, then he is to be arrested and imprisoned. That will prevent many desertions and help greatly to avert misfortunes which otherwise we shall certainly encounter.'

Daun had anticipated the route of the Prussian retreat through Silesia and made preparations accordingly. It then came as a shock to find that instead of going back to Silesia the Prussians were heading for Bohemia and Leitomischl and that Daun was now two whole weeks behind them. James Keith took his wagon train into Leitomischl on 8 July as the King went on ahead to clear the road and take Königsgratz. Keith's part in the retreat from Olmutz has been recognised as being militarily brilliant. While the retreat continued Keith had taken personal command of the rearguard and, although ill, kept the probing attacks from Laudon's marauding Croats at bay. Laudon was nothing if not determined and this type of action against Keith's convoy was the sort in which he had gained distinction and a recognised expertise. When Keith was still a march from Königsgratz, Laudon and Hoiltz he launched a heavy attack on the leading wagons.

Hearing the cannons open up ahead, Keith quickly gathered his cavalry and proceeded to clear the hilltops and surrounding cover from which his wagons had been taking fire. In Keith's estimation, his wagons had been allowed to take fire for far too long and retaliatory measures should have been taken against the Austrians much more quickly – he considered that one of his generals had been far too slow to respond to enemy fire. Keith told his aide-de-camp in French to take a message to the erring gentleman which went as follows: 'Tell Monsieur from me, he may be a very pretty thing, but he is not a man.'[†] James Keith himself told the Olmutz story, in letters to his brother:

[†] 'Tell Monsieur from me,' said Keith to his Aide de Camp, 'he may be a very pretty thing but he is not a man (*qu'il peut être une bonne chose, mais qu'il n'est pas un homme*)! The excellent vernacular Keith; – still a fine breadth of accent in him, one perceives! He is now past sixty; troubled with asthma; and I doubt not may be, occasionally, thinking it is time to end his campaigns.' Thomas Carlyle, *Frederick the Great*, Vol. 3, p. 288.

We opened the trenches before Olmutz last night, at 500 yards from the place, without losing a single man, the governor not having perceived what we were about till it was daylight, by which time we were already covered by our works. All this morning he has been firing, but not vigorously, and almost entirely with small cannons. If he does not increase his fire, I reckon in three days on being able to bring to bear upon the place twenty-four great guns, and sixteen mortars. If we are lucky, I hope in four or five days more to extinguish a great part of his fire; for having the advantage of the ground over him, we see the inside of several of his works. On his side he does not spare labour. I see from the top of the house I am living in, that he is opening a battery on our right, in an island that you will see on the other side of the river. We must therefore plant one to oppose him. Adieu my dear brother.

Another letter reads:

I have received my dear brother's letter of 4 May, and have shewn it to the King, who was much pleased with the part relating to the canton of Berne. The taking of Scheidnitz did not exactly occur in the way that it is reported. There was neither a breach, nor a piece of the wall fallen down: but a deserter gave information, that the soldiers, who were placed to guard a certain fort, were all below in the casemates, in account of the quantity of shells which we threw there. The resolution was, in consequence, taken to scale that part, which was done without resistance. The entrance of the casemates was then taken possession of, and those within were obliged to beg for quarter. The possession of the fort remained to us; upon which the town, of which all the strength consists in the forts which surround it, capitulated. We found fifty-one Austrian cannons in it, besides those we had ourselves left there. I wish I could also give you an account of the taking of Olmutz; but the Baron de Marschall, who commands there, does not approve of my doing this immediately. He is a very brave old man, seventy-six years old, dextrous and experienced in this kind of warfare. He is in a very good place, provided with everything he wants, and having, at his disposal, all the cannons and ammunition destined for the siege of Neisse, provisions in great abundance, and an old engineer named M. de Rochpine, who assists him admirably in his defence. His garrison consists of eighteen battalions, and three squadrons of dragoons, but there is a good many recruits among them. I see, that, for the services of danger, he trusts principally to six Hungarian battalions, who are with him; for in the three sorties he has made, hardly any one but Hungarians have appeared. In the last he has given them a good dose of *acqua magnanimitatis*, as Lacy used to call it. They were all drunk, and in this state rushed into our batteries, and nailed up six pieces of cannon and three mortars, but so ill, that four hours afterwards all of them went off as well as before. Our people killed 100 of their soldiers, and five officers, with their bayonets; and we took an officer and forty-seven men prisoners. The deserters assure us, that, with the wounded, they have lost 300 men, out of the 1200, of which the last sorties consisted. In consequence for the last three days they have attempted nothing. I tell you nothing of Prince Henry and Prince Ferdinand of Brunswick, because they are nearer you than us. All that we know is, that they are both in motion, to try and execute the projects they have concerted with the King. I am obliged to you for all the good things you send me. I can only send you plans in return. By that of Olmutz you will see how far we are advanced; and as Weideman did not send you that of Scheidnitz, I have begged Balbi to make me one, which I will send you in my next letter. The King, who covers our siege, came yesterday to see our lines, and to receive a hundred or two cannonshots. Lieutenant-General Fouque received a contusion on his thigh from a twelve-pounder; but it is not a dangerous wound. I see that the King will be glad to receive letters from you from time to time. You can send them inclosed in those to me.

Adieu, my dearest brother. The Swiss officer's remedy against danger made me laugh heartily, and the King also. Fermor and Browne have not been recalled. You know the Russian generals sufficiently well, to be aware, that they are not anxious for commands, where blows may be expected, so, probably, they will remain.

A letter to Marischal described the failure at Olmutz:

You must have already heard, by the newspapers, of the raising of the siege of Olmutz; but as I am persuaded that many false circumstances will have been added to the detail of that event, I am going to relate the whole transaction to you, with that accuracy, which you know I always adhere to. I must first allow that we had by no means a true idea of the strength of the place or of the garrison; and that, consequently, we had not brought with us enough ammunition to take it. This obliged the King to order a great convoy from Silesia, under an escort of eight battalions of infantry and of about 1100 horse. The enemies, who perceived that everything depended upon the arrival of this convoy, and who, being in their own country, were well informed of every step we took, collected several small bodies of our men, which had already been posted in the mountains behind us, with the view of cutting off our communication with Silesia. With these they attacked our convoy on 27 June, but were repulsed with the loss of 200 or 300 men. As soon as I heard this I sent Lieutenant-General Zieten, with five battalions of grenadiers, (not very strong ones, I allow), and three regiments of cavalry and hussars, to meet the convoy, which was already within three leagues of us. The day after (the 28th) the attack was recommenced by the enemies, with the same troops as the day before. But while Zieten was occupied in repulsing them both in front and rear of the convoy, for they attacked in both parts at once, General

Saint-Ignon arrived with 4000 grenadiers and 3000 dragoons, and fell upon the centre; so that our forces and convoy were divided into two parts, one of which arrived at camp, but the other was destroyed; and Zieten, who was in the rear, was obliged to return to Troppau, with whatever scattered troops he could collect. You will readily perceive, that after the loss of our ammunition it was impossible to take any other part, than of raising the siege, which we did on the morning of 2 July. I was obliged to leave a single cannon and five mortars behind us, which are the only trophies the enemy has to boast of; for I brought away with me all the sick and wounded, except twenty-two who were actually dying. As soon as the siege was raised, the King resolved to quit Moravia, as all the provisions in it, both for men and horses, had been consumed, during the two months we had been there. He determined to march into Bohemia, where we hoped to find a fresh country. We arrived here without any difficulty from the enemies, except that the day before yesterday Laudon and Saint-Ignon, with a corps of 10 000 men, wished to make an attack upon the baggage of the troops under my command. Instead of succeeding, however, they left them about 500 dragoons either killed or taken prisoners, and only got possession of four or five carts of flour. My health has been very feeble ever since the month of April. The fever pursues me, but I cannot tell you what sort of fever it is, as there is nothing regular about it. The gout also takes its part, and at one time fixed itself in my right foot; but it has since risen into the body, where it gives me great pain. I have need of repose, but our situation does not permit me to hope for it for some time, so I must drag myself along as well as I can. Adieu, my dearest brother, I will try to send you news of myself, as often as I can.

Only four weeks earlier, James Keith has passed his sixty-second birthday and now gout and a sporadic fever added to his lifelong battle with asthma. Keith did get some respite from the war, for Daun and his army stood rooted to the spot at Königsgratz, unable or unwilling to test their strength against the Prussians. From James Keith's own hand we read that a lifetime of campaigning had taken an increasing toll of his heath: in addition, too much claret, port and brandy, in liberal quantities as remedies against the cold, illness and pain, had brought him gout. Gout, like death, was an occupational hazard for senior commanders in the armies of the time.

During the siege of Olmutz, Fermor and his huge Russian forces had begun to move into Prussia from the north, scarcely hindered or checked in their advance by the far inferior Prussian forces standing in their way. On 16 June, Fermor made his headquarters at Könitz, while his Cossacks and regular troops went on a rampage of killing and burning. They showed no mercy to the civilian population and committed atrocities on a hitherto unheard-of scale. So desperate was the situation that the Prussian General Dohna, who had been standing guard with his men over a Swedish army locked up in Stralsund, was forced to leave the 7000 starving Swedes to stagger out of captivity so that he could slow the Russian advance. Elsewhere, in Saxony, Prince Henry was waiting with 50 000 men to meet an expected Austrian advance through the Metal Mountains while Duke Ferdinand was even then scattering a 47 000-strong French army after inflicting 4000 casualties on them.

By their cruelty to the civilian population, the Russian army had become absolutely intolerable to Frederick and he had decided that they must be dealt with as a priority.

On 2 August 1758 Frederick marched his army out of Königsgratz towards Landshut at precisely the same time as Fermor and his army set off for Brandenburg. On 10 August, Frederick drew up a set of directions for Prince Henry, telling him what to do in the event of his death, since he expected to meet up with Fermor shortly. Frederick took only half of the Prussian army away with him while James Keith still had nominal command of the other half. But Keith's health had taken a knock from a severe asthma attack and he was given orders to rest and recover his strength at Breslau.

On 20 August, Frederick arrived with 15 000 men at Frankfurt-on-Oder; the King stayed the night with a clergyman's widow in the Lebus suburb. During the course of the evening, and even into the night, Frederick was often seen to go out of doors to listen to the sound of cannonfire coming from the direction of Custrin, where the town was being reduced to a smoking ruin. Everything around the Russian army was being turned into a desert as they burned and looted, ruining the very food supplies they were going to need until their own supply lines could be made secure. By the time Frederick awoke the next morning, after listening to a night of gunfire, both Custrin and its castle were a smoking pile of debris.

By 22 August Frederick's army had been reinforced to a strength of 30 000 and he was ready to march. After bombarding the Russian-held fortress at Schaumberg, in a feint attack, he crossed the Oder with his army twelve miles further downstream and, with his army intact, marched on Zorndorf. His plan was to pinfold the Russians between the Mutzel and the Oder. As his army marched it destroyed all the bridges behind it, for this was going to be a battle of annihilation, of do or die; there was going to be no way out and away from this battle for anyone.

Intelligence of his enemy's whereabouts had not been getting through to Fermor and his Russian generals. But on the night of 23 August Fermor finally got to know what was happening and began to make his own preparations for the coming battle. After some shuffling about, Fermor had his Russian army arrange themselves on open ground, in a quadrilateral formation two miles long by one mile wide: muddy quagmires afforded some protection against Prussian cavalry. It was a repeat of Munnich's successful Schiltron battle formation.

To Fermor, it seemed as though he had anticipated everything, but what he did not know was that the Prussian army had used tree cover to circle round behind to his rear. As Fermor's Russians hurriedly turned about, to face south rather than north, the protective anti-cavalry quagmire was now behind them, and all bridges leading away from the battlefield were burnt and gone.

The Prussians began their action on the south-west corner of the huge Russian army and, after deafening cannon barrage smashed up that sector, the infantry marched into it with bayonets fixed. The cannonfire was so concentrated that when it hit a solid mass of men it did frightful damage. On this occasion, for example, forty-two men from one regiment alone were blown away with just one cannonball. As the Prussian divisions closed with their enemy, a gap appeared between the two columns and Fermor, scenting an opportunity, directed his troops into the gap. It was a ghastly mistake for they soon found Seidlitz with 5000 cavalry charging down on them and, those Russians who were not trampled into the ground by horses' hooves, were cut down by Seidlitz's sabre-swinging cavalry. As the horsemen hacked and trampled them in the middle, the Russians were simultaneously taking musket volleys and bayonet thrusts from the flanks as the infantry closed in for the kill. For the heaving, panicking mass of confused Russians it had become 'payback time' for all their atrocities.

Siedlitz's sabres swung until only tiredness itself slowed the bloodbath which engulfed half of the Russian army.

A rapid regrouping then took place before the Prussians started forward to deal with what remained of the Russians. But suddenly, in a mad, uncontrolled charge of infantry and cavalry together, a Russian tidal wave of men swept forward in a desperate counterattack which swept whole Prussian battalions away in a surging mass. Only Seidlitz, it appears, kept calm and took stock of what needed doing to rectify the situation. With sixty-one squadrons of horse he went driving into the Russian cavalry and destroyed it. This bought all the time the Prussians needed and, with their usual discipline, they regrouped once more to march into the Russians with fixed bayonets.

Bridges all gone and bogs behind them, there was nowhere for the Russians to go: they just stood helplessly, taking the endless bayonet and musketfire like animals in a slaughterhouse. While Prussian forces, disciplined as they were, could always be recalled to battle order, the Russians had no such discipline to save them, and they were simply shot and bayoneted to death.

Incredibly, even as the battle was going on, Cossacks were pillaging and murdering in surrounding villages. At the hamlet of Zicher, Prussian Hussars caught up with one band and 400 Cossacks died in a fire of their own making as the Prussian Hussars stood awaiting their end in a surrounding ring of steel. When it all ended, the Russians had a total of 21 529 casualties among which, the dead amounted to 7990. The battle cost the Prussians 3680 dead and 11 390 casualties.

Beaten he may have been but Fermor still had about 29 000 Russian troops left. The next day, 26 August, Fermor proposed to General Dohna that there should be a three-day truce to allow burial of the dead. To this appeal Dohna replied: 'It is customary for the victor to take charge of burying the slain: that such a proposal is surprising and quite inadmissible, in the present circumstances.'

Fermor then restarted hostilities and bursts of cannonfire came from both sides although the two armies were equally weary and short of ammunition. Shortly after this exchange, the Russians pulled out in retreat with Dohna seeing them off Prussian soil as they made their way back to Russia.

One enemy had gone but another still remained to be stopped before autumn turned to winter and a temporary peace could return to central Europe. By 2 September Frederick was marching on Saxony where he planned to meet up with his brother, Prince Henry, who was holding the passes through the Metal Mountains into Prussia. Waiting his chance on one side of the mountains was Daun, with a numerically superior Austrian force poised and ready.

James Keith's period of recuperation at Beslau had come to an end and, barely recovered, he was also on his way to rejoin Frederick, Henry and the Prussian army in Saxony.

15

·

A Soldier's Death

·

FROM THE POINT AT which his army held the Saxon passes leading into Prussia, Prince Henry could only watch helplessly as the Austrian Marshal Daun – with a huge army – struck across the Bohemia–Silesia frontier to take Zittau on 17 August 1758. Daun's intention was to fortify Zittau and use it as a forward base from which to supply his army in a war against Prussia. When Zittau fell to Daun, it became apparent to the Prussians that they were witnessing a disaster in the making. If Daun managed to combine his army with that of Fermor, whose still-large Russian army was licking the wounds it had received at Leuthen and within a reasonable distance of the Austrians, then a possibility too terrible to contemplate was looming before them.

Some time between 17 August and 12 September, James Keith left his convalescence in Breslau. While Frederick and his army were hurrying along to join Prince Henry and confront the Austrian threat, Keith had arrived at Grussau to resume his command of the 25 000 men quartered there under the temporary command of Margraf Karl. Shortly afterwards the Prussian and Austrian armies began testing each other out in a chessboard of moves.

One of the last letters James Keith penned to Marischal went as follows:

I received, two days ago, two letters from my dearest brother; one of 10 August, the other of 10 September. In one of them was a letter for the King, which I delivered immediately. You see, by the newspapers, that the Russians continue always to claim for themselves the victory in the late battle. I wish them, with all my heart, such another victory; for you may rest assured, that their loss in that one was at least 25 000 men. I must, however, do them justice; they fought very well, especially their infantry, which threw the King's left wing into the greatest confusion, and was the cause the victory was not more decisive. But if they gained a battle, why have they profited so little from it? Since, instead of advancing, they have retreated behind Stargard; though the King was obliged to return, with all the troops which had marched with him. It was, indeed, time that he should do this, for Prince Henry began to be very much pressed by the two armies of Daun and the Prince of Deauxponts. He is now in a better situation, for the King has obliged Marshal Daun to quit his position at Stolpen, and, consequently his communication with the Elbe, and to retire towards Zittau, where we have pursued him step by step, but without ever having had an opportunity of engaging a combat. He remains always among the mountains, and encamps in places so inaccessible, that it would be the greatest act of rashness to attack him. And it is only by secret marches, that one draws him out from his position. It was by a march of this kind that we turned his right flank, and thus obliged him to abandon his camp at Stolpen. Now the devil has sent him to the top of the hill near Lobau, and we must contrive some means of drawing him out from thence, or he will stay there till the snows drive him away. It is true that this would not be a peculiary great evil, for we are now placed so, that he cannot receive anything from Saxony, and that he is obliged to bring all his provisions etc. from Bohemia, which is behind him. One sees clearly that his intention is not to give battle, but that he want to live as long as he can at the expense of Saxony, and so save Bohemia for his winter quarters. On our side we want to prevent his foraging in Saxony, because we mean to winter there. Here you have the secret of the rest of this campaign, which, according to all appearance, cannot be long; for it is already as cold as if we were in the month of December, on account of the nearness of the mountains, from whence, by the way, it is not possible to draw this tiresome man, in spite of all he must suffer there. For we see, by the desertion, that he must suffer a great deal; for in a single night we have had 150 deserters come to us from his army, and not a single day passes, that there do not come thirty or forty. Make many compliments from me to the dear chancellor. I am as anxious for peace as he can be; for my health can no longer sustain the fatigues of war, especially in the way that we are now obliged to make it, against so many enemies, whom we are forced each campaign to run after, from one end of Germany to the other.

Two days before the Battle of Hochkirch, Keith was sitting hunched before a fire, wrapped against the cold in a fur coat, busy writing what was to be his last letter to Marischal and saying 'As to your Epitaph, I advise you to belie it by a big fire and a good fur coat, as I do here.'

From the tone of Keith's correspondence it seems he was contemplating retirement from the army and its never-ending campaigns; for here he was, suffering from old wounds and gout, not to mention his recurring chronic asthma, saying that it was all getting too much for him. Perhaps he would have left earlier, had he had the security of an adequate pension to protect him against penury; but Keith was never able to hold on to money. He had his sons to support and it is probable that Eva was also being sent regular sums of money to keep her. At this time, the necessity of retirement must have been staring Keith in the face, but he still had bills to pay and may not have had any expectation of post-retirement resources that would match his needs.

Daun's army was far from sitting still, however; a part of it reached Sonnenstein where it circled around Prince Henry with the intention of taking him in the flank. As Frederick came up with his relieving army, Henry's forces were having to pull back to Dresden to avoid entrapment and, by 1 September, Daun was within ten miles of the Meissen Bridge.

Without even halting on his arrival, Frederick instantly moved on to a flank attack on Daun's right, by the road to Bautzen, highlighting the logical military follow-up of a march on Zittau and the capture of the Austrian's supply base. Daun knew that if Frederick reached his Zittau objective, then Neisse and Harsch would fall in quick succession after Zittau. On 1 October, Frederick's vanguard under Retzow entered Hochkirch, after capturing all the hills of any significance on which to place cannon and cover the army's line of advance. He took them all except for one, the Stromberg, and very soon it had strategically-placed Austrian cannon sited on its slopes which then began to direct an uncomfortable fire down onto the Prussians.

Daun may have been slow to make decisions but it did not take him long to grasp that the fate of his army hinged on the safety of their supplies in Zittau. If Zittau fell, the whole Austrian army was finished. On the dark, wet and windy night of 5 October, he pulled his army back to a better defensive position, ahead and east of Bautzen which also served to block Frederick's advance to Zittau. When Daun's army had completed their digging in and fortified their new positions, the Austrian army stretched across the Zittau road at right angles and in a north–south line.

The Prussian army came to within a mile of the Austrian line; both armies were now placed on a pair of parallel heights. Frederick told his adjutant, Marwitz, to mark out his army's camp. Unusually for a Prussian soldier, Marwitz protested, pointing out to the King that Austrian cannonfire was even then reaching into where the King wanted his army to encamp. Poor Marwitz had gone too far in questioning an order from the King and was put under arrest while another officer was found to carry out the command.

Probably still irritated by Marwitz's insubordination and the reality of cannonfire reaching the site he had chosen for his army camp, Frederick had General Retzow called before him to explain why he had not taken the Stromberg when clearing defence lines up to Hochkirch. Frederick berated Retzow for his negligence, against the sound of incoming Austrian cannonfire, before finally placing him under arrest.

If it was clear earlier to Marwitz that the site was the wrong one it was soon to become evident to everyone else, including the King, that a monumental mistake had been made. Privately, Frederick realised his blunder and planned to evacuate his position on Saturday 14 October. James Keith, in well-chosen words of thinly veiled criticism told the King: 'The Austrian generals deserve to be hanged if they don't attack us here' to which he heard the reply: 'We must hope they are more afraid of us than even the gallows.'

Hochkirch itself was a village sitting on an exposed hilltop position and visible for miles, with the ground falling away from it on all but the south side. The houses must, at that time, have been wholly constructed of wood and had thatched roofs. From among these houses and other buildings, the steeple of Hochkirch church with its belfry reached up above them. Hochkirch was a typical alpine village, in a setting of small woods and arable pasture, from where little streams descended to join the Lobau water on its way to meet the Spree.

The military position was that Daun's left wing threatened the Prussian right wing at Hochkirch and the Austrian General Laudon, with 3000 grenadiers, was awaiting his orders. Opposing Laudon and the Austrian left wing was Frederick's right wing commanded by James Keith, whose responsibilities stretched up to Hochkirch village and beyond. Covering the ground lying south of the village was a twenty-cannon battery, whose muzzles pointed towards the wooded area on the near, southern horizon. Between the cannon and those woods, were bushes and some trees which hid a light screen of Prussian troops. Frederick himself was in quarters more than two miles away from Hochkirch. The opposing armies were separated at some points by only half a mile and, in hard numbers, some 40 000 Prussians were looking across the intervening valleys at 90 000 Austrians.

Cautious as ever, Daun had also thought to pull out of his position on 14 October but suddenly realised he had a heaven-sent opportunity awaiting him, if he could only just pluck up his courage and get on with it. After being prompted and reassured by his generals, Laudon and Lacy, who had also seen the chance of a victory, Daun started to make his plans – this General Lacy, by the way, was the son of Peter Lacy, Governor of Riga and Keith's good friend.

Daun and his generals soon completed their planning, timing the offensive at Hochkirch for Saturday, 14 October 1758. The agreed signal for the first assault wave was when the bell at Hochkirch church pealed 5 a.m. This would be followed by some 30 000 men, who were expected to roll up the extremity of the Prussian right wing.

From the moment the battle plan was completed Daun set to work. He had his army felling trees which were then laid down to form roadways through the woods to facilitate the rapid movement of his troops and equipment when they attacked the Prussian right wing, but he always ensured the retention of sufficient trees to screen what he was doing from the watching Prussians. They heard and saw something of what was going on but thought that the tree felling, the sawing and banging, was only the Austrians reinforcing existing defences. For two whole days the Austrians cut and sawed frantically, until at last their leftward path was cleared and ready for the movement of troops, horse and cannon.

During the night of Friday 13 October, the Austrians began to move out of their positions and circle up towards the last tree cover that lay between them and the village of Hochkirch to the north.

Over at Hochkirch not everyone was asleep. Sentries and pickets were out, keeping watch as night wore on to morning. Around the twenty cannons, in a protective role, were four battalions facing south-west while yet another four, together with Zeithen's cavalry, looked southwards with some of the cavalry's horses left standing, saddled and ready throughout the night, in case of an emergency. Among these sleeping troops stood sentries, who occasionally warmed themselves at watchfires, as they waited for the dawn to break into a new day – and, all unknown to them, the clock hands in the Hochkirch steeple were moving inexorably towards a rude and noisy awakening at 5 a.m.

It was an accepted fact of army life that, in a tense situation like this, some sniping and testing of defences would be the night-time occupation of their Austrian enemy. Only on this occasion an artillery subaltern, whose duty had kept him on watch since 3 a.m., noticed it had all been unusually quiet; much too quiet, although he never voiced his suspicions or disquiet to anyone else.

A first warning of the impending assault came with a crackle of musketfire out in the darkness, among the pickets and sentries stationed near the woods to which the cannon pointed – it was 5 a.m. Through the thick mist of morning the Austrians had begun their attack and, although nothing could be seen of them, the unmistakable noise of troops on the move and the nearing sound of gunfire, was enough to tell the seasoned Prussian artillery what to expect. Correctly guessing the direction of the attack, the artillery loosed their cannon off blindly into the mist, only to find themselves minutes later being overrun by large numbers of Austrian grenadiers who came charging out of the mist at them.

As the infantry of both sides locked in battle around the cannon battery, the Prussian cavalry came hurtling up to repel the Austrians. Battalion Margraf Karl had taken up a position within the Hochkirch church and the surrounding churchyard where it was dealing out death in a steady stream of musketfire, cutting the Austrians down as they came. The battalion stood there unflinchingly, until its ammunition ran out, after which it attempted to cut its way out of encirclement with bayonets. Only a very few made it and their major was fatally wounded. Prussian military discipline demanded that under no circumstances did troops retire; it was the duty of those under attack to fight to the death, if necessary, in order to give their comrades a chance to regroup and come back to the rescue.

Because of the blanketing mist, it took a vital hour for the Prussians to fully appreciate the scale of the attack upon them. As the Austrian troops advanced, and battalion after battalion flung itself at the enemy, only Zeithen's cavalry had any success in repulsing the attackers. By calculated and targeted charges, Zeithen's horse managed to stop the Austrians completely on the west flank.

It must have been about 6.30 a.m. when James Keith was awakened from his sleep to be made aware of what was going on high above him at Hochkirch; to be told that his battery of twenty cannon was already lost. Mounting his horse, he then ordered the Kannacher Battalion and every other man immediately available for battle up to the battery. Hurrying straight up to the lost guns, Keith's soldiers went on to recapture them.

The guns were not to be in Keith's possession very long however, for a surging tide of Austrians pushed Keith and his men back. At this point in the battle, James Keith looked around to discover his two aides-de-camp had gone. He repeatedly asked for them but they had already been lost in the fighting, nor were there any reinforcements to help him stem the flow of Austrian infantry. By this time Keith had taken two bullet wounds to his right side and, surrounded by enemy troops, he tried to take out what men he had left in a bayonet-fighting retreat. As they started to fight their way back, Keith took yet another bullet and fell dead from his horse into the arms of John Tebay, an English soldier who had been attending him as his groom.

The Croats fighting with the Austrian army were in the vanguard at Hochkirch and they went on to strip the dead of anything and everything of value, so that a Field Marshal now looked no different from all the other dead lying around the battlefield. But the stand taken by battalions Margraf Karl and Kannacher, aided by Zeithen's terrifying cavalry charges, had been enough to buy the Prussians sufficient time to reorganise and fall back in a disciplined manner to fight another day.

As we already know, it was the custom for the victors to bury the dead and no doubt the Austrians had been warned to look out for the body of James Keith. Searching through the piles of dead at Hochkirch and looking for one body among a mass of bloody dead must have been a difficult task and it took the Austrian General

Lacy, Peter Lacy's son, to finally identify the body of the man he had known from childhood. Lacy was visibly shaken and shed a tear when looking down at his father's friend and sometime comrade-in-arms.

With a dozen Austrian cannons roaring three salvos in salute to the dead hero, Keith was lowered into a soldier's grave at Hochkirch with full military honours. Today his death at Hochkirch is commemorated in the church by an inscribed marble urn.

Four months later Keith's body was exhumed on Frederick's orders and taken back to Berlin. On 3 February 1759, while the church bells dolefully rang out their farewell to a fallen hero, Keith's cortège made its way to the garrison church and his final resting place.

The Prussian state did not allow the services of this Scottish soldier to be forgotten with the passing years. In 1786 a statue to Keith's memory was unveiled on the Wilhelmplatz in Berlin, joining others in tribute to Frederick's supporting circle of generals. On 27 January 1789, Wilhelm awarded Keith's name to the First Upper Silesian Regiment.

Epilogue

·

WHILE LACY, THE SON of James Keith's friend, was walking through the piles of Prussian and Austrian dead up on the Hochkirch battlefield, searching for Keith's body, Frederick the Great and his army were now some way distant from the scene engaged in a tactical withdrawal. Frederick himself had been anything but a passive observer at Hochkirch and during battle his horse had been shot from under him. Despite the immediacy of all the military problems confronting him, the King still found time to send a letter breaking the news of his Field Marshal's death to Marischal.

Catte, Frederick's secretary, wrote at the King's direction as follows: 'It is with deep distress my lord Marischal of Scotland, that I inform you of the death of my brave Marshal Keith; and as if all misfortunes were joining to overwhelm me, the Princess of Bayreuth, the most cherished sister, and who most deserved it, has also been snatched from me. God preserve you and have you in his holy keeping.' Written in the King's own hand was an added postscript: 'What sad news for you and for me.'

James Keith's death must have been a devastating – although, given his brother's military career, unsurprising – blow for Marischal. Marischal, however, was not a man to give way to displays of uncontrollable grief, at least not in public; he maintained his aloof, aristocratic and unflinching composure through all the days that followed Hochkirch.

He wrote an incredibly cold and cynical letter to Madame Geoffrin, a Paris socialite, in which he said: 'My brother has left

201

me a fine heritage. At the head of his army he laid all Bohemia under contribution, and seventy ducats in his sole fortune.' Marischal did not need any part of James Keith's estate for himself, for he was comfortably off in his own highly placed employment with the Prussian government. That comment to Madame Geoffrin might just be an indication of how much he resented the financial support James Keith had given to his mistress Eva Merthens. Even more curious was his refusal to link James Keith's death with Frederick the Great's inexplicable decision to take up such an exposed and vulnerable position at Hochkirch, a position which simply begged attack. Marischal wrote a letter to one of his friends which exonerated Frederick from any blame whatsoever and it read: 'I cannot doubt, in this last affair, when a wing of his army was surprised, that it was the fault of him who commanded that wing, and not the King's . . .' When the newspaper reports reached Marischal, and some at least must have described the Hochkirch battlefield, his letter clearing Frederick of all responsibility begins to look very strange coming from someone of military experience. Then again, nothing was going to bring James Keith back and his own aristocratic code of conduct probably demanded unswerving support for the King.

Some weeks after Hochkirch, on 23 November 1758 Frederick wrote to Marischal from Dresden.

> There is nothing left for us, my dear milord, but to mingle and mix our tears on our losses. If my head contained a reservoir of tears they would not suffice for my grief. Our campaign is over, and nothing has come of it on one side or the other but the loss of many good men, the misfortunes of many poor soldiers maimed for ever, the ruin of some provinces, the ravaging, pillage, and burning of some flourishing towns. Such, my dear milord, are the exploits which make humanity shudder, sad results of the malice and ambition of some powerful men who sacrifice everything to their unbridled passions! I wish for you, dear milord, nothing at all resembling my fate, but everything it lacks. It is the only means for you to be happy; I am more interested in this than any one, being your old friend, a designation I shall retain till the tomb.

Frederick, as a close friend of Marischal, had long been aware of his bouts of homesickness and was now approached by Marischal to use his influence with their British ally to lift the attainder which had been imposed on him after the 1715 rebellion. This would not only allow Marischal to go home to Scotland for a visit, it also allowed him to inherit the Kintore estate from his cousin whose death was thought to be imminent. Prussian intercession proved to be effective, allowing Marischal to return to Scotland in the wake of a pardon to take possession of his inheritance. He returned to Scotland accompanied by Emete Tulla.

After his arrival he made the journey north to Peterhead intending to visit the family home at Inverugie Castle. News that George, tenth Earl Marischal of Scotland, was home preceded him and extensive preparations were made to welcome him. A huge banquet was prepared in his honour at the Keith Masonic Lodge and on the day of his arrival it seemed the whole town had turned out to line his expected route through the streets. Marischal's carriage duly arrived as expected and, flanked by an escort of local gentry on horseback, it eventually came to a halt among a surging crowd.

As he scanned the sea of faces around his carriage, seeking out familiar faces from his past, Marischal soon saw that of a Mr Forbes who heartily responded to his recognition by grasping Marischal's outstretched hand. Forbes, a boyhood companion and friend of Marischal, then went on to read a welcoming address from the town as the assembled folk hurrahed and roared their own approval of the visitor.

Then another familiar face was spotted as she struggled to get through the crowd – it was Mrs Gordon, Marischal's old nurse, now bent and grey with the years. Tears welled in both pairs of eyes as Marischal enquired of her health and welfare before pressing some money into her hand as a parting gift, apologetically saying that he only wished he could have given her more. Mrs Gordon had sold her cows to realise twenty pounds (Scots) which she then sent to aid Marischal when he returned for the 1719 Glenshiel rising.

Escorted this time by a huge crowd, the last Earl Marischal set off for Inverugie Castle. Along the two-mile route, at the Collieburn – which feeds into the Ugie near its mouth – the procession found a house blazing while its tenant was even then throwing his rent money into the fire and declaring he 'wid thack his hoose wi' gowd.' The poor man was so overcome by an overwhelming sense of occasion that he had rendered himself homeless.

203

Delayed by the milling, jostling crowd and the most likely still-appalling road, it took hours for the carriage to finally come within sight of Inverugie Castle. As his carriage halted Marischal stood up to get a better view of his family home, only to see that it was now only a ruined, roofless wreck. Overcome by emotion, he gave a cry and slumped back into his seat before taking one last lingering look and ordering a return to Peterhead.

Inverugie was indeed a ruin and Argyle's Hanoverian troops had blown Dunnottar to bits. Marischal did not need any memorials to the decline of the Keith fortunes under his stewardship: he sold the Inverugie estates to his neighbour Lord Pitfour and Dunnottar was sold to a relative at a knockdown price. Marischal left Scotland for the last time in 1764, and returned to Prussia.

On 23 May 1778, the last Earl Marischal of Scotland died. Carrying out his deathbed wishes – that no money was to be wasted on an expensive funeral – his weeping servants buried him in Potsdam's 'God's Acre' in a burial that cost just three louis.

Emete Tulla

The little Turkish girl whom James Keith had pulled to the safety of his saddle at the Siege of Otchakow was left almost the whole of Marischal's fortune, as he had adopted her as his daughter. Before his death she made an unfortunate marriage to a Frenchman who had obviously cared more about her financial prospects than for Emete herself. As Emete Tulla de Fromert, after her marriage to Colonel Denis Daniel de Fromert had failed, she returned to Neuchâtel, where Marischal had served as Prussian governor. From then on she took up residence in a little villa with a garden that stretched down to the lake, living the life of a virtual recluse and becoming more eccentric as the years passed by. She died in 1820 and, although no one could say for sure, she was thought to have lived for almost 100 years.

Mocho

After Keith's death at Hochkirch, his faithful black valet Mocho returned to Marischal's household to rejoin Ibrahim, Stepan and Emete Tulla. On Marischal's death, Ibrahim, Stepan and Mocho all received an annuity of 500 livres each from an investment in the Hotel de Ville in Paris.

The Empress Elisabeth

In 1759, the year following Keith's death, Russian and Austrian armies met up with Frederick the Great and his Prussians at Kunnersdorf. Frederick's 'oblique order' of battle failed to work as planned and the Prussian army suffered heavy losses in a devastating counterattack, leaving 20 000 dead on the battlefield. In 1760 Berlin was captured by the Russians and, after a joint naval and military descent on Kolberg, Frederick contemplated suicide.

He was saved from suicide by Elisabeth's death, real this time, in 1761. Elisabeth never did find anyone like Keith to marry and sit beside her on the throne. She was succeeded by her nephew who, as Peter III, promptly took his army out of the war with Prussia. Peter had always been an admirer of Frederick and actually returned a detachment of his forces to help Frederick against his former allies, the Austrians.

Frederick the Great

Long years of war had taken their toll when the French minister, the Comte de Segur, saw Frederick on 29 January 1785 and reported what met his eyes:

> With a lively curiosity I gazed at this man; there as he stood, great in genius, small in stature; stooping, and as it were bent down under the weight of his laurels and of his long toils. His blue coat, old and worn like his body; his long boots coming up above his knee; his waistcoat covered with snuff, formed an odd but imposing whole. By the fire of his eyes, you recognised that in essentials he had not grown old. Though bearing himself like an invalid, you felt that he could strike like a young soldier; in his small figure, you discerned a spirit greater than any other man's.

Frederick maintained a frantic work schedule in spite of deteriorating health. By January 1786 he was suffering from asthma and dropsy, living in constant fear of a recurring 'suffocation fit'. Switching doctors and medicines, he searched in vain for good health. At 2.30 a.m. on 17 August 1786, Frederick's last great battle, for life itself, ended after a reign lasting forty-six years. He was seventy-four years old.

At 8 p.m. on the evening of his death, his washed body clothed in the uniform of the First Battalion of Guards was conveyed in its coffin to the palace with an escort of guards officers to lie in state. All the next day tearful thousands filed past the coffin to pay their last respects. At 8 p.m. on Friday 18 August, his coffin was taken to the garrison church, where it joined that of his father in a vault behind the pulpit.

Eva Merthens

Just why Marischal claimed a 'fine heritage' of seventy ducats from James Keith's estate in his letter to Madame Geoffrin is hard to explain. The truth was that James Keith had left his whole estate to Eva.

After Keith's death Eva turned up to claim what she knew had been left to her. It seems Marischal did not want any of his brother's money but did want some of James's effects as keepsakes. The matter was put to a military court for a decision and they went on to decide in favour of Eva. Prior to the court hearing, both Eva and Marischal had feared the decision might go against them and, since the dispute was about personal effects rather than money, they both destroyed Keith's letters and other memorabilia rather than face being ordered to hand them over by the court. Eva was to treasure her memories of James Keith and had been given an oil painting by her late lover. The King offered her a large amount of money for the painting but she refused to sell it at any price, allowing us to assume the portrait is an accurate likeness of Keith. That painting now hangs in the Dahlemer Gallery in Berlin and it is reproduced in this book.

Some time after Hochkirch, Eva married Schlosshauptmann von Reichenbach (Captain of the Palace Guard), scion of an old, noble German family which had made its first appearance in the eleventh century. She spent her later life at Stralsund, in what has been described as a satisfying marriage, dying on 15 October 1811.

Nothing very much of Inverugie Castle is now left to us and what remains is surrounded by modern bungalows forming a grotesque backdrop to this piece of history. Dunnottar, or what is left of it, is in a better state of preservation and gives us a more accurate idea of the power and position of the Keith family through the centuries. In art galleries and private collections, other carefully maintained paintings and memorabilia still exist. At Hochkirch church a marble urn on a plinth remains as a memorial to Keith and at Rheinsberg there is an obelisk dedicated to him by his comrade-in-arms, Prince Henry of Prussia. On the Wihelmstrasse in Berlin, alongside that of von Winterfeld, Schwerin, Seidlitz, Zeithen and the old Dessauer, stands a statue of James Keith; it is a copy of this statue which stands in Peterhead's Broad Street today.

Even in death, James Keith was not to be given an undisturbed rest from war. The French entered Berlin after the Battle of Jena in 1806 and allegedly entered the garrison church to raid the tombs of the dead lying there in peace. Rings were said to have been taken from Keith's fingers, leaving one to wonder what happened to his Russian sword – or all of his other presentation swords for that matter. When fire swept the garrison church in 1908, Keith's coffin was opened and there he lay in full uniform, in a near-perfect state of preservation; recognisable and curiously with a still-tanned colour to his face: this remarkable preservation was a result of a number of factors peculiar to the church's environment. Keith's upper lip was seen to carry a bullet wound where the last fatal shot entered to carry on up into his head. The Croat who pulled the trigger must have been shooting upwards from a fairly close range.

After the destruction of Berlin's garrison church at the end of the Second World War, the vault containing the mortal remains of James Keith was again plundered, although the body itself was left intact. In 1948 James Keith was uplifted and taken to Staunsdorf Cemetery where those searching for his resting place will find him today.

All the main characters surrounding James Keith in life have been accounted for in these pages, or can be found elsewhere in other books dealing with this period of history. There may, however, be others close to James Keith who have slipped away from the gaze of history in the years following Keith's and Eva's deaths. I refer, of course, to his family. For myself, I like to think that somewhere in Germany today a 'happie offspring' is delightedly playing practical jokes on family, friends and whoever happens to come within range. Or it may well be that a young soldier, of squarish build with a heavy tan and dancing blue eyes, is about to embark on an army career . . .

Appendix:

·

the Last Earl Marischal and the Jacobite cause

·

GEORGE KEITH WAS CONSCIOUS that future historians would be
seeking reasons for the Jacobite failure in 1745 and feared
that somehow he might become an easy target for at least some of
the blame. To set the record straight he left papers explaining
what had happened in the lead-up to the 1745 rebellion; his minor,
advisory role and his reasons for finally turning his back on what
was now clearly a lost cause, but a cause he, and his family, had
until then unquestioningly supported through success and failure.
Marischal's papers, written in French, are as follows:

Aix la Chapelle,
30 May 1746.

I must be satisfied with no longer being blamed by a small number of
honest men who know me, for I cannot claim that of those who have
deliberately blackened my character, nor of those who could believe
they needed persuading that I was wrong, because my opinion was so
different from theirs: I have not changed at all because I have followed
Truth and the demands of my party have been my guide, I said in
honesty (and in good faith) how things appeared to me and the
outcome only justifies overwhelmingly that either I knew the country
better or that I was more honest than the others. I have finally made
up my mind to retire for our affairs are in tatters, even though one
would want to do the right thing, I will simply tell you some true facts
in order to convince you that I could take no other action.

Since the 1743 Dunkirk business it was clear that I was no longer
wanted, nor was the Duc d'Ormond, for not only was he not consulted
about anything, but the letter summoning him from Avignon was sent
from Paris only on the Monday whereas on the Thursday of the same
week they were intending to embark and set sail for Dunkirk: I was

then in Paris, the secret was carefully kept from me. I was only allowed an audience with the Prince about a fortnight after he arrived in Paris, although lots of people had already been accorded that honour. The first time I saw him his Highness ordered me to go immediately to Versailles to give my proposals about Scotland. I did this, giving the proposals in writing (as M. Amelot asked me), I was urged to set off right away for Dunkirk without the slightest reply to my requests, being assured however that I would receive them the next day in Paris, or that I would find an answer waiting for me at Dunkirk with the Marshal of Saxony. I never received it.

It is said that after this business had totally failed M. Amelot did me the honour of writing to me saying that he was considering my requests, and that he would soon give me an answer. I returned to Paris where his Highness, the Prince, came several months later. But I was no longer accorded the honour of seeing him. Those around him were not even allowed to see me or to have any correspondence with me. In Avignon I rejoined my friend, the Duc d'Ormond. However my compatriots asked the Prince that I be solely consulted about their affairs: this I had in writing from Mr Murray of Broughton who spoke in the name of all the party in Scotland, and it wasn't the first time that I can say that the Prince owed this kindness to listen to me, to a nation so faithful and so devoted to its Royal House.

If they had found my advice so worthless the party would have said to His Royal Highness not to consult me anymore, but if it was only that the French Ministers wanted to exclude me (an excuse which I had been given) I doubt that was sufficient reason, and I am convinced that a wise prince must rather listen to the general voice of his party than the secret Council of a few individuals, or even that of Ministers of a nation currently at war with his country and at all times its enemy.

I have found in H.R.H. the Duke of York the same prejudice against me. He didn't recount affairs to me correctly – 5 000–6 000 men were 15 000 men. If I gave advice according to what H.R.H. told me I was betraying the cause and my friends by giving incorrect advice. If I gave advice according to the true number, strength and situation of the Prince's affairs I was accused of making difficulties. At Boulogne when he intended to embark towards evening he didn't say to me, 'just be ready to leave', although I had, that day, the honour of dining with him and spending four hours with him. And some time later when disappointed to see all hope towards England fail and carried along by love and pity for my poor compatriots, and by the good opinion, friendship and respect I had for the Mrs Fitzjames and Lord Clark who was, from what I've heard, to command the troops who were going to Scotland, I asked the Duke's permission to willingly go with them, he refused saying he was keeping me to go to England with him.

I suffered a lot from rheumatism in Boulogne. I came back to Paris for a change of air. I found that I had been accused. I'm speaking about some French Ministers, to betray them. It had already been said that I should reveal all that I knew to M.L.D. Morton. Since then I thought, as did the Duc d'Ormond, that it was a pretext in order to tell me nothing. It is clear that by all this and a thousand other things that they didn't want me at all, that I can't do anything and that if I continue to involve myself in the affairs I lay myself open to being accused of all that could be revealed by the dishonesty or rashness of others. From Boulogne I wrote to the King that I saw the Duc warn against me, that I was not in good health and that I would retire first of all because there was no longer any hope of success. H.M. seemed to approve my intentions, did not oppose them at all nor showed any desire that I continue with my services, nor offered to advise the Duke to make allowances for me. He wrote to me, however, not only politely, but even kindly.

I came to these quarters here to be at hand to receive advice from friends in the country and to still continue my efforts to help if I could. I carried out faithfully the tasks I was given and I was ready, notwithstanding all that had happened, to return to France if they could have given in good time what our party asked for, for, for I only know those who can judge this, but since the affair is obviously without resources, and since I have H.M.'s permission, I retire from this business forever to see if I can regain my health which has been ruined.

Farewell I embrace you in the most tender friendship and I am faithfully devoted to you for all my life.

Please show this to those who visit and to our oil merchant when you have the opportunity.

Marischal had distanced himself from the Jacobite cause: his honest appraisal of Prince Charles's chances of success had been right on the mark. Associated with past failures, in poor health and approaching his fiftieth birthday, George Keith had little to offer the Jacobite cause but his realistic assessment of their position. It could not be what they wanted to hear.

But if the Earl Marischal felt so deeply about the numerous slights and snubs and took the trouble to set them down on paper for public inspection, so must he also have communicated them to his brother James in the steady flow of letters passing between them. The Jacobite cause was now well past redemption and Prince Charles beyond any hope of return to Scotland. However, with the departure or 'retirement' of George Keith the Jacobites would almost certainly have lost the services of James Keith, now one of Russia's leading generals.

In the rest of George Keith's fragment of memoir and its appendix, he further explains why the Keith brothers walked away from the cause which had cost their family everything. The memoir reinforces other source material for this book and, because the story of James Keith is inseparable from that of his brother, the second fragment is also reproduced:

I have written to you with several reasons for my retiral from everything since 1745, but I have not given you them all. For a long time I have seen the Party attached to the House of Stuart as being destined, it would appear, to be nothing but the puppet of foreign princes, especially of France. The events of 1745 confirmed my opinion.

Some years ago in Spain I knew that Patino, a cunning Minister, had told one of my friends that he would never consider restoring the Stuart family, but in case of a break with England, he would arm, and pretend to arm, the fleet in the Atlantic ports, that he would march the Irish towards these ports, that he would send the Duc D'Ormond and myself there. By doing this he would alarm the English and make them send a large fleet to these ports, thus having lots of ships at sea at great expense for no reason, and that he would risk nothing.

This plan was partly carried out in 1740. Spain pretended to arm in Galicia, summoned the Duc D'Ormond from Avignon and myself from Valence to Madrid. The Irish were to march to the coast, and the artillery, weapons, munitions, pontoons, everything in fact necessary for a landing in England was prepared. The General of Artillery gave the Duc D'Ormond the list of everything. I knew that everything was false that there had been no preparations, but I knew for sure that preparations were being made in Barcelona and that by little sixty cannon were secretly sent to Majorca. There was a fleet in Carthaginia within range of escorting troups from Barcelona to Minorca. I didn't doubt then, nor do I now, that the true plan was to attack Portmahon, while they attracted the complete attention of the English towards Corunna and Ferol, where the Court ordered the Duc d'Ormond and myself to go immediately.

I warned the Duc d'Ormond of my true suspicions. I pointed out to him that we weren't mercenary adventurers come into the service of Spain to devote ourselves to it, but that we had been called in the time of Alberoni for an expedition that we believed to be for the good of our country, and that we were not at all obliged to serve Spain against our country, to facilitate the taking of Portmahon, and that I would not go to Galicia. I said we should say to the minister, the Duc de Montemar, that, although everything was ready, it wasn't advisable for us to be in Galicia and that he should sound the alarm and draw the English fleet in to block these two ports. The Minister urged our departure, and we stated that if he kept on insisting on it, we would hand in our resignations and ask for our passports in order to withdraw from service to Spain. We were asked to stay on and no more was said about the Galician expedition. The arrival of English ships in the Mediterranean made the Potmahon attack impossible.

The Duc d'Ormond went back to Avignon. I stayed in Madrid. Some time later they spoke to me about a second scheme, that of going into Scotland and right afterwards or at the same time France would send a company of soldiers to England. This scheme came from France. I had orders from Rome to agree to whatever France and Spain planned together. I pointed out in vain, to tell the truth, how little you could count on the promises of France, that she had misled Spain about the expedition that she had encouraged Spain to mount, for a transport of troops from Italy, while assuring Spain that these troops were ready, as were the ships in Marseilles and Toulon. Spain spent a great deal of money on the expedition and when everything was done, France didn't want to do anything, nor had she made the slightest preparation. I reminded Rome of the way France had played with the Poles and Stanillas, and that one could never trust the promises of Cardinal de Fleuri. I pointed out that there was less risk in carrying out all the arming from Spain than one in Spain for Scotland, and another from France for England. I said that Spain had enough troops and ships, that there was a lack of money because of the financial troubles, that Cardinal de Fleuri could have provided money and if he refused he was not acting honourably. I also said that for my part I would go wherever the King sent me, as a Spanish officer. If he sent me to Scotland I would tell everyone not to make a move until the French landing in England.

After this clear declaration that I made I never heard another word, either about the French going to England, or the expedition to Scotland. The great ministers we had in France who served France by providing plans were Mr Daniel O'Brien, Lord Sempel and Mr MacGregor of Balbady.

A little while later something gave me a lot of doubt, if I had never had it, about the dishonesty of the old Cardinal although it has nothing to do with the subject I'm talking of. I'm putting it in here to show the double dealing of the priests and Ministers.

When I returned to Valence I received a letter from Don Sebastian de la Quadra, Minister of the King of Spain, ordering me in the King's name to write to my brother saying that the King had received his letter in which he asked to return to the service of Spain. His Majesty had agreed to his request, and as a result I had to write to my brother saying that the King had taken him back into his service. I was astonished. I suspected something, without being able to work out what it was. I replied to M. de la Quadra, asking him to convey my thanks to the King, for the kindness the King had just granted him. But, since up till then my brother had never had any secrets from me, he must have had very good reasons not to risk his plan to leave the service of Russia being discovered. I was not to write to him by ordinary mail, that I therefore was to ask M. de la Quadra to let my brother know the favour the King had done him, by the same channel my brother went through to ask it. La Quadra replied that he knew nothing whatsoever of this; and that it was a concern of the French embassy, i.e. that everything came from the French Ambassador. My brother later discovered that it was a plan formed by Cardinal de Fleuri, along with the Swedes, to make the Russians suspect my brother, who in the absence of Marshal de Lacy commanded the Russian Army. The plan was to have him arrested and to attack the Russians in the absence of Lacy and my brother. The Swedes were also hoping to have arrested as suspects the generals Stuart, Brown and other foreign officers of distinction. The letter would have been intercepted, and the plan, if I had written it would probably have been successful. The Russians are so jealous of foreigners that they wanted to get rid of all foreigners in their army. Mr Volken, the Swedish minister at Petersburg at that time, confessed all of this conspiracy to my brother later. The French ambassador was the Bishop of Rennes.

Nothing happened until 1743 when there was equipping of the army at Dunkirk. I have never been able to decide if France was acting in good faith, or not, at that time. They spent a lot of money, embarked about 9000 men and the Count of Saxony was to be in command. The necessary orders were given to the troops, engineers etc. That made me think they were acting honestly. On the other hand I know that the fleet at Brest was ordered to intercept a convoy of ships coming from England, whether war was declared or not. Tell me, did the arming at Brest have a double or hidden reason – to cover the Dunkirk expedition and to take the merchant fleet? But what can be said about making ships come from several ports to take on troops, when in the port of Dunkirk there were enough small ships to embark 14 000 men, which were much more suitable for a landing. The others were much too big to stay in port and were obliged to stay at La Rade and raise the alarm early. They were lost in a storm.

France gave Prince Edward £20 000 for his retinue, journey and his aides de camp etc. That was soon spent and he let the Count of Saxony know he had no more money. The Count told him he had no authority to give him any but that his own funds were at his service. The Count had a note, from the French court, authorising Fitzgerald & Co, to give Prince Edward the money when he was in London. This is true, although it appears ridiculous. I doubt they would have treated the Prince so meanly if they were really thinking of a landing. The day before I was sent to Dunkirk (for up till then the secret had been kept from me) they told me to travel incognito under an assumed name, but to take care however, to let it be known who I was. If I had been sent some time before the expedition I would have thought they wanted the English to change their minds and make them march their troops towards Scotland, but I was sent to Dunkirk only two days before the expedition was to leave La Rade.

In a letter of which you have a copy, you have the reasons for my retiral. In 1746 I resigned from Spain so as not to be put in the embarrassing position of having to refuse to serve Spain in whatever way she wanted, while I was on the payroll, or to be a tool serving France or Spain against my own country. I thought that by leaving for Russia I would live for the rest of my days peacefully with my brother. Prince Cantemir, my friend, to whom I had frankly explained my reasons for leaving, assured me that I would be welcome in Russia and that the Count Voromsoff also assured me of that. I had enough money to live in the Ukraine, not anywhere else, as my fortune consisted of a life annuity of about £120. My Lord Hindford took it into his head that I was coming to Russia as a kind of minister in order to work against his court. I think he regarded me as an emissary of the Devil, of the Pope, of the Pretender, and made this known at the Russian court. It refused me permission to enter Russia. This made my brother leave its service and I went to finish my days in Venice where I once more received my pension from the Old Chevalier in Rome. When I decided to leave everything and go to live in the Ukraine, I decided never again to take anything from anyone I no longer wished to serve and it was he who said to me in Venice that there was fourteen months of my pension due and that he had ordered that I be given it.

The arrival in Berlin of my brother made me go there. The benevolence of the King, which I had not sought or thought of, made me enter his service. He sent me to Paris. I saw the necessity of no longer thinking about the affairs of the Young Pretender. He came to Paris while I was there. I saw him two or three times. He had advisers who proposed such ridiculous things to him that I could hardly believe anyone could think them up. One of the marvellous plans was to marry an English princess, to have as a dowry 14 000 men, a fleet of ships and go and have himself made Emperor of Peru. There was also another impracticable project, although not quite so absurd. He put it to some party members in England and they sent it to me for my approval. I threw the ball back into their court, but eventually I was urged to give my own opinion about it. I did so, saying that I believed it to be as impractical as taking the moon in your teeth, but that didn't prevent him sending men to pursue the plan and to tell them it was on my advice and with my approval, which was far from the truth. Poor Cameron was caught and hanged.

The conduct of Prince Edward had not pleased the wisest men of his party for some time. In England, amongst other things, they tried to find fault with a mistress that he took everywhere with him. They believed that could easily lead to his discovery and have him traced to his hide-outs. His mistress had a sister at the English court. She offended a lot of people who thought she might reveal her lover's secrets to her sister. I am convinced these fears were unfounded but in her unfortunate situation it would have been wise to remove all suspicion by staying away from all situations that could give rise to suspicion. The girl herself would willingly have agreed, being quite unhappy with him. Representatives were sent from England, which was thought the most appropriate thing under the circumstances, and in particular he was advised to put his mistress into a convent with a suitable pension. They assured him they would look after his interests on all occasions and try to have him restored. The person chosen to convey to him the feelings of the leaders of his party (of whom the two main ones were the Count of Westmorland and Dr King) was a man of whom Prince Edward had the highest opinion. He told me that himself two weeks before he went to Paris. He spoke to me on the orders of those who sent him, for, since they had come to the opinion that the Prince was not very tractable, they didn't think their remonstrances would have any effect. So they told their envoy to consult me as to whether it would be necessary to speak to him or not. My advice was that they should let him know the feelings of his friends in England. I even said that if he was really in love with her he would perhaps go to see her or take her away later but he would give his supporters the satisfaction of putting her in a convent once.

I found the envoy to be a gentle, polite man, of good sense and integrity. He gave the Prince the message he had been charged with, telling him by way of introduction that he knew the message was unpleasant, that he had been charged with it out of zeal and devotion to his service at the risk of his life, since it was of the greatest importance that the Prince should be informed of the views of his supporters. When he suggested putting his mistress in a convent the Prince told him he wouldn't send one of his dogs for them all, and that the messenger had only to carry this reply back to them. The envoy replied that he would not do this, that the Prince's situation was unfortunately such that he should treat his friends carefully, that if he had nothing to ask them he couldn't grant them anything. The envoy used all possible arguments to calm the Prince. He pointed out the risks his friends had run for him, that they were ready to serve him at the risk of their lives if such an occasion arose, and that while waiting their funds were available to him. He said that without them he could do nothing, that if they got tired of it all he would be without resources and if he didn't please them on this occasion they would have never have anything to do with him again. Several times he tried to soften him up, but to no avail. The Prince had at his side Mr Goring, one of the good men who had always been with him and who had served him through everything. After the envoy went away, the Prince, speaking about those who had sent him, said that they were a lot of wretches and that he was of a good mind to send their names to England and have them all hanged. When Goring (who was a bit of a John Bull) heard that he said to him, 'Sir I have suffered a lot since coming into your service, but by God, this takes the biscuit. There is not a highway robber in my country capable of such thoughts. I resign. I don't want to remain any longer with Your Highness.' In fact he did leave, entered the service of the King of Prussia and died soon after.

I wrote to the Prince to tell him that having willingly become mixed up in this and having mistreated all these friends that I knew in England too much, it was impossible for me to serve him any longer. I was forced to write to him, since otherwise he would have summoned me to the first plan despair put in his head, and when I refused he would then have said that I was betraying him. That's why I let him know that he could no longer count on me. All these friends in England were sincerely renouncing Jacobitism. The Prince tried to join with them again but they no longer wished to listen to him. Dr King, to whom he spoke, replied that he could no longer serve him, and that even if he could, he would no longer do so. People were wrong if they believed that the minister, up to now, had involved the Jacobites in the affairs of the King. There were some who did, but today they are the furthest from him.

A little while after this scene between the Prince and the envoy, I met, while out walking alone, Mr H, a man as famous for his integrity as for a witty book. He had been an enthusiastic supporter of the Prince. I knew this. Although he had never said anything to me, and the Prince secretly stayed with him, we walked along together. I introduced the subject of Prince Edward into the conversation. He said to me 'My Lord, I don't want to deceive you, but don't deceive men. A little while ago I would have gone to the gallows for him but now I wouldn't give a farthing to pull him out of the bottom of the river.' He had heard his tirade about a heap of miserable wretched etc.

As I no longer wished to serve Prince Edward I didn't want to listen anymore to these suggestions to collude with him. I couldn't do anything even if I wanted to since he had broken forever with those of his friends that I knew in England.

I stayed quite apart from the Chevalier and his children and also from the Dhanovre family, thinking only of living as a good Prussian. One day the King of Prussia took my hand in passing, drew me aside to a window and said 'I want to arrange your affairs'. I replied, 'I beg you, Sire, do not think of that at all. You have already arranged things so that I am rich. I don't need anything.' He said to me, 'I see that you don't understand me. It's your own affairs I want to sort out and I have already done something about it.' I thanked him. That's how I had my pardon. The King of Prussia knew that benefits would come to me as a result of the pardon.

From being 'Bonnie Prince Charlie' the Prince went on to lose the friendship and respect of all his supporters and to die much later a drunken, ruined wretch. One wonders how he had ever managed to capture the love and respect which had taken thousands out into battle, many to die for him. In an Appendix to the Marischal's memoir he sheds some further light on the rebellion:

217

I was no longer in the secret [of the 1745] since 1743. However since I saw a lot and I was told of things by others, I'll give you a brief account.

I was in Avignon when I received a letter from Prince Edward, after his embarking, ordering me to go to the French court to plead for help, and then to join him in Scotland. I was with the army camped at Liploc, where the King was. I made a rule of obeying as much as I could, this being the advice of the leaders of the party in Scotland. I had letters for several people, asking for a considerable body of troops, money, arms, ammunition, and saying that on these conditions they were ready to declare themselves for him, adding that if your Highness undertakes any hasty steps, and badly thought out ones, you will ruin forever the interests of your House and all your friends. These letters came from France, three weeks after the Prince left, and since he would never have dared carry out the plan they involved him in, if he had seen these letters, they didn't allow the messenger to give him them, nor to let him see them, although he came on behalf of the main Lords of the party in Scotland.

I asked this gentleman what they meant by a considerable amount. He said they were asking for 10 000 men. I adjusted the amount and asked the Minister of France for 6000. He gave me so many weak excuses that I didn't see my request succeeding.

My cousin, Lord John Drummond, and Lord Sempil urged me to write to Scotland, giving assurances of France's good faith, and that they would be strongly upheld. They themselves had already written and told me that the Spanish ambassador and the Duke of Bouillon had also written to Scotland. I replied to them that since apparently they had written what they believed I had nothing to add. I said that if the Spanish ambassador with the assurances of the Spanish court that would add weight, but his opinion on the part of the French and about their good faith had no more authority than any individual. The Duke of Bouillon was a very honest man but not at all consulted or instructed. As for me I was quite convinced that France was tricking us and therefore I couldn't write to Scotland to urge the friends I might have there to sacrifice themselves in the interests of France.

While I was with the French army M. L. Clancarty arrived. A priest called Croix had assured the House of Stuart supporters in England on behalf of France that in addition to the expedition to Scotland there were 10 000 men with arms, munitions, etc., ready to put to sea. M'Lord came as a pilot, being a seaman. I took him to the Minister d'Argenson who said to him first of all, that all that la Croix had said to him was lies and that la Croix a no authority whatsoever. M'Lord who is quite quick-tempered became annoyed and complained to the Duc de Richelieu, who said to him 'What the devil do you want to listen to that fool (speaking of the Minister) for? I'll talk to him.' In fact after dinner when I came back with M'Lord to the Minister we found him completely changed. He agreed to everything, although everything, wasn't ready but they were quickly preparing things.

I think that if M'Lord had asked for 100 000 men and 100 warships they would have agreed to it. M'Lord wanted to withdraw to the French borders and hold himself ready there to return as soon as everything was prepared for embarking. The Minister urged him to stay with the army. He didn't want to but he was made to come a little while later under various pretexts. They didn't allow him to remain unknown. They made public his stay in Paris. France hoped that by pretending to prepare an expedition they would bring about the return of the English troops from Flanders.

I returned to Paris under the pretext of consulting with Maurepas, sent by the Minister of France, on the means of getting 6000 men to Scotland, but really to be rid of me. I had suggested to the Minister to consult with M. de Bart, a skilled seaman, but he didn't want to, de Bart was at Dunkirk. A little while after I was in Paris, the Duke of York arrived. He listened and let himself be influenced by Mr Daniel O'Brien, and madame, who were less worthy than Lord Sempil and MacGregor. You can't imagine the absurdities, the lies that were told and carried out. They produced texts to encourage the Jacobites, to call attention to the actions of Prince Edward and to get some Swiss money from Mr O'Brien. One of these texts contained an account of 600 Orcadians who had joined the Prince. They were almost as big as giants, they were dressed in wolfskins and bearskins, they spoke a language unknown to other men, they had terrifying faces, they were armed with enormous axes. Each man had two auxiliary mastiffs. They were detached with another corps under the command of the Duke of Perth. They attacked the Dutch by night, massacred them and ate almost all of them. I have used the expressions of the illustrious Swiss writer almost word for word. The Duke of York had told me that his brother at the Prestonpans business had 15 000 men. They couldn't impose this upon me so crudely but they forced me to be silent. I said however sometimes that we should tell France exactly how things were – that if she were acting in good faith, as claimed, it was necessary to tell the truth, so that she could take the right measures. I said that if she believed that the Prince already had 15 000 men, France would correctly believe that he had hardly any need of aid, and that if France were not acting in good faith, we would not get her on our side by always telling lies. When I pressed them they replied that you had to draw France in subtly. I replied you can draw your friends in too far but you can never draw France in further than open war. She's there and she will do what she judges best for her own interests.

They prepared the expedition from Boulogne. The Duke of York summoned me one morning and told me that he was to go to Boulogne that day and that I had to follow him, that he was going to raise the alarm at the wrong time that the expedition would not be ready in ten days. I spoke in vain. He didn't listen to me. He told me that the court of France wanted it, so it had to be. She made him go to Dunkirk to raise the alarm quicker. The cannon, ammunition etc., was to go from Dunkirk to Boulogne, Dunkirk being blockaded. The day after he arrived twenty-two frigates crossed in front of Dunkirk which pleased his Highness very much.

The French view was to make the English troops in Flanders cross the sea again to facilitate the military operations in that country and in particular the siege of Brussels. The reason why the French court had hastened the departure of the Duke of York from Paris was that the weather was very frosty. They hoped to move the heavy artillery towards Brussels, to attack it. That was obvious to anyone who wanted to see, for the same day that the Duke of York was forced to leave, all the officers were ordered to rejoin the Marichal of Saxony's army in Flanders While we were in Boulogne France had secretly sent to London, to try and make England neutral. I really think that the Duke de Richelieu would have liked to have crossed the sea to get the Marshal's baton, and go to London if he could. The French in Boulogne wondered what contributions could be raised by the city of London. They estimated about 100 million. That was good for the French and perhaps also for some of their pensioners, but hardly agreeable to me, who was neither one nor the other.

*While the Duke of York was in Boulogne he made a novena to the Virgin who had come there in a little boat at some time. Whereupon Lord Clancarty said to me – 'I don't know if that's a way of getting to paradise, but by the devil, it's not the way to go to London.'

With George Keith's help we can see how a gullible Jacobite party and their Prince were used as pawns and decoys in the bigger wars of Europe. Apart from Keith, none of them ever appears to have realised just how much they were being used by a cynical French government and we now have an explanation why, when Prince Charlie landed in Scotland, he did so without any French forces behind him. The venture was hopeless from the outset and only sheer bravado and ignorance of the odds stacked against the Jacobites carried them on until the final showdown at Culloden.

Bibliography

Records of the Marischal College and
  University of Aberdeen
                                        Anderson, Peter

Studies in the History of the [Aberdeen]
  University, New Spalding Club Historical Papers 1699–1750
                                        Anderson, P. J.

Memoir of Marshal Keith   Anderson, Robert

'Old Inverugie' 1885 lecture to Peterhead
  Mutual Improvement Society   Boyd, William

Memoir of Field Marshal Keith (presented to the Spalding Club by Thomas
  Constable)

Frederick the Great   Carlyle, Thomas

Crown and Gown   Carter, Jennifer J.
                                        and McLaren,
                                        Colin A.

The Life and Times of Queen Anne   Curtis, Gila

The Scottish Friend of Frederick the   Cuthell, Edith E.
  Great

Jacob Keith   Ense, Varnhagen
                                        von

A History of Peterhead   Findlay, J. T.

William Meston, A. M. Buchan Field Club Findlay, J. T.
  1902–3

The Scots in Germany   Fischer, Th. A.

Castles & Domestic Architecture in   Gibbon and Ross
  Scotland

221

Barony and Realm	Gray, John
An Echo of Olden Time	Gregor
An Aberdeenshire Estate 1735–1750	Hamilton, Henry
Castles of Aberdeenshire	Hay
Neue Deutsche Biographie	Kafka-Kleinfercher
Memoir of Field Marshal Keith	Keith, James (presented to the Spalding Club by Thomas Constable)
The Covenanters in the North	King
An Economic History of Modern Scotland	Lenman, Bruce
Russia in the Eighteenth Century	Lentin, A.
The Clans of Scotland	MacDonald, Mitchell
Peter the Great	Massie, Robert K.
Buchan Field Club Vol. XV	Moir, D. G.
The People Above	Murdoch, Alexander
Peterhead	Neishs
Soldatisches Führertum	Priesdorff, Kurt von
A Memoir of Marshal Keith	Scott, David
Marischal College Buildings 1594–1844	Shewen, J. S. Brown and Beattie, C. I.
Dunnottar Castle	Simpson, W. D.
Inglorious Rebellion	Stevenson, Christopher Sinclair
The Jacobite Cess Roll, 1715	Taylor
Some Chapters of Church History	Wilkinson